TO BLOSSOM OUT FROM HIDING

Especially for Women

By
Gloria Mangum Glasgow

To Blossom Out from Hiding

Especially for Women

Written By: Gloria Glasgow Mangum

Edited by: Able & Willing Editing

Cover Design By: Aaron C. Butler

Second Edition 2024

ISBN: 9798991412162 (Paperback)

ISBN: 9798991412179 (eBook)

Library of Congress Control Number: 2024923182

Printed in the United States of America

BookButler Publishing Company

Upper Marlboro, MD

thebookbutler.com | info@thebookbutler.com

Dedication /Gratitude

There are many to whom I owe gratitude; however, I dedicate this particular writing to five women who have made positive deposits into my life, leaving lasting and loving impressions. They are my five sisters, Necie, Willie Mae, Louise, Alice and Gladys; often, the wind beneath my wings.

In memory of my sisters: Necie – the eldest and motherly one, deposits a sense of family connection; to know that to bond with one another becomes the backbone of the family. I shall fondly-remember her unique sense of humor. Willie Mae - the adventurous one, deposits a sense of appreciation for the joys of life; food, travel, and all people. And I shall always be mindful of her wise advice; "Trust in the Lord and wait on Him to guide you." And, Louise, one who exemplified courage and strength-deposits a seed of bravery and an awareness to maintain calmness and a smile even in times of adversity. The memory of her infectious laughter warms my heart.

To Alice - the business-minded one, and Gladys the intuitive one; respectively, I cherish your presence in my life. Please know that I can always depend on your love, support, and prayers. I am so proud to call you sister.

In fondness - my dear friend Grace, one who is like a sister; thank you for your encouragement and cheering me on to complete this book.

In loving appreciation to my immediate family, I am immensely grateful for your unfailing love and support.

Preface

"*To Blossom out from Hiding*" – *Especially for Women*; is a book of personal testimony, and hopefully one which inspires and encourages to live life in fullness - engaging one's true essence, unveiling hidden desires whereas to bring together heart and mind into a wholesome balance; rising above certain imposed expectations and traditions which stifle personal growth and development. For those needing to receive, "*To Blossom out from Hiding*" aims to motivate to go inside self and pull out the authentic one which personifies true spirit; thus, uncovering hidden elements; talents, dreams and passions; to realize that amid responsibilities and obligations, a true sense of self is to be maintained and lived so as to experience a purpose-filled, joyous and content life.

Contents

Introduction
A Wish

Somewhere in the midst of it all, woman decides to hide in a fog of responsibilities, expectations and traditions. It is not fully a conscious decision, but a decision settled into as she relents to the perceived demands of life as being a woman. In the midst of these demands; her mind, body and other bits of her identity are widely distributed, overshadowing her sense of self. As time passes, the fog invades her presence, she is overtaken, and self in the truest sense, becomes hidden.

Everything is well with responsibilities, traditions and expectations, but at the center, must woman lose focus of her inmost self? In losing sight of self, she exchanges her fundamental nature for a predetermined and expected model. With it, she feels obligated to accept this model above and beyond her own personal truths. As this model becomes her way of life, as personal truths are forsaken, and as responsibilities and obligations mount, it becomes complex and improbable to delight in herself as an individual. This is not to suggest neglecting responsibilities and obligations, but in their fulfillment, why abandon self-distinctiveness, joy and contentment?

Woman compromises herself for others, and often deserts her personal goals, dreams, aspirations, and interests, as if neglecting herself makes it better for others. But, does it really? She supports, promotes and defends others, yet requires less for herself? Why not have priorities and be one of those priorities? Why contain that which burns within-innate traits and attributes which

1

makes one who they are? Why does a woman perceive such behavior as required for being woman; and equally as important, why do others expect it of her?

Furthermore, why is woman susceptible to societal mores and concepts which demand a code of conduct, impose double standards, and yet hold her answerable to that which is dictated; as if that mandate is primary and personal choice secondary? Why has she accepted these conditions? Not that woman isn't to live by standards – most definitely so – but shouldn't there be equity in standards for all?

All these questionable "whys", are valid queries drawn from personal experience, noted observations, and varied reports. They are ones which I perceive as truths, yet have come to believe need not be the case. Even though traditions, societal stipulations, and role expectations all have their proper place, I do not believe such should dictate who one actually is, and encroach upon your life. Although in many cases it remains unspoken, women "in general" take issue with such encroachments, yet remain steadfast to the expected "role".

It appears woman "in general" has become complacent in the "role", allowing the "role" to define who she is, even when she knows it is not her true definer. Yet she settles into it anyway, and daily functions under its stipulations. And as she settles, and settles into the "role", bit by bit, her true self becomes more and more hidden and fails to fully blossom.

I believe, many women live life one dimensionally (family/work/home), negating to activate and develop their other core attributes, while inwardly desiring to engage those attributes. Why is it that way? Why it is that a woman simply settles? I have given much attention to this matter, and it has sparked an interest to explore the reasoning behind many of the whys. Subsequently, my discoveries

afforded me a better understanding of the traditional path of woman as well as a better understanding of established mindsets and perceptions. In that light, I have been given information to share and heartfelt wishes to propose.

While the wish list may seem long and perhaps in ways unattainable, I believe possible for each woman to achieve, and rightfully, should achieve. To succeed however, to move beyond prior established beliefs, convictions and views, I believe it is necessary to proceed differently - to amend certain mindsets and perceptions which become captors and hold personal joy and development hostage; to realign certain ideology, tradition, and training which forge their way into the psyche and become disablers more so than an aid.

The wishes I propose, I endeavored to bring to fruition for myself, and now I extend the same to you. As you read and meditate on the information which I offer, I trust you will become enlighten and encouraged. Heart wishes need not simply remain in your mind, but rather to become your reality.

If it is your heart desire to refresh, to renew and reinvent, then, I wish for you:

- To bring back to the surface the core elements of self which have lain dormant.
- To reclaim your just position in daily existence so you may experience contentment in self as an individual aside from all the other which encompass you.
- To experience true joyfulness – not succumb to its portrayal, but to actual experience joyfulness; distinguishing between the joy imposters and true joy.
- To wear a smile on your face – not merely portray a smile on the outside, but actually possess an honest smile from the inside that radiates outwardly.
- To enjoy laughter, not fake laughter, but true laughter from the heart and gut.
- To view self as important, a priority, and first class. Not to assent to subordination solely due to gender. But to view self as gender different; first-class different and first-class valued.
- To shed the "at your service" mindset, and embrace a mindset of possessing your own as a gift to be offered and to be received; presenting self as a choice and priceless jewel.
- To seek out that which lies rooted within and explore your God-given make-up - talents and desires which have been unexplored. Instead, go inside self, and realize the woman that lives within. Embrace her and learn to enjoy living with her.
- To appreciate and savor the breath of life, and accept the responsibility of cherishing joy in the life which is breathed.

- To exude vivacity – to take courage to do what is required to embody wholesomeness inwardly; therefore, emitting wholesomeness outwardly.
- To love self for self, and project an image of self-love; one to be respected and appreciated.
- To engage life in a manner which is personally fulfilling- in your Lord, your loves and self; and to hold yourself accountable to experience the presence of real joyfulness.

I wish for you as I wished for myself, to journey to reclaim that which has been hiding within. To blossom to the fullest, achieving and living out the essence of your true character. And if you're one discovering your essence is indeed hidden and that you've lost the sense of who you are as an individual, then my wish is that you find the path which leads you back to self – authentically. I know it can be done for I am a testament of this fact.

Welcome our Lord to guide your way; to be a lamp unto your feet and a light unto your path; to reveal the beautiful innateness of His special and unique design – you.

Come along with me as I unfold "To Blossom out from Hiding" and hopefully it will inspire and encourage you to fulfill your own heart wishes.

Hope deferred makes the heart sick,
But a longing fulfilled is a tree of life.
A longing fulfilled is sweet to the soul…

Proverbs 13:12; 19

Chapter One
The Quest to Reclaim

The slogan, "I am Woman" encompasses a range of meanings, and often carries with it the sentiment, "I can do it all" and of a mind-set, "I'm expected to manage it all". It is this sentiment and viewpoint which form the basis and establish the outline and platform for which I support in writing; examining these impressions and exploring many of the facets.

By nature, gender, tradition and practice, women are faced with enormous and seemingly unending responsibilities day in and day out. And for the most part, they try their best to meet these daily demands as wife, mother, caregiver, housekeeper, cook, household manager, errand-runner and other things, in and outside the home. There are a lot of intricate pieces to position and manage on a daily basis.

Often, these tasks are performed while maintaining full time employment, creating even more of a challenge to function amid daily undertakings. Yet, a woman attempts to accomplish everything expected of her and adjusts her mindset to match that which she perceives is her required role; a role for the most part, predetermined by customs.

In woman's attempts to measure up to this pre-established mode of conduct, she often falls short in exercising freewill; freewill to embrace that which is personally needed and desired. As tradition has it, she aspires to hold fast to the pre-established standards.

Therefore, to embrace inner-self and fulfill what is needed for self is overlooked as being a primary focus.

As wife, mother and caregiver, she perceives herself to be the anchor of the family, a constant force cheering on each member to achieve their dreams, goals and aspirations. For that reason, if anyone's ambition is to be suspended, she views it to be her own. She accepts this stance in the belief that it personifies an accountable and nurturing woman.

In her willingness to perform accordingly to this established order of conduct, this interpretation of her role, one which dictates how she should or should not perform, and as she surrenders to its scrutiny, suspending her own wishes, interests and goals, she actually lays aside individuality; the very essence representing her true self.

Even when desiring otherwise, she goes forward regardless, attempting to be consistent with that which is expected of the role. She perceives it her place to do so. And in lieu of holding true to individuality, her special design, her true voice; she succumbs to this preset mode of operation, feeling the need to follow the pathway of the predesigned prototype, traditional ways and practices; sort of a one-size-fits-all woman's mold of conduct. Often, her worth, productivity and actions are measured by these pre-existing standards.

Possibly, this predetermined, one-size-fits-all pattern of conduct had its acceptable place at one point in time. Whereas, in earlier years - a different era, it was customary for females to remain in the home to take care of the family and household matters, while males went out into the workforce to earn the household income. In this regard, a wife honored her husband's way of doing things, supported his endeavors, and therefore, would live vicariously through his dreams, wishes, and aspirations.

Overall, at that time, this arrangement was an acceptable lifestyle. It was considered the standard and was practiced by the majority of households. But even then, Perhaps recognizing that the customary view of a woman's role, the one-size-fits-all mold may have been appreciated and accepted, however, the mold didn't include her other needs and desires. Existing outside the parameters of this mold, woman possessed other traits which didn't characteristically line up with the one-size-fits-all. Possessing an audacious spirit, something seated deep within just wouldn't allow that audaciousness to be contained. So, with courage, and most likely a measure of apprehension, these pioneer women made a choice to pursue something different, venturing to seek distinctiveness; to engage and embrace the fullness of self.

I'm sure as these women pursued other ventures; others looked upon them as being different. And, I suspect more often than not, they were looked upon unfavorably, for they were pursuing something other than the normal practices. I also suspect that as well as being viewed as different, they were also viewed as society's "abnormal". Perhaps, many of these women even thought of themselves as abnormal, feeling they desired different than what was typically projected as for woman. Nonetheless, for these pioneers, something within would not allow that bold spirit to be squelched.

In consideration and defense of these pioneers, for the most part, I don't believe it was a matter of their disclaiming customary ways or denouncing age old practices and traditions. But rather, I believe they simply desired a more inclusive lifestyle, one engaging other aspects of self; one engaging more of the total person; and to live out what represented the essence of their being. I believe they felt a sense of entitlement to claim and declare it. I believe they were venturing to claim ownership of self.

As brave as these pioneers were and although this declaration appeared to offer them a sense of liberty, associated with that liberty was hardship. Being ahead of their time, their present social order, they would find themselves faced with public disapproval and criticism. Many were ostracized for their actions, and labeled as society's misfits.

I'm certain many other women desired to step out and follow the example of the pioneers, realizing too that taking care of household and family only represented them in part. But, seeing the criticism and harsh treatment the pioneers underwent curtailed their actions of stepping out. It was easier to simply adhere to traditional practices, and adjust their mindset to fit the classic mold. But inwardly and silently, they would continue to experience inner-conflict; individuality and personal desires tugged against the predetermined mode of operation.

In present-day however, conditions are not quite the same. Many cultural aspects have changed. Women are not faced with the same rigid role of previous eras. Today, women are in the workforce the same as men, and in similar professions and positions. Not that home and family don't remain utmost important to them, they most certainly do. But today for many households, women are needed to join the men in contributing to the family's financial security. And, in many cases, women are the financial providers, especially in single-parent homes. Of course, today it's not all about family need, there's more a matter of freewill and choice. Many women choose to extend self beyond home and explore life's interests, as today's culture is more accepting and promoting.

Unfortunately, however, I believe there still remains a disparity and shortfall. Amid all the positive changes in views concerning a woman's position in society, for many women, individuality still wars against age-old practices and traditions. Women are moving forward in one way and basically standing still in another. The reason for this is the expectation of her role remains basically old-school tradition. The same old-school benchmarks continue to measure her conduct and presentation.

Although woman now extends herself beyond the boundary of home, engages other aspects of life, actively seeks employment and career, still yet, in many homes, she's looked upon to be the primary caretaker of family and household daily operations. Now, instead of one full-time position, she has two; the one away from home, and another awaiting her when she returns home. The perception she holds for herself, as well as what others expect of her is, she is "woman", one to manage it all, and one to fulfill all expected responsibilities. So, she takes on both full-time positions and strives to do both without fail.

There are times; however, when she falls short in meeting these expectations and she feels pressured. Veiled remarks of family members and society's traditional gauges resound that she is not measuring up to the pre-established model. She's expected to juggle all areas and meet expectations without a hitch or complaint. She's expected to maintain a strength she may or may not be able to maintain, to juggle and master a schedule she may or may not be able to master, and take care of situations and needs she may or may not be able to effectively handle. Yet, she tries to measure up to what is expected of her.

As she relentlessly continues with these daily demands and expectations, juggling work, home and other involvements, personal injury lurks. Nonetheless, her eye remains on the perceived ideal model; the measurement of what she perceives as a true woman.

She thinks she is supposed to handle it all, and others look to her to do it all. So, she presses on to reach the mark. However, as she continues on in this manner, something gives way in some form or fashion; for she is simply human, not a device. But the "model" of how she is to perform has been carved in her mind. This perception overshadows everything else, believing, "I am Woman - I am supposed to do it all, and I'm supposed to do it all - well. And furthermore, I am expected to do so."

Over time, becoming wiser in experience, I realized that I too had succumbed to this model; this ideal woman. Along the way, I didn't realize that step by step, I was surrendering my own individuality. Hook, line and sinker, I had gotten on the pathway of predetermined practices; woman's unspoken code of ethics; the one-size-fits-all customary woman.

She is who I perceived I was supposed to be, she is who I felt assured I was expected to be, and I had worked hard to become that model woman. She was my measure of success. However, and unfortunately, in striving to fit the prototype, I abandoned distinctiveness and privilege assertiveness, as I fused with the many roles I was expected to fulfill. I allowed myself to be shaped and molded by tradition, practices and expectations, as if I were pliable clay and outside of me was the controlling potter. I was subconsciously flowing with the movement of the potter.

I hadn't understood that amid it all, I was to maintain a sense of self as a distinct person. But, in the course of responsibilities as wife, mother, homemaker, employee and other obligations, having the many roles and wearing the many hats, how was I to preserve my distinctiveness? How could I possibly keep up with it all, and still safeguard a sense of self? As wife, a woman takes on her husband's way of doing things, as mother she serves as nurturer and caregiver, as homemaker she strives to uphold a domestic standard, and as employee she takes on a job description. So then, in the midst of this and trying to manage it all, where is individuality?

Yet, for the longest time, I continued to prevail against the odds, striving to fulfill the predetermined role. It was not forced upon me; I had consented to all of it; maybe not by conscious approval, but certainly by subconscious willingness and acceptance. And in the process, I had gone far off the mark of what actually represented me as a defined individual. I traveled this course for a long time, becoming wearier, and more and more irritated within myself. It was as if I was on a wheel, consistently going round and round. Barely allowing myself time to get off the wheel to nurture and replenish.

I was traveling a course by dictation, influenced by expectations; the must-do, and the need-to-do. All along, the inner-self was warring against the outer professed self, and I arrived at a place which I didn't desire to be; a state and place of discontent and weariness. But from the outside view all appeared well. And, I had convinced myself all should be well. So, I conducted myself as if all was well. And I moved full speed on a path heading toward an emotional collision.

As I loved and cared for others, participated in undertaking after undertaking, and relinquished privilege

after privilege, I did not maintain my own overall emotional, mental and physical well-being. I hadn't seized control to secure all areas of my well-being. To a degree, I depended on such nurturing and safe-guarding to come from without. If I'm doing for you, the same should be reciprocated. But it doesn't work that way unless you require it. The outside doesn't deliver unto you unless you demand it, and I hadn't. I was too busy making sure I measured up to the mold.

Life experiences and time however, have a way of bringing matters to awareness. Over time, I became aware of my actions and began to evaluate them. I realized so much of me, the individual representing me as a separate and distinct person had become disengaged; masked amid a perceived role as I walked in the shoes of the customary woman.

Women have a tendency to push themselves. We do when we don't want to do. We do even when we're feeling too tired to do. We say yes, even when the mind, body and spirit are yelling "no, I don't want to". It's customary, so women just do and do. Why it is that a woman feels she is supposed to do regardless – even if no one else is doing? Why it is that a woman accepts this as required?

Over time I began to realize the customary shoes weren't personally designed and customized for my feet. Well-designed perhaps, but weren't of my selective design. And the more I walked in those shoes, the more I became aware my toes were cramped. And for whatever reason, even with cramped toes, and for the longest time, I kept walking in those shoes. Eventually, the shoes of customs began to squeeze my toes more and more. As I became more uncomfortable wearing them, I knew I needed to adjust the shoes. I needed shoes that didn't cramp my toes. I needed comfortable, tailor-fit, of my own special design.

In other words, I needed to redesign my day-to-day lifestyle, from a customary, one-size-fits-all, traditional fit to a more personalized-fit and tailored made for me.

Subsequently, and step by step, I began to customize my fit. I took a long look at the "model" shoe of "customary" and dissected it. Then, running on a parallel track, I took a long look at my personal shoe – needs, desires, wishes, thoughts and actions, and I began to dissect it as well, comparing the two shoes. Following the dissection, I started to make some changes and adjustments. Prior to this point, I accepted the model as primary and placed myself as secondary. Actually, I needed to have flipped that switch long before. But, as I gained insight, I also gained a renewed strength and focus.

In doing so, I began to release myself from the firmness of needing to hold true to pre-determined standards; the prototype of woman's conduct. I began to separate my own ideas from the imposed ones, and determine what I needed to lead me to a more content individual from the inside out.

Grasping a better understanding of self and circumstances, I realized I needed to regain self-management; to better control what I needed and wanted. I had to nourish myself back to an overall state of well-being. I knew in order to do so, I had to make significant changes which included slowing my speed, rethinking my position, mentally readjusting and revamping my course. But even in knowing this, how was I to achieve it?

First, I allowed myself to accept I wasn't solely a one-size-fits-all customary woman. I was not going to abandon traditional training and practices, for I actually appreciated certain aspects of traditionalism. But to realize there were other ways, other privileges and other avenues. I accepted I wasn't bound to those practices simply because it was the age-old way, or simply because I had been operating in a certain manner for so long. Realizing, it is okay to change regardless of age and time invested.

Next, I had to grasp an understanding of my emotions. Understand why I was questioning my position in the first place. What was the nature of my discontentment, especially when family, employment and the general conditions of life were just fine? So why was there a problem? Yet a problem existed; significant elements were missing from my daily living; disquieting from within. External factors most definitely had impact and influence, but the root of the problem lay within-my perceptions of it all.

As I began to take long looks at the factors surrounding me, I understood I no longer wanted to measure up to a model of how I was expected to be, rather, measure up to the self I desired to be. I wanted to seek out and secure that distinction which actually embodied my nature; and to do so become my quest.

Somehow, during the course of life, women more so than men, seem to get off track of self. We empty ourselves so much into others. We become merged into their lives, their ambitions, goals, mannerisms, practices and interests, especially when it comes to our families. We enjoy and appreciate much of what we do, and in some cases would have it no other way. But we don't put the same type of energy and effort back into ourselves. As we merge into others, we abandon traits of ourselves. Initially, it seems like the very thing we should do, but later, we find out that it is the very thing we should not do.

As I came to this realization, and continued to figure things out, I better understood my position; many of the whys, whats, and hows. And without a doubt, I understood I needed to reclaim the bits and pieces of self-essence I had allowed to fall by the wayside; those elements which personally offered me peace, joy, satisfaction, and contentment; those elements of my nature which made me; my special design; the part of my design which was not contained in the one-size-fits-all model of a woman. But I desired to recover those missing traits. I wanted those elements to resurface, be acknowledged, and furthermore, be exercised.

One cannot maintain a true sense of self when operating opposite one's true nature without experiencing personal conflict, side effects, and possibly personal injury. Your well-being emotionally, mentally, physically and spiritually becomes at risk. In spite of, women generally continue down this path anyway. For the perception of; this is what I need to do, this is how I need to act, this is who I'm supposed to be and this is what is expected of me weighs heavily on the mind. Actions are dictated by these thoughts, agreeing or disagreeing.

On the other hand, however, it is hard for woman to say, "I'm not doing well" when all outside appearances indicate you should be well, general circumstances indicate you ought to be well, and the portrayal is you are doing well. It's very hard to cross that barrier and expose self; to convey to self and others that in spite of what it looks like, I am not all that well. The "ideal" model really isn't ideal for me after all.

Women become consumed though. Their focus is to perform ideally according to what is expected; to perform in a certain manner, to accept this and that, to take care of this one and that one, and compromise here and there. They forge ahead on this path, even if there's an inner-voice whispering, cautioning her to beware, or an internal warning, signaling she is approaching a danger zone.

Unfortunately, too often these signals and warning alerts are dismissed, disarmed or ignored. But ignoring them, doesn't make the whispered alerts and alarms go away, rather, silences them. By silencing them, the real issues remain hidden and danger zones still lie ahead.

It took years, but I learned to pay attention to the whisper of my alerting inner-voice. But before I actually listened, the whisper had to turn into more of a resounding thump. I had been so accustomed to disregarding the whisper, forging ahead as so many do. But finally, after a few severe thumps, viewing danger zones ahead and actually going through a few of them, I listened. And as I listened, I was able to grasp a better understanding of the alerts.

I felt I was basically doing well concerning my body. I ate selectively, took vitamins, exercised, and kept up my appearance but, I wasn't applying the same efforts to stroke and nourish the inner-me, my soul. I wasn't giving my core what it virtually needed. I knew I had to retrieve my fundamental nature; to recapture what I needed and release what I didn't. My inner self and my outer professed self, needed to be the same.

I desired the two to agree and come together in fullness, enabling me to go forth as an overall balanced well-being; more energized, joy-filled, and intra-purposely directed; going inside self and bringing forth authenticity, no longer fragmented, but more whole. To achieve more wholeness, I needed to uncover and reveal hidden elements – my distinctiveness, self-determination, aspirations, interests, and soulfulness; to rearrange perceptions and uncover the unique sense of self which I had allowed to become subdued.

Following and most imperative, once these elements were uncovered, and as I put them into practice, I had to rework the circumstances of my daily living, yet create a satisfying balance. I didn't want to abandon who I was at that point; instead, I wanted to unify who I had become along with who I desired to be. But, how was I to conquer this feat? It wasn't going to magically happen. There were a lot of unknowns to process, but what I did know was my course of action would be a process. My journey to rediscovery, renewal and reclaim would need to be explored inch by inch and step by step. I was excited to start the journey, but little did I know how involved the journey would become. It wouldn't be a journey in haste. As I journeyed, I would encounter periods of highs and lows. I wasn't expecting the lows. I had a false sense that the journey would be this exciting venture of finding me. But to find "yourself" you must scratch through some briars and thistles in getting there.

As I continued on, changes began to occur. Gradually, I shifted my mental processing from one of total traditionalism; the one-size-fits-all model to a more customized model. I began to allow myself to accept other viewpoints. I allowed myself the freedom to explore other avenues. And most importantly, I began to yield to the coaching of my inner-self.

Through it all, the highs, lows and indifferent, a path has been determined leading to a more self-embracing and enhanced reality. Along the way, I examined many perceptions, uncovered many hidden elements and released them from hiding. Purpose, direction, and inner-joyfulness were restored, and in some cases a transformation occurred.

I ascertained a new and clearer prospective, as well as a new sense of freewill.

This journey was not a simple or overnight process. Rather, a journey traveled step by step, and discovery by discovery. As I journeyed, it was important to pay attention to the manner of how I did things, how I received and dealt with issues, and how I reacted to situations. My goal was to realign and readjust self. It could not have been achieved unless I first conducted self-examination. I had to focus on which elements required reworking, which ones required restoring, and which ones required abandoning. I somewhat compare the journey's experience to that of a transfusion, whereas the old passes through and out, and fresh replenishes the body; more sustaining and more vigorous.

I did not have a mentor in place to guide me along the way as I journeyed from hiding. Mostly, I had to rely on my own strength and draw from inner-resourcefulness, which became the best course for me. Through the processes, I realized the greatest strength comes from within. But most assuredly, I leaned mercifully upon the guiding of the Holy Spirit. I was determined to go forward, for I knew it was a journey I had to take. Not just for myself, but for others like me.

When I first began my journey, I thought it would be one of an outward change, changing others and circumstances that surrounded me. I wanted others to change to fit me, to fit my needs, my desires, and my wants. But surprisingly, it has been the opposite. This journey has been one of a personal change; circumstances which surround me have remained basically unchanged.

The more I discovered regarding my inner-self, and listened to the voice of my inner-self, the more I managed to place everything in a right prospective. I was once again able to recognize myself as an individual entity, having shed certain misconceptions and predetermined expectations.

Gradually, as I continued to forge ahead, that heavy weighted, subdued place of existence faded into non-existence, replaced by a brightened and heightened place of existence. I had managed to change my function setting from one of a typical, preset mode, the one-size-fits-all customary woman, to one of a more personal setting. Still maintaining responsibilities and obligations, but from a change of prospective.

I must emphasize though, before I journeyed forward, I had to take a glimpse backward. I believed I couldn't go forward successfully without grasping an understanding of what lie behind; to understand previous actions, thought patterns, the what and the whys. I don't believe lasting change can be achieved without awareness and an understanding of how you arrived at your present.

Another key factor was to understand the nature of the journey. Understand where I was planning to travel, and why? What's the purpose of the journey? What will be the mode of operation? What are the goals and objectives? What decisions need to be made? Simply put, where am I going, why am I going, and how am I planning to get there?

To actually get going, and come up with a definite travel plan can become mind boggling. Making changes aren't always comfortable or easy, particularly if you have been used to doing things a certain way, and especially if you're going to venture into unfamiliar territory. There needs to be a strategic plan. But, the initial effort to get going can be exasperating. It's sometimes just easier to leave things as they are than to change.

I however, was no longer willing to maintain the status quo. I desired to make changes in my life. In decency and in order of course, I was most willing to do whatever required getting me to the other side. It was a journey that was critical to my over-all well-being, and I wanted to be restored to self.

Still, I didn't know how to begin. I needed motivation to be jolted from complacency. Just thinking and wishing weren't going to make it happen, regardless of how much I desired it. Blessedly, I received the very jolt I needed; the right thing at the right moment. It was the book *Fresh Wind, Fresh Fire*. Reading this book gave me the motivation I needed to get going. More importantly, I received direction. *Fresh Wind, Fresh Fire* gave me a definite focus; prayer.

This book proved to be exactly the very source I needed to initiate my quest, guiding me to a purposeful direction, and a renewed spiritual vitality. I definitely wanted change, but not simply to make changes, but rather, to make the right changes, the right way. *Fresh Wind, Fresh Fire*, reminded me as well as commanded; I needed to first consecrate myself in prayer. I needed spiritual guidance to receive the best results for the whole. It wasn't just about me, but about family and all the circumstances surrounding me.

I began to engage vigorous, unyielding, soul stirring prayer. Within this sacredness, I was allowed to bear all without judgment or popular opinion. I could just unload as I needed and welcome spiritual guidance and revelation. That is exactly what I did, and that is how I began my quest *To Blossom out from Hiding*.

It has been somewhat of a turbulent journey, this journey to renewal, because I basically traveled it alone and

in silence. Nevertheless, it has been a journey worth all the efforts; having arrived at a renewed place where I am self-assuredly present in my own right as an individual. I know who I am, what I represent, and what I desire, while possessing the persistence to grab hold of it; no pretense, no masks and no hiding.

I don't know all the answers, but I do know a lot more than when I first began the journey, especially about myself. It is like the heavens have opened to me, and breathed a fresh wind and fire upon me, and given me a clear direction and a transformation for which I shall be eternally grateful.

If you too determine you have become entangled in the trenches of daily activities, entrenched in expectations, traditions, obligations, and circumstances, and realize that, within this entanglement you have lost sight of what represents you as a distinct person, then it is my wish for you to begin your own quest to reclaim self. And if you are realizing you have lost your wind and fire, and have become stagnant and perhaps robotic to a lifestyle of preset and mundane tasks, then I encourage you to reclaim your wind and fire and find a path of return; a path designed to meet your personal specifications, enabling you to be a well-balanced being.

Please know that, the only way to get moving is to get moving. The path is right there in front of you, ready and waiting for you to get on its track. As I needed, you too may need a nudge in order to get you moving in a different direction. My nudging force was a message and revelation received through reading a book that reminded me, encouraged me, and directed me to pray.

Over the years, even though I had been mindful to pray, much of my prayerful times were as a matter of course. I

realized the importance of prayer, yet I was somewhat methodic in doing so. And as I prayed, I was not listening to God speak in return. Therefore, I wasn't yielding to the guidance of the Holy Spirit. I was sending up prayers, but still operating on my own.

Through the blessing of *Fresh Wind, Fresh Fire*, I received a new prayer anointing and was reminded that prayer is not and should not be a matter of course, but rather, heartfelt splendor, as we speak to and receive from Almighty God. Prayer is power, prayer is worship, prayer is connectivity to God's channel, His purpose and His will. And yes, prayer is most definitely a forerunner to initiate change. Prayer truly changes things.

Prayer became my starting point. Through prayer, I was able to meditate, seek direction, and receive divine revelation. But along with prayer, I had to invest much time and hard work in order to regain an understanding of myself, as an individual. Bits of my essence had been scattered – responsibilities, expectations, traditions, family life, church life, work, and other things. I found I needed to collect those scattered pieces, and restructure them as necessary in order to regain wellness. I wanted to gather those pieces and arrange them into a unity that made sense to me, enabling me to produce a more contented me, to conjoin the inner-me and the outer-me, establishing a balance. Through prayer and works, over time, and point by point, I gathered the scattered pieces and allowed them to be placed in perspective personally desiring of my heart, and satisfying to my soul.

It is amazing how bits and pieces of your life scattered in various directions can begin to come together into wholeness and formulate something very good and

satisfying. Yet, we have to take what we may consider the bad, along with that which we consider good, and reshape it, mixing it all together. Similar to forming clay, we collect all the fragments and imperfections then mold them all together. Then if the first shaping is not the desired one, we can reshape, and if necessary, reshape again until we arrive at the desired finished product of satisfaction. We are all as clay, and it is okay to own-up to needing to be reshaped.

"And we know that all things work together for good to them that love God, to them who are called according to his purpose."

Romans 8:28 KJV

I'm mighty grateful to the author of *Fresh Wind, Fresh Fire* and the blessings imparted. I'm also grateful to my son Lemont for the gift of caring enough to share with me a book which he viewed as a blessing to himself. It was exactly what I needed in a time of uncertainty; to receive direction, a fresh wind and fresh fire. I have become grounded in a new prospective and direction.

From my own experience, and now having gone through my quest to reclaim, my eyes have become like detectors, readily to detect others in similar distress. And, I'm willing to share my journey as testimony of victory

In sharing, it is my aim to serve as a guiding source to others finding it necessary to take a similar journey. To be to you a guiding source which I did not have the benefit of, but needed; someone to shorten the steps and soften the travel.

It is my wish that my testimony will reach, edify, and hopefully, emotionally release others to accept their own feelings and thoughts. Not only to accept, but to realize that your feelings and thoughts are valid.

For this purpose, I am retracing my path, to first record the feeling of a place where I once privately existed, and now, as I have transformed, to record the renewed feel of a livelier, healthier, and more assured place, a place where I now wonderfully reside within self; a peaceful and joyous existence, from the inside out. All that I state, I can personally bear witness to the dynamics of each step of the journey.

I hope you will find whatever you need to be your nudging source or force, something to motivate you to move in a direction your heart desires. Believe me, prayer is a wonderful starting point. God knows all about you and your circumstances. His spiritual guidance will allow you to arrange it all in the right prospective.

Share with God. He's forever present, and always near to extend a supportive hand for you to grab hold to direct you wherever you need to go. He is an excellent problem-solver and life coach. What He has placed in you, I believe He desires for you to live out.

As you go forth on your own journey, be aware, once you begin to make significant and perhaps, radical changes, you will also change the sculpting of others involved. For a season, circumstances may appear more mystifying and dimmer, but keep in mind the brightness of the sunny day is surely to arrive- just stay on course. I can assure you, once the path is traveled, and transformation transpires- days are enlightened; a fresh newness overshadows your presence.

I wish you courage as you journey. However, be mindful and have a clear understanding of what it is you desire. Allow God to be your center focus and guiding force. Then, if you follow His guided path, your change will be the right change for you. Your quest to reclaim self will be right directed. And your journey out from hiding will be blessed! Go forth on your journey until you find that which your soul needs; your identity in self; your deliverance; journeying from obscurity to clarity; from dimness to light.

It is this story of deliverance from dimness to light which God has rooted within me and given me a compelling passion to share with those needing to hear; the ones whose mindset and perceptions run parallel to that which I once possessed.

I self-battled to overcome the infrastructure of a particular mindset. But by God's amazing and saving grace, I am winning the battle and have released myself *To Blossom out from Hiding*.

Most certainly it is not of my own strength to publicly share my feelings and thoughts, as I am one of a private nature but, it is of God's power that I receive courage to shed my cowardice skin and to openly share intimate parts of my life. This compelling desire to share overshadows my cowardice nature and the Holy Spirit gives me strength and boldness. Through it all, it is the Holy Spirit that guides me in this mission and it is my service to humanity.

As I see it, if these pages impact and benefit one, then, that one can influence another. For our life choices and decisions don't just impact self, but extend to others and through generations. So, if my testimony shall help one and that one filters to impact another, and the chain continues, inspiring in a manner that transforms unhealthy perceptions to healthy perceptions, and unhealthy mindsets to healthy mindsets, so that the quality of lives are enhanced, then my mission's purpose is fulfilled.

Now, engage as I share in portion my quest and journey, sharing experiences and revelations. It is not a tell-all recording, disclosing dark secrets. Nor is it one of shame, blame or remorse. But rather, you will find it to be one that is God inspired, sharing wisdom; inspiring and guiding to overcome a particular negative driving force that directs the actions of many women; a negative force I personally have had to war face-to-face.

Overcoming the struggle, I have been directed on a path which led to a most beautiful ray of light; inner-peace and joyfulness from within. I was able to rearrange a few things in my life, amend a few perceptions, adjust mindset, and allow myself certain liberties that had long been forfeited. Through lessons learned and blessings received, God has commissioned an assignment for me to reach, teach and edify.

I feel assured that many of you will be able to relate to what I have to say. For I have had an opportunity to observe many of you that are wounded, hurting, angry and tired. You exist in a state of submission to life's demands and expectations, and are mystified about what is needed to rectify circumstances.

Although I speak from the aspect of having become overwhelmed with obligations and tasks; and of falling subject to traditions and expectations, there are however, many causes and circumstances as to why a woman may find herself in a similar position of hiding. Even though causations may vary, however, the effect in the long run is so similar. It is that similarity on which I focus.

So, ladies, settle in as you continue to read these pages and absorb what I have to share. Think of us as friends, just chatting. Listen as I share with you some of my experiences and God-given insights. I know women need to release and dialogue, so in the process, talk to me as you read. Record your thoughts for later assessment. And at the end, prayerfully and hopefully you will be enlightened *To Blossom out from Hiding*.

Hear; for I will speak of excellent things; and the opening of my lips shall be right things.

For my mouth shall speak truth; and wickedness is an abomination to my lips. All the words of my mouth are in righteousness; there is nothing froward or perverse in them. They are plain to him that understandeth, and right to them that find knowledge. Receive my instruction, and not silver; and knowledge rather than gold. For wisdom is better than rubies; and all the things that may be desired are not to be compared to it.

Proverbs 8:6-11 KJV

Chapter Two
Instructed to Pray

"When you pray, ask God for wisdom, knowledge and understanding." I was just a young girl when my father first gave me this most valuable instruction. And, as a child kneeling in prayer each night, I recited in my prayer, "God, grant me wisdom, knowledge and understanding."

Growing up I didn't give much thought to the meaning of such instruction, or to why my father thought it important to guide me in this particular manner. But now, matured in my own spirituality, and as I reflect on his words, what better instruction for a parent to gift a child than to teach how to pray.

My family however, wasn't particularly one united in daily prayer and devotion. So, I cannot claim a family united in worship. Yet, within my home, my parents instilled a reverence for God which established a foundation of belief. I would hear my mother softly humming and singing spirituals, observe my father in daily Bible study, and they made sure my siblings and I were present in church services each Sunday. Yet, and unfortunately, we didn't perform these valuable practices together as a family unit. Still and without a doubt, my parents guided their children to God. We respected their guidance, and were obedient to their instructions.

For that reason, for me to receive instruction from my dad on how to pray hadn't appeared foreign. Besides, he was one of much authority, so I just received his instruction, prayed it without question, and without fail. I was simply obedient. As children, we generally do as our parents' request, even when we don't clearly understand what is being communicated. We simply trust and do. Therefore, my father's directive had not been questioned. I simply followed his instruction, allowed the prayer seed to take root and continued to pray in blind faith.

Now, rooted in faith and biblical knowledge, I clearly understand his instruction. I also feel I recognize the source from which he received his incentive. I feel certain his instruction derived from his study of those in the Bible who appealed to God for the favor of wisdom; particularly King Solomon's request, noted in 1 Kings 3.

I believe my dad understood that God hears and honors such requests. Perhaps, passing prayer instruction to me, and most likely to all his children was his way of equipping us for the journey of life. I think he believed if God would hear and honor the request of kings and others in the Bible, surely, he could and would do the same for his children. Certainly, in the experience of life, we need to be equipped and armored in wisdom. My father no doubt knew this.

Over the years, as I prayed the words, "God, grant me wisdom, knowledge and understanding", they resonated within my spirit. Even though at times, I prayed as a matter of course. Nonetheless, I continued to pray, "God, grant me wisdom, knowledge, and understanding." But we know even prayer, being as important as it is, and even when faithful to pray, it can become routine or a ritual, as we move in motion with the busyness of daily life. We believe we are to engage prayer, and we wish to honor God, so we pray. Even when our thoughts are focused somewhere else while we are actually praying, we still follow through with the ritual. Even though we are serious to pray, nevertheless, it can become a formality.

There are times though, when we are faced with special concerns and needs, we become more fervent in prayer, more focused and more in tune with God. But often, when the crisis is over, unfortunately, we return to praying as routine, as though prayer power is available particularly for crisis. But actually, the dynamics enclosed in prayer, the ultimate communication with the Almighty, is available to us for all times.

Prayer should be more than merely routine and formality. But sometimes, we become stuck in the practice and fall short in receiving the greatest benefits; the most intimate communication and divine guiding force. Often, in order to become unstuck, and to awaken us to the realization of prayer dynamics, we must experience a shake-up, an upheaval, such usually occurring at times of troubles and pain. This is why *"Fresh Wind, Fresh Fire"* impacted me so greatly. It served to awaken me to prayer dynamic.

Its message reached out, and served as my shaking source and force. Its message allowed me to realize I was stuck in a prayer formality. While reading and meditating on its message, it planted within me a fresh seed, inspiring me to fervently and purposefully engage in prayer; reminding me to recognize God's grace, mercy, and mostly, His power. To truly understand that He's willing to listen, embrace and provide whatever I may NEED; maybe not exactly as I wanted, but surely as I needed.

Since my youth though, I've been mindful of the fact that God responds to prayer, and I've conducted my prayer life in this awareness. But even so, I came to realize, awareness verses real relationship are totally different levels of prayer worship. In unawareness, I had limited God to my mind, with words of faith and love, appreciating Him from a distance; conceptually; somewhat keeping God in the abstract. Yes, I believed He could, and I had personal testimony He would, but I didn't trust Him in all situations.

Over the years, as I prayed, I hadn't been faithful to wait on His response and guidance, I trusted in myself more. I depended and trusted God for the high artillery matters; when I could see no other way in my own limited view. But He's omnipresent, omnipotent and omniscient. He's everywhere, has all power and knows everything, so where is there limitation?

From the message received through "*Fresh Wind, Fresh Fire*", I realized I needed to allow God in closer; release Him from the conceptual and allow Him to penetrate my mind and heart with understanding. I needed to accept His grace, mercy and supremacy and be in close relationship with Him. Not just in crucial times, and certainly not in the abstract, but an actual real, intimate relationship; God, Jesus Christ, the Holy Spirit and me, unified in divine partnership. I wanted to remove the barrier of limitation.

Although I'm most grateful to my dad for passing on his instructive words regarding prayer, I know now it was God at work for my purpose. My earthly father had simply been a vessel, a channel. "*Fresh Wind, Fresh Fire*" reminded me of his instruction, the root of my prayer life. Its directives guided me to a totally different height in prayer worship – with faith, wisdom, knowledge and understanding.

It is astounding to know that through God's provision, spiritual seed is planted at times when we don't even recognize it is being planted. And if cultivated, that seed eventually sprouts and later blossoms. In my case, my father planted the seed through his instruction to pray, and prayer became rooted in my spirit. The seed within me was being cultivated even when I didn't realize it at the time. It was that prior seeding that positioned to accept its importance and dynamics at a most needed time.

It is through prayer I began my own journey out of hiding. Through prayer, I gained patience, mind clarity, prospective and guidance. I began to better see my place in the whole scope of things, and better understand my position. Emotionally, mentally and spiritually I became untangled, arranging things in right order; becoming anchored in self; and establishing a real intimate relationship with Christ.

My journey started out as a selfish pursuit, but most assuredly, the more I prayed, the more the pursuit manifested differently than what I was expecting; different, but so much better. I allowed myself to be spiritually fed and guided. Even though my pursuit was of a personal nature, God revealed to me that my discoveries are to be unselfish and shared.

Now, I believe I have been granted an insightful channel into wisdom, knowledge, and understanding regarding a particular strife facing many women today. He has given me a perceptive passageway which I believe has been commissioned directly through His workings. He actually does answer prayer, and now, I believe He heard me throughout the years, even when I didn't realize the purpose for which I was praying, nor the mission which was ahead.

Now as I reflect on the path of my life's journey, my experiences, adventures, challenges, disappointments, repercussions of certain choices favorable and unfavorable, a story unfolds; a certain testimony permeates from within, and a mission is now set in motion. Amazingly, God takes our errors in life, and if we are willing, He corrects and reshapes them in a manner that is used for our good; He then positions us for His service. My service at present is to speak out to women needing to hear what I have to say; and I have no doubt there are many.

Through employment and other areas, I have been surrounded by women of all walks, ages, and cultures; different, yet similar, who seek direction and life coaching. It seems each position has been centered on a common theme – concerns of women. God situated me as a drawing force for many that were confused and going in misguided directions. I found myself in a position that many, mostly younger, but not all, were somehow drawn to my presence and counsel; a force of magnetism that sometimes became overwhelming. It was as though I had a neon sign on my forehead which read "Welcome to Counsel". It was not I, but rather, the Holy Spirit's presence within me that was the attracting force. I was simply a vessel and channel; a small branch of the Vine, commissioned for a mission; a mission which I obediently accepted.

This position and mission didn't come overnight. It evolved over time, having experienced a few personal hard knocks, wounds and bruises, while all along becoming sculpted, molded, and shaped in experience and awareness; becoming knowledgeable and educated about certain modes and fashions of life. You don't always know when you are being equipped and positioned for a mission. Years roll around so quickly, and you are steadily undergoing experience after experience. In your mind you think you're at one place in life, only to find out that years and experiences signify you're in a totally different place. All of a sudden, you find yourself in the midst of an undertaking and on a journey, one you didn't even realize you were preparing to take.

I did not seek this mission, rather the mission found me. Frankly, I would rather not have experienced some of the things I did in order to get to this point. But just as in preparing for battle, one must receive proper training before entering the line of fire, having to undergo training you wish you didn't have to endure, but is necessary. Once prepared and equipped, training is matched to the operation. And from what I understand of the workings of God's assignments and missions, you can either go forth willingly, or be sent under duress kicking and screaming. Personally, knowing His authority, I choose to go willingly. Even so, first, I had to undergo proper training as God lined it all up for me to utilize my training, experience and spiritual gifts.

"There are different kinds of spiritual gifts, but they all come from the same Spirit. There are different ways to serve the same Lord, and we can each do different things. Yet the same God

37

works in all of us and helps us in everything we do. The Spirit has given each of us a special way of serving others. Some of us can speak with wisdom...."

1 Corinthians 12:4-8 CEV

I believe God has entrusted me with a voice to share what bears on my heart. For this mission, I believe wisdom through God's working and blessings anchor me, life's experiences position me, and the workings of the Holy Spirit direct me as I speak with conviction regarding a particular quandary numerous women face today. I believe many have renounced self-ownership; and fail to live out the inner-person that lies within. They continuously give outwardly and fail to grab hold to what is needed within.

Many live out their life without experiencing personal joyfulness, and sad to say, many live and ultimately die without acknowledging the true self. It has been woman's belief that she is to place herself after everyone else. And while she is deferring her own desires and needs, much of life's joys escape her. She fails to realize that joyfulness in self can be attained along with all the other things she finds necessary to do. I am a voice to attest you can, and an advocate to promote you should realize your own dreams and desires.

I believe for the most part, it's the mindset that prevents a woman from seizing this privilege, and the chief force preventing her from attaining it is – self. There are varied contributing factors, some more dominant than others, but in either case, the results are similar. Self is hidden.

I realize there are always exceptions and not all women experience the same, nor do they have the same concerns. But I've seen evidence that many actually experience silent struggle and hardship striving to measure up to a perceived model; a model which doesn't characterize who they actually are.

Woman should not be expected to, nor accept existing in part, but strive for a wholesome balance. She need not strive to be super human; and she need not carry the burden of having to become a super hero. She should simply do her best. I believe your best in any given situation is all that is required. But in the process of doing your best for others, you must do your best for self as well.

Unfortunately, a woman can become her own worse adversary. Often, she doesn't own up to her true feelings. She projects one thing, but desires another, expresses one thing, but inwardly yearns for something else, and does one thing, but actually wants to do another. Why is that? What is the portrayal all about?

Just because woman accepts others into her life, and takes on ensuing responsibilities, it shouldn't make her less of a person; less distinctive. It shouldn't stop her from totally investing in self. She must advocate for herself; be her own best supporter, and her own best defense. It doesn't mean that others in her life won' be as important, but still, she needs to be her own enthusiast.

So, women, as you nurture and care for others, recognize you must nurture and care for self as well. Your life and individuality are to be appreciated and celebrated. No one, for any reason should rob you of that. You are to appreciate and celebrate self; the innate being that you are. I believe God wants nothing less for you than to live out all aspects of self, the self He has entitled you to be.

I speak to those who are in midst of such struggle and dilemma. Those who have chosen to accept the expected code of conduct over their own personal truths; those who have chosen to travel a course opposite of what their inner-person desires; those who fail to balance responsibilities in conjunction with personal needs and desires; those who perceive life requires you to compromise self; those for whatever the personal reasons, have lost sense of self, and forsaken individuality.

I can't say at what point I became the voice of an experienced one. Nor do I know if I'm ready to be that voice. Scripture tells us, "To whom much is given, much is expected." And really, it seems like only yesterday I too was one seeking life direction, and requiring a similar kind of counsel. But it wasn't yesterday. Time has passed and I have encountered much. Still, I am a work in progress, years in the making, and the making continues on.

Through it all though, I have become a willing vessel, realizing that along the way God has been preparing me to be to others that which I once desperately needed for myself, a life coach and counselor. In the process of this journey, and while being shaped and molded, I have received exactly what I needed, as the Lord became my personal and inimitable counselor and coach.

I don't know why God has chosen me for this particular mission, but Jeremiah 1:5 states; He knew us before we knew ourselves. He knew my prayer request before I knew I would be praying it, and even why I would need to pray it. He knew I would need to be anchored in prayer worship, and I would need to know how to call on Him. My earthly father had instructed me, as my heavenly Father guided him.

I believe one's mission doesn't remain the same focus indefinitely, so I have to share this testimony while it weighs on my heart. I believe we have a season for a mission, and it is now my season for this particular one; a mission to speak out to women needing to hear insightful revelations regarding strife that many face. .

We don't always know when seed is being planted, why it is planted, or for whom it is being planted. Regardless of the reason, if the seed is allowed to take root, grow and blossom, the harvest becomes available to share.

Jesus being the True Vine, He uses us as branches, planting within us seed to sprout so that we might blossom and branch out - if we are willing. I trust my planted seed, which has now blossomed, may be shared to strengthen others; particularly that of a certain woman.

As you begin your own journey and quest to renewal, first and foremost, pray and seek God's guidance, then, allow yourself to delve inwardly. Meditate, meditate, and meditate some more. Understanding self is important. You need to know who you are fundamentally, what you want, and where you want to go. You need to understand your current position, mindset and perceptions. What is your current stance, and why? What is your actual mindset and perceptions? Have you ever really thought about the whys of what you do, or don't do for that matter? Understand why you want what you want; its benefit; and its purpose. But beware; don't make changes on a whim. Be patient, think things through and be certain of the direction you desire to take.

Perceptions and mindsets are powerful forces, and it's important to identify and understand the nature of your own.

Now, let's move along and take a closer look into perception and mindset.

Chapter Three
Understanding Perception and Mindset

It's incredible to realize, whether justifiable or not, whether fact or not, how we perceive our experiences actually determines our mindset, which in turn molds and shapes our behavior; establishing thought patterns that propel and dictate our actions and directions. Our perception becomes truth in our minds, and that perceived truth is what directs us.

As I continue to share my experiences, disclosing my own established thought patterns, be mindful, it is not the actual experience to which I bring focus, but rather, my perception of the experience, my personal truths and views, ones that I chose to accept and live out. Believing as I went that, I was conducting myself as I thought I ought to; later to discover, much of what I thought I ought to be was actually unnecessary.

I have been greatly blessed during the course of my life for which I am immensely grateful. But I cannot deny the fact that, interlaced amongst it all, I took upon myself mental and emotional battles and struggles which I need not have labored and warred. A type of laboring and warring, a tugging of the true self against the ideal professed self that many women face today; operating within a realm of expectation, which in turn becomes the perceived truth. I believe women too often accept circumstance as it appears and as presented, rather than explore alternatives; therefore, settling for the expected over the preferred.

Within "normal" circumstances, we all have the freewill of choice. Sometimes however, we don't fully realize over which choices we actually have dominion. Often, women negate choice, and instead go along with the expected. They alter their mindset to accept something other than what is actually desired and fail to recognize the factor of choice is almost always present. But, to repeatedly ignore choice and disregard personal needs and desires will eventually impact mental and emotional well-being.

Mindset makes or breaks, enlarges or limits. A mindset to conquer all, to do all, and to be all can prove to be one to break rather than make. You become so absorbed in responsibilities and other attributing factors, while mainly striving to measure up to a role perceived outside of self; the superwoman; the fallacy; wearing and tearing down the body, mind and spirit.

There was a time when I too tried to do it all as I perceived a "strong" and "total woman" is supposed to do. Engaging full time employment, trying to maintain the house in tip-top condition, preparing meals on schedule, obliging the wishes of others, going here and there, and the list continues. Then at the end of the day, I was just ready to collapse from exhaustion, my mind overwhelmed. This happened day after day.

During that time, my thoughts were that, a woman is to do as a woman is supposed to do, regardless. Continuing this trend, point by point, I arrived at a place where daily living was becoming stagnant, patterned, predictable, and in some ways, paralyzing. Outwardly I was a tower of strength, but inwardly, the inner-being was weakening bit

44

by bit. At first, I didn't realize it was happening. I was too focused on the expected and the model. My mindset was to follow through with what I thought was required as woman.

The occurring of such a mindset had been years in the making. Patterned behavior had been etched in my mind by previous training and examples. I went about life performing as I had seen, as I had heard, and as I thought I was supposed to. My thought pattern wasn't so different than most women I associated. They talked and complained of similar concerns. Yet, we continued the trend anyway. We apparently felt compelled to measure up to the "ideal model"; but why?

Women are genuinely appreciative and grateful for their families. They love their families and want to do good for them. Most women I associate with fall into this category; they are grateful, appreciative and loving; unquestionably. But, within this lot, only a few express joyfulness and contentment in self as an individual. When I examine my own personal circle of friends, the list is short in number of women that is content and joyous in self. And if you were to examine your own circle of friends, how many can you say are joyous and content with self in their day-to-day lives? Not in outward accomplishments and productivity, but in self as an individual, aside from all the other.

Being nurturers, women are busy concentrating on everyone else's needs, wants and even their demands. She has tendency to believe that is her purpose. Others tend to believe it as well. As she rallies around them, she doesn't get rallied. But to live day-to-day denying self and failing to capture contentment within self is an unwholesome way to exist. I strongly feel there are many women experiencing a similar kind of unwholesome lifestyle, and many struggle day after day to attain inner-peace. I believe many are boxed in a role and don't know how to become unboxed; silently struggling, just warring - true self against ideal self.

I am not ashamed to say, I faced such struggle for years; inner-tugging. Somehow over time, it softens your voice of expression; not passively, but devotedly; and not coerced but submission. And for the longest, I didn't really understand my quandary, or even why I was experiencing such a dilemma. I even questioned if I had a right to feel what I was feeling. Thinking something was wrong with me, questioning if I should do anything about it or just remain silent. I thought that all women were supposed to perform similarly. Aren't we supposed to do what is expected of us regardless of our personal feelings? Aren't we supposed to make sure everyone else is taken care of? Aren't we supposed to overlook self? Mindset and perception are powerful forces.

Trying to make sense of it all, and in sharing my thoughts and feelings with those closest to me, it didn't seem to connect, because my outward appearance portrayed differently than what I was trying to communicate. Outwardly, I appeared solid and without a care. Outwardly, I didn't appear in personal conflict, or to have reason to experience personal conflict. Just because something appears all okay, doesn't mean it is.

When the ones you're reaching out to don't seem to get it, and question your reasoning because what they see in you doesn't match what you are saying to them, you just slither back under your rock and quiet down. Then you keep things to yourself and try to figure it all out on your own; or you simply continue to complain to your friends, the same friends which are experiencing similar concerns, each of you taking a turn in the complaint arena, exhaling a bit, but at the end of the day, continuing on as is.

Another element to consider is that there's also a matter of pride. Prideful women will avoid the appearance that all is not well at all cost. It's something about women and their pride; we allow pride to keep us from speaking what is real while holding on to appearances. What appears as truth overshadows the actual truth. On the outside we portray as if we are "all that" but on the inside, we're wondering – "who am I really."

Keeping it real, nourishes the inner-person; the soul. Ask yourself, what happens to any living being when it does not receive proper nourishment? Does it thrive to potential? No. So, understand that it's the same with you. And the only one that has ultimate control to make sure that you receive proper thriving nutrients is you. Realize what it is that will make you healthy in mind, body and spirit? What is needed for you to be joyous in self? Answer this question – to yourself.

As I look back, it is obvious to me now that for years I chased the wrong goal. And, it seems like the goal post kept moving further and further away as I chased it. I was aiming in the wrong direction. I was in the ball game, but I was running hard and fast in the wrong direction on the playing field. I knew it wasn't quite the way I needed to go, but I felt it was proper to go in that direction, even if the play strategy was designed for another player.

I followed suit with the proposed game plan anyway, going in a direction I perceived a woman is to mirror. So, I continued to chase that "predetermined" goal and dream. Until, and it was over time, I realized I had to establish a few game rules of my own. Not only to change the game, but also to become my own coach and designer of the plays. I decided I was going to run the field going in a direction of my choice; a direction mapped out especially for me.

Inner conflict and struggle, especially when silent, are powerful forces of negativity. But women feed into negativity by revealing only what they want others to see, and participate in game play when they don't agree with the game strategy. We disguise reality whereas conditions appear to be one way when they are actually another. We become crafted in projecting the opposite of what we actually feel; the essence of our true feelings. Why do we believe we need to do this? Why not just express what is, as it is?

It is like we operate within a type of secret code of behavior, and within the confines of these encoded messages, we establish a certain mindset. We perceive we must take care of the needs of all others; we must put ourselves last, we must maintain a spotless home, we must maintain order in the home, we must maintain attractiveness, we must maintain an appealing weight, etc., etc., and etc. Who established these codes of ethics? Yet women still try to attain the unattainable, failing to realize the harm being incurred while trying to measure up. Man

48

doesn't put such stipulations on himself. Why does woman feel the need to do so?

I too, for the longest, operated within this same established code of behavior. I was a strong-willed person by nature-no doubt. Yet, I allowed my perception of what was required of my role to hinder me from ensuring my own well-being; placing myself last in the spectrum of things. I didn't really agree with this position, but I accepted it. Now, sad to say, I realize I had become a "role" conformist; one walking in the shoes of a devout customary woman. But I wasn't totally customary. Yet I accepted it.

It wasn't a conscious effort to do so; it simply evolved. I got caught up in doing for family, trying to oblige requests, needing to take care of household affairs, needing to meet perceived appointment, serve on this and that committee, participate in special projects, and on and on; sacrificing self-time after time. All along, thinking I was doing as required of my role.

Eventually however, as life happens, I recognized it wasn't working well for me. I was beginning to see signs of detriment-physically, emotionally and mentally. In addition to that, I felt like I was stacking more and more onto an already over-stacked deck. In time, and as I continued in self-talk, I began to understand I hadn't taken time to develop me. I realized my personal interests and needs had been held captive, by my own mindset. I had not allowed myself to experience certain freedoms, to enjoy certain interests, or simply handle matters in a manner of my choosing. Why hadn't I? Although external elements had influence upon my actions, the force that had hindered me, mostly was me. I placed restraints on myself, I allowed myself to be cornered and pigeonholed.

It was my mindset holding me captive and in "hiding"; perceptions which I had allowed to distort what was realistically required of me. Along the way, I hadn't exercised liberty to handle me amid my circumstances in a manner that rendered the best for my over-all wellness. I had allowed my distinctiveness to be overtaken by the mold of tradition and expectation. Aspects of me that represented my individuality had gone somewhere far, far, left.

It wasn't so much what was going on outside of me that was concerning, but more, what was happening from within. I simply hadn't held true to self. I had bought into the "expected" preset model of how a woman is supposed to conduct herself. But fortunately, along the way, I awaken, and I began to understand that self also has to be in right order and a main focus. Not just appear well and fit, but to actually be well and fit.

There comes a time when you're faced with a need to make changes and do things differently. The first place to start looking is within self. It's important to meet self, face-to-face. There is where authenticity lies, and also may answers. That is if you can be honest enough with yourself to receive your truths. And in order to be raw honest with self, I believe, is something a woman has difficulty handling. We don't want to own up to some of the answers. We don't want to expose the façade. We become masters of camouflage.

In general, I don't believe maturing girls are taught and encouraged to understand self. More so, girls are encouraged and influenced to meet expectations outside of self; to become givers and supporters to others. In the process, her identity becomes somewhat diminished; almost like becoming disarmed. But one shouldn't extend self to another and other causes to the point of experiencing personal upheaval. When you do, ultimately, in its midst, you become hidden; busily doing everything, for whatever reason you view as important at the time.

I discovered myself to be that case in point. Hardly ever did I place myself at the top of my own to-do-list. And somewhere in the mindset, I thought it would be selfish to do so. I guess I felt time was on my side, and sooner or later I would get around to me. But time doesn't actually stand still, does it? Time moves on and we cannot recapture those moments. Over time, you discover that busy works and a busy lifestyle are no substitute for personal joy and self-contentment.

No doubt, everyone has to sacrifice at points in time. That is life and is to be expected. But it does not need to be one sided, and become the norm of one's daily operations. When that is the case, those around you grow accustomed to your sacrifices. And as you continue to sacrifice, it becomes their norm, and over time, a norm expected of you.

Of course, it has to be put in a right prospective. No one needs to focus on self at all times. We must consider others in our lives as important. But self has to be placed on the priority list, and that fact has to be established amongst the whole. Women must view themselves as a priority; expect to be viewed as a priority; and do so without feelings of guilt.

I was fortunate to arrive at a point of realization. And trust me, it was a process. But I accepted the fact that my heart and head were going in opposite directions, performing one way, but actually desiring another. It takes honesty to arrive at this point. After facing a few facts, I began to understand the nature of my interpersonal tugs; and following, I began to adjust my perceptions and mindset.

It takes courage and honesty to acknowledge truth to self. And women are so accustomed to disguising their feelings to a point of becoming lost to what is actually real. But I figured out that heart and head must come together and establish a sense of oneness and balance. It is this sense of balance which my soul craved. Yes, I loved my family; yes, I loved my home; yes, I wanted a comfortable and attractive environment; and yes, I wanted to maintain it all. But I would go forth differently.

It's not a simple task to become reacquainted with the true self when you've gone far left for so long, and you're

no longer sure who the true self really is. But I continued my quest to find out, and step by step and in due course, I arrived at a point of rediscovery. It is crucial to know yourself and it is equally important to be true to self.

It has been through God's amazing grace, self-actualization and assertion; I have overcome the silent inner-struggle and its shadow. I got on a path which has led to a most beautiful ray of light; inner-peace and joyfulness from within. I was able to rearrange a few things in my life, adjust a few perceptions, adjust mindset, and allow myself certain liberties I had long ago forfeited.

I wish the same for you. But keep in mind, most of the answers and solutions lie within self. Examine your mindset and perceptions. Understand them. Tweak, adjust and renew. Release the strongholds which keep you captive. It doesn't mean you will lose anything, but you most certainly will gain something-strength, liberty and courage to blossom out from hiding.

Chapter Four
Devotedly Submitted
The Heart of Her

Thus far, I have spoken of a woman in general, while sharing a bit of my own inner-struggle. It is obvious by now; I believe there is a certain woman existing which is in dire need to LIVE. That this particular woman over periods of time has allowed the essence of her true nature to be tucked away, embedded deep inside for reasons and circumstances involving her unique and accepted lifestyle. Now, let's delve deeper into who she is and further understand why she is who she is; the core and the heart of her.

First understand that social status, ethnicity, creed, race or age, doesn't classify this particular woman. Her determining factor isn't a single aspect, but rather, a culmination of different facets and phases, many images and messages, direct and indirect, effectively binding her to an ethical code of action. She's astute in many forms, and likely, she doesn't exhibit any obvious signs of a private struggle. Yet inwardly, she struggles. Although she may feel she's alone in such a struggle; let it be known there are many like her (like you) amongst us. But, since she believes she's alone, she hides within; her thoughts, desires, and voice.

Circumstances may vary from woman to woman, so her outward description isn't a fixed one. Since women are good at hiding what's real, this particular one may not be distinguishable with a mere glance, but she's there amongst the crowd. There is however, one thing that connects them, one thing that's in common with others, a common thread shared between them, which is her essence; unique and defining attributes tucked away claimed and overtaken by obligations, responsibilities, and expectations, whereas to become disconnected, and even desensitized to her own needs and desires.

Even when circumstances are unfavorable, this particular woman generally manages situations well, generally looks well, performs well, and goes about her daily duties in what appears to be the normal fashion, using her God-given talents, gifts and compassion to serve. She stays busy nurturing and giving relentlessly to those she loves and to activities to which she is committed. Amid it all, and as time passes, it escapes her to experience the fullness of life for self. As a result, her true spirit becomes hidden deep inside as if in waiting; waiting for the opportune time to resurface. Although, on the surface she portrays all is well, but beneath the surface there is unrest.

Years in to the process, and sooner or later, her soul silently begin to cry out, "What about me! ME!" But circumstances dictate she remains busy, so she does, enriching the lives of others. Unfortunately, she gives minimal time to nurturing her own true needs, and those near and dear to her are not in tuned to what she actually needs. They want too much of her for themselves. She's a valuable resource to them. Inadvertently, they become blinded to the fact that she too is in need, and that she too requires nurturing and up-building. Inevitably, as she continues this course, she begins to notice she is losing herself in the midst, and she starts to feel an overwhelming sensation to restore, retrieve, and more importantly, to release; she wishes to return to self.

Nevertheless, weary though she may become, she is loyal, so she continues her routine, while her essence as a distinct individual, silently and gradually shifts into a position of hiding. She wishes to engage her own interests and desires, but doesn't really know how to, while at the same time remain loyal to family, responsibilities, and traditions without distracting from what she feels is required of her as woman.

Sadly, however, after going through the motions for an extended time, her true nature becomes unrecognizable to others, and eventually, unrecognizable even to herself. Bit by bit, she surrendered passions that once breathed exuberance into her soul, and without a doubt, she feels void within. There is an empty space, and its affect is suffocating; hindering character free flow. Yet, she continues on as her essence becomes suppressed, because she is functioning in opposition of what is soulfully desired. Over time, a false identity invades her presence, gains control and takes over.

Most certainly, there are women amongst us, who are experiencing such a lifestyle; wives, moms, caregivers, those of religion of varied walks; and others of various circumstances and situations. I used to think it was the older, old-school, married, and traditional woman to which this applied, but now, I've learned that's not the case. The more I delved into this matter, the more I discovered its far-reaching range. Surprisingly, I found it to extend to the young as well as older and to the single as well as the married; because it's a mindset rather than social classification.

Regardless, what is certain about this particular woman, older or younger, single or married, is that she dedicates and devotes her life to acts of pleasing and fulfilling the needs of others. Furthermore, those others have become dependent on her dedication and sacrifices. It serves as the cohesive factor that makes it possible for their environments to operate smoothly.

She is bound to her beliefs, and dutifully strives to fulfill her expected role. Because of her love and nurturing nature, she becomes dedicated to fulfilling this role at the cost of her own personal joyfulness. But eventually, she becomes consumed and her daily existence becomes a huge blanket, full of expectations and obligations. Daily she is captured and gets entwined; becoming more and more buried underneath and more hidden within. Amidst all her doing, she neglects to take time to experience those things in life that afford her self-fulfillment. Still, she doesn't resent having the responsibilities she has, nor does she resent serving the people she serves; she loves them. She is devotedly submitted and committed.

Generally, this particular woman receives surface gratification and is admired by family and others for her efforts and good works. In part, this surface gratification is what keeps her going. However, eventually and unavoidably, after years of denying self, she gradually changes into someone she doesn't recognize. She has set aside certain interests and aspirations and perceived it selfish to indulge in interests of the heart. As a matter of fact, her established routine doesn't allow time for self-indulgences; there is simply not enough time and too much to do. On the other hand, she observes others enjoying areas of life she too desires to experience. It becomes almost like viewing a movie and she's merely a spectator,

not a player. But she busily provides good works, so life moves on as she grows older and more tired.

Silently, she begins to ask herself: Who am I? Where am I headed? At what point did I go into "hiding", and why? She finds herself desiring answers and begins to feel a deep desire to find answers that will enable her to return to self. If she's daring, she will begin the search to retrieve self. She realizes she doesn't want to continue as is and continue to allow her essence to remain in hiding.

Some time ago, years ago now, I was all too familiar with these feelings. For years, I allowed myself to exist as though I was hidden from myself. Not that I wasn't aware of my feelings and my heart's desires - I was. However, I allowed daily functioning and certain influences to overtake me. I became interweaved with matters and actions I believed were necessary at the time. So, I would buckle under and yield to the demand of circumstances and do what I perceived was required of me. I took on a face that really wasn't my face, an attitude that really wasn't genuine to my nature, and a voice that was subdued. What, how and when all became circumstantial. As a result, my deepest wishes slithered into hiding. Nonetheless, I was handling things as I felt was required of me.

It didn't really interfere with my overall daily performance. I performed well in many areas and was highly productive. But, as time passed, as I began to understand what was happening from within, and as I gained boldness to face my reality, I realized I could not continue the same. For years, I had sensed my true self fading- fading- fading. It was as if the essence itself was slowly draining from my being.

I remembered, prior to this point, I had actually appreciated the *individual* who once embodied my nature, the one who rejoiced in laughter, possessed an adventurous

spirit, enjoyed spirited conversation, appreciated time with a good book, showed excitement about learning new things, prided herself on physical fitness, and more. But somehow, engaging in those things became less and less important, as I busily performed doing whatever. I began to wonder where that person had gone. And I missed the spirit of that person.

I had surrendered more and more of myself to traditions, expectations, and causes of which I was involved. My distinctiveness was actually disappearing as if I was tucked in a barrel and more and more was being dumped in on me. I was becoming more and more concealed, more and more hidden.

As a wife, traditionally, a woman takes on the ways and desires of her husband. That's simply what she is expected to do. That's the understanding of a "good" wife's role; she plunges into the matters of her husband. He expects her to do so, and she obliges. It is not so much of a concern whether or not she's interested in those matters, or even that her individuality is likely to become masked in the process. But because she's his wife, his interests are to become primary. As his wife, she's to build him up and support him in becoming all that he is to be.

As a mother, she continuously forsakes self so her children receive what they need, when they need, how they need and as often as they need. I don't believe children see their mother as one with needs of her own. They just see a mother, one to love them, one to supply needs, and one to be available whenever they need.

In the case of a wife and a mother, her output often outweighs input. It appears so much relies on her actions and sacrifices; and she performs accordingly; placing

herself in a position of sacrifice that no one else in the family is expected to hold. She not only sacrifices in actions, but also in mind. A woman often acts as though she doesn't see what she actually sees, she doesn't feel what we actually feel, and repeatedly ignores what is actually happening as though it's not really happening. Understand too, it's not a matter of her being passive or timid; although it may appear that way. Women are generally expressive; pointing out what they want in a given situation. But, when she accepts the opposite in spite of, then becomes expected of her to accept in spite of.

Within my own family unit, I would generally express my wishes and needs. In fact, I thought of myself as tenaciously spirited in this regard, even to the point of personal frustration. But to express yourself is simply not enough if what you are expressing is not bringing about positive results. In fact, if you are not enforcing what you say, it just becomes a matter of spitting out words, and after a while, your words lose power. This is what happens in the lives of women. We lose voice power because we compromise what we say and mean.

What stops a woman from making certain she gets what she needs? Not necessarily what she wants, which in part, is also important. But why are women so compromising and so accepting to the point of neglecting their own needs? With me, in cases, even when expressing myself with those in my family unit, often my requests weren't delivered as desired. What I desired may have differed from what another family member wanted or needed. And since I had taken on an "accepting position", many times my requests were modified, delayed, delivered in part, or overlooked for the time being. I know now, it happened that way mostly

because I didn't see need to enforce what I said, nor enforce my requirements. Rather, it was understood I would accept and compromise. I was woman –isn't that what we are supposed to do?

Family members look upon wife/mother/caregiver as being an instrument to help meet their wishes and needs, but not necessarily to be a recipient of the same. For the most part, she is glad to be such an instrument to her loved ones. But in doing so, since there's only so much time in a day, and only so much energy to expend within a day, she foregoes her own wishes and needs. And because she does, she is taken for granted by others. Whether intentional or not, the result is the same. She is the giver more so than the receiver. She becomes largely satisfied in daily accomplishments, and the family is satisfied she has accomplished what is meaningful to them.

She often accepts her family's wishes and needs over her own because of her devotion. I did. But actually, in doing so I projected that my sacrificial actions were the standard. I would support their agenda and allow my own to be overlooked – in devotion to my family. So often, a wife/mother's agenda gets lost in the crevice. And, if you think about it, a woman is known by her husband and children's agendas- so and so's wife, or so and so's mother. Often time there is where her identity lies and she accepts that position. But when or if she becomes dishearten with that identity, as her only identity, and feels the need to voice her complaint in that regard, her family simply looks upon it as if she needs a moment of "me-time". Just let her get it all out and she'll be alright. To them, it's a matter of providing her time to get through the episode, so things can return to their normal. They care about her, so, they show their caring by listening, and backing off for a spell, hoping she hurriedly gets through the episode so things can be as they were.

Simply listening to her and giving her a moment doesn't actually cure the problem. It only serves to band-aid the issue; appearing as though she's being heard and her issues addressed. As a result, they expect her to be as she generally is – doing and accepting. To take it a step further, if she's really agitated about an issue, again, acting differently than her usual "accepting self", then her agitated state is looked upon as though it's just "that time of the month", as if she doesn't have real concerns or real issues but rather an emotional moment. As if "that time of the month" could be the only factor attributing to why a woman acts as she acts at a given moment. Therefore, the meaning behind her words is most definitely not understood, and more importantly, her issues are not truly resolved. So, life moves on as usual.

The irony in my own situation is that, it wasn't I didn't feel appreciated in the midst of it all, I did, and I was; it wasn't that I didn't feel respected, I was. But I do feel, that many of the times, my good intended nature was taken for granted - my sacrificial mode of operation was viewed as the routine practice. However, we women place ourselves in this position; performing as we think is required, allowing others to impose expectations, and sacrificing ourselves, when most of the time it is unnecessary. But we perceive it as necessary and perform accordingly.

Usually, this stance is not forced upon us. It hadn't been forced upon me. I had simply followed a mode of tradition. I hadn't considered it a priority to make certain my expressions were heard, received, and enforced. I was so devotedly submitted. I hadn't asserted my own right. But I didn't realize that to be devotedly submitted didn't require the need to forfeit my assertive privileges.

All along though, I should have been doing just that, asserting. I had possessed such a trait once upon a time, but somewhere along the way, as I took on obligations and responsibilities, I misplaced that part of me. Significant character attributes were missing from my daily functioning, and laid dormant, and became an inactive part of my character.

Over time, because those traits were inactive, yet in my spirit, I began to grieve for those elements. Initially, I didn't recognize it as grief, but I was experiencing a sense of loss. Since those distinctive elements were inactive, they hadn't been fully developed along the way. But life moves on anyway and we just keep moving along with it, failing to grab hold of fullness. Resulting, we grab hold of a pseudo-satisfaction, and claim it as truth. Women are notorious in doing so – right, settling for one idea while emotionally and soulfully desiring another.

Understand that, early in training, girls fail to grasp the understanding that they are to live self-fulfilled lives, even in the midst of taking on a family and other responsibilities. Girls at young age are taught to be nurturers and supporters of others. And that in part is okay. But we aren't taught to nurture and support ourselves equally. Therefore, we take on the mental weight of needing to keep everything else together, and in order. But really, we should be taught to do the same for ourselves. We don't need to view it as required to surrender self in order to love and care for another.

For me, somehow in the midst of my daily living, I became fixated to the flow of traditions, expectations, and the perceived need to sacrifice, and accepted this flow. I

felt pleased with what I was doing for family, home, employment and other projects. But there came a time I began to realize, I didn't have to adhere according to the established script and that, I could actually write my own script, personally designed.

It is possible to become a dedicated wife, mother, professional, involved in church and community, yet be dedicated to self. Devotion shouldn't cancel out your own personal zeal, nor should it soften your voice. You shouldn't need to position self lastly in the line-up. And if you are one to view yourself as a priority in your life, it doesn't mean you are less devoted to others. Why not just line everything up more even-keeled from the start? Others can enjoy and appreciate what you have to offer, and you can appreciate self in what and how you offer it. You don't have to do all things perfectly at all the time. In fact, you don't have to do all things; be selective.

You are personally responsible for your own well-being and happiness. Accept that. Own it. You must appreciate your own thoughts, feelings and actions as you allow yourself to appreciate others. Don't allow circumstances to siege your essence, or allow it to be taken for granted or misused.

As you lend yourself to the development of others, and support their efforts, you must also do the same for self. God has created each of us to be unique. He creates each of us as a distinct individual with our own talents, gifts and interests. And that is exactly how we need to be, even among the whole, separate and different. It's similar to a fingerprint, separate and different from all others. And because you assume a "role" with many responsibilities and obligations, it doesn't mean you have to relinquish

individuality, and abandon the many facets that make you who you are.

Women, as we devotedly submit ourselves to others; and we should, for this is what love and devotion is all about. But amid it all, we should also be devotedly committed to our own individuality - engaging special interests, expressing uniqueness, and asserting our voice with the insistence of fair consideration. Your voice, desires, goals, skills, and talents, are all inclusive of the total person. We should not ignore our unique make-up.

As we incorporate others into our lives, as we develop and experience our families, and as we engage other involvements, we shouldn't stop being who we started out being. That person should be developed and enhanced. We must project individuality and liberties should be respected, and will be engaged; conveying that as I serve and nurture you, I will also serve and nurture myself. And furthermore, as I serve and nurture you, I require it to be reciprocated.

We must embrace the difference of self, and not alienate it, surrender it, and most definitely, not hide it. Why not experience the total you?

If self-fulfillment in life is to be achieved, then you must grab hold of it. Simply put, you should fully live life as you live the life given you, not merely exist. Don't feel you cannot serve others and grow in self at the same time. You can and you should. Ask God to guide and bless what He has placed in you.

Chapter Five
Hiding?

Hiding? Why have I continuously used this term to convey feelings and actions? What does "hiding" mean in this context? Why have I associated this term and concept with my own experience? What is its implication? And, why is the term "hiding" used as the center-focus of my theme and platform?

In response, I would like to explain its meaning, its inferences, and the process which brought me to this account. Once explained, I believe it will provide you an understanding of the premise of the hiding concept as being presented. So come along with me as I unfurl the meaning of "hiding" – as I see it.

In retrospect – during the course of my journey in finding my way back to self, and of unveiling personal feelings and precepts, I came to terms with certain realities. I quickly realized it wasn't all about external circumstances. As well as having to examine matters outwardly, I also had to go inward to face some things. I had to probe deep within and conduct an honest and thorough self-check. It was important to do so in order to decipher the fallacies; separating true from the not-so-true.

My self-check revealed many things, and among the revelations, I received understanding of how and why I had fallen short in maintaining my own welfare; and realized I had become somewhat character-malnourished. Over the years I had allowed myself to become boxed-in, and had only permitted myself to experience life in part; a fraction of what I could have been indulging and enjoying.

Certainly, this is no different than what many women experience. Many women experience a similar existence of engaging a fraction of what and who represents the total person. However prior, I hadn't considered myself to be one of those women. But I was because I had not invested in myself to the degree that brought about overall well-nourishment.

As time passed and my quest continued, I examined my total mode of operation from a practical point of view. It became obvious to me I had assumed an identity that wasn't quite me, and I had substituted my essence for one of an assigned role.

As I journeyed on, I began to weigh actual requirements against perceptual requirements; a fundamental process to undergo and a fundamental factor to grasp in understanding the "hiding" concept; to understand why it is a woman permits herself to hide and the contributing factors; facts and truths, and necessary versus the unnecessary.

It became apparent I had been overshadowed and tangled in daily undertakings. I was busy fortifying more outward endeavors, while neglecting the inward. I was so busy performing between home, work, and other obligations that I hardly had time to even think about my own interests and desires. I was involved in this and that, going here and there, pleasing this one and that one, obliging in this area and another, and compromising here and there, while the days whirled by; days eventually turned into years. I wondered how am I to wean myself from all that are keeping me inside the whirlwind.

As the process continued and I began to understand more of the whys of my actions and long-established precepts, I began to release myself from some of the preconceived "expected" mandates and open my mind to other options as I searched my truths.

There are times in discovering your truths when you need to have a conversation with yourself and call it as it is even if it pinches a bit. Then, you need to allow yourself freedom to accept you as you are at that point in time. However, to shake off preconceived mandates you have been adhering to for so long, is easier said than done. It really takes practice to do things differently. At first it feels a bit strange, because what has been your usual action and reaction is now trying to undo itself. You still feel like you should do a certain thing, yet you don't want to, but you feel as though you ought to regardless of your desire not to. So, there will be that tug for a while until you adjust to the desired change.

It is unfortunate though, when you lay aside the very attributes that represent who you are as your own person. For the sake of being "a true woman", and. "super woman", many women perceive it is necessary to do just that; to put aside the very traits which offer personal joy and self-contentment.

A woman tends to have this inner-notion that circumstances will fall in their rightful order at the appointed time. She believes by happenstance; everything will majestically arrange and align itself as desired; that

69

what is personally needed and desired will eventually come to fruition. In the fog of such a notion, as she with hope waits for this arrangement to majestically take place, efforts to assure its happening are abandoned. As time passes, she becomes older and somewhat disenchanted with what is, she notices time and opportunities are passing by. In realizing this majestic happening may never occur, fear and regret begin to flood her presence. She begins to question if such an alignment will ever take place. Unfortunately, in hopelessness, she simply surrenders to the status quo.

At a point, I too questioned the timing of this presumably majestic happening, since it wasn't occurring. And to simply wait and hope didn't make it happen either. I understood if I wanted this alignment to occur, I needed to make changes, seeing the majestic happening wasn't likely to occur. I would have to become proactive. I needed to apply action to my hope. *"Faith without works is dead." James 2:20.*

I wanted to recover the parts of me I had allowed to fall by the wayside. I wanted to retrieve traits I had forsaken in the midst of it all. I wanted the person which represented those traits to be front and center and engaged in my life. I wanted my inner-spirit rejuvenated.

In regard to the saying "take time to smell the roses", it became clear to me I had neglected to take the needed time. Not only had I neglected to take time to smell the roses, I hadn't even taken time to identify which roses I particularly liked. Even with roses in hand, I hadn't taken advantage of the time to actually smell and savor their sweet fragrance and beauty. It is the savoring which is most important, not mere possession.

Case in point - when ladies receive beautiful flowers, we go as far as to place them in a special vase and position them in a special spot to be admired. We are pleased to receive them, but shortly after receiving them, we may soon forget the roses are in our presence. They become a part of the scenery, and their special appeal fades into their surroundings. The next thing we know the blossoms have withered and it's time to throw them away. We allow their beauty and sweet savor to escape us.

Aren't women much like this? We become like the roses as we allow our fundamental nature to fade away into the scenery of our lives, later to wither away. We allow the beauty and sweet savor of our distinctiveness to escape. We allow ourselves to be viewed as part of the scenery; aware of our presence but the appreciation of our presence fades.

For me, as I performed within predetermined mores, and compromising my own wishes, I knew that in the backdrop, my fundamental nature was disappearing. I was present, yet I felt absent, and I was noticeable, yet I felt hidden. After self-assessing, having examined my thoughts, feelings and actions, then allowing myself to acknowledge those thoughts, feelings and actions, I realized if I was to return to self, to recapture my fundamental nature, I would need to claim ownership and accountability of what I wanted for myself.

It is said we all have at least two sides to our character make-up. Being so, women often allow the most spirited and adventurous side to remain hidden within self. This hidden side is generally experienced in the mind; mostly in daydreams. Women are notorious daydreamers, and the dreams very often remain within. But, if that vigorous and adventurous side is alive in the mind, and it is one which self could appreciate and enjoy, then why not allow those attributes to surface and be experienced? Why not live it out?

Why do we allow a most desired side of self to remain hidden within? Why not integrate all sides of what represents your true spirit? Why do women allow the "perceived role of conduct" to become the primary governor of behavior? Why not just be the person that lives within as well as the one portrayed without, that is, if the one portrayed without is actually representative of who you are. Why not exercise character balance?

To achieve such character balance can be challenging. The degree of challenge is determined by how deeply embedded preconceived thoughts, actions and circumstances are. Since women are trained to be helpers, nurturers and supporters, therefore, we take on much that is not our own. The more we take on of others, the more difficult it is to determine what is yours versus what belongs to someone else. After years and years of performing a certain way, thoughts and actions become engrained.

It isn't easy to make this separation when there are so many parallel strands operating together. Some strands are more closely interweaved than others, therefore, even more difficult to separate. After all, we're not only trying to unravel our own precepts with understanding, but also, the precepts of others which have impinged upon us.

For me, it became important to make this separation. I wanted to understand the process which brought me to a point of self-surrender. Why had I felt it necessary to compromise my fundamental nature? What had actually been the controlling factors? What was my part in the scope of it all? What in fact was I feeling, or not feeling? I wanted to give myself freedom to explore and acknowledge what those feelings actually were. I needed to validate those feelings, to claim ownership, and then, do as needed to resolve the issues concerning those feelings; therefore, altering my actions.

Why hadn't I allowed myself such freedom, I don't know. Why had I contained my wishes? Why had I allowed the outer-me to be more in order than the inner-me? Why had I not secured my contentment? Not a circumstantial joyfulness and contentment, but a way-of-life joyfulness and contentment. Why had I operated under restrictions; restrictions which needed not have been the case. There were no outside forces to mandate such restrictions, yet I operated as though there were. Of course, there were influences, but not controls.

Continuing to filter through my thoughts and feelings – such an awesome process – it became evident I indeed had hidden significant portions of my true self; veiling certain passions, yearnings, aspirations, joys, and yes liberty; good old self-liberty. It was an evolving occurrence no doubt, yet one which I allowed to take place. What I had been doing to manage things outwardly had far exceeded what I had been doing to manage self inwardly.

During this process, the word "hide" kept coming to me, and I began to personally associate it to my own actions and behavior. It became a focal point. As I explored the word "hide", I discovered meanings such as: to hold back, to conceal, to cover up, to shield, to disguise, to sweep under, to blot out, and to lie low. Wow! My feelings were confirmed. These phrases actually conveyed my actions, or more so, the lack thereof. These words became a comparative representation for which I could begin to place things in perspective. The word "hide" and its connotations served as the core element for me to formulate a concept to address a point of view; and to use as a symbolic description to exemplify a frame of mind and a standard of living.

In using this concept as a descriptive framework, it serves to give understanding regarding a state of existence; my state of existence; a mindset and a mental and emotional place I once resided. This conceptual description, of course, will not be found in any other resource regarding the same point of reference. I have simply coined the phrase and concept as a meaningful expression to use as a descriptive comparison.

In using my personally coined phrase in this context, it is my hope it will offer clarity and an in-depth look into the primary focus for my entire writing. Accordingly, *"hiding"* in the context used hereafter, is to reference and signify a state of existence, and to be viewed as–a *perpetual state of mind-conditioning, which leads to withdrawal, denial and confinement of the True Self, having been influenced by environment, personal experiences, lifestyle demands, and traditional views.* This is the point of reference that "hide/hiding" is used in the remainder of my writing.

In reference to this phrase and concept, understand that "hiding" is not to be looked upon as a way to gain control or manipulate another. It is also important to understand it is not to be viewed as a means for which one can retreat from insecurities and fears. It's not an intended course of action. Rather, "hiding" is to be viewed as an unintended happening, one which creep in inch by inch, bit by bit, and layer by layer; one which eventually, gains dominance of mindset; an evolving process which inadvertently, influences one's actions, and ultimately, the letting go of distinctive attributes and personal desires and wishes. Those attributes and wishes are shifted into a hiding mode. They are out of view and perhaps out of mind. I've offered a lot of words, I know, but if you would allow yourself to digest them, the concept will make sense.

Although this "hiding" concept may be applied to man and woman alike, because both to a point may deal with similar issues, but I cannot speak to the perspective of man, only to that of woman. Therefore, as I speak on behalf of woman, this symbolic reference, "hide/hiding", is used to represent a mindset and a lifestyle that many women accept and embody; a lifestyle which in the long run, is very likely to become her adversary.

"Hiding" in and of itself doesn't necessarily hinder productivity or achievement. One can be a great achiever. But it does rob of the fullness of life joys and inhibits the pursuit of inner-peace and emotional well-being. Personal needs and wishes are placed on the back burner as everything and everyone else's are moved to the forefront.

Being so, the inner-self becomes compromised and the true nature is forsaken.

At a point in time, I began to understand that, I was one in "hiding"; assuming a mindset which mapped my directions and dictated my actions. A mindset derived through a number of forces and dynamics forming together-upbringing, training, tradition, and mostly by prototype; examples of the women before me, paving and directing the way. I simply followed suit with their example.

Even though in today's culture, many new and different trends have taken place, but a woman's basic approach to doing things as expected of her remains relatively the same. She in many ways, and for many reasons, continues to do things similarly to that demonstrated by the women of yesterday's circumstances and culture; a standard of living demonstrated by her mom, which had been similar to that of her mom's mom, and her mom's, mom's, mom; therefore she becomes the product of her mom, her grand mom, and great-grand mom; carrying yesterday's approach into present-day; a trend which doesn't promote or support the release of natural tendencies to develop and appreciate individuality. She is trained to be reserved and predictable, while males are trained to explore and release.

There may be many differences between male and female, and rightly so in many ways, but should there be such disparity between the two when it comes to exercising individualism. What makes it okay and natural for a man to exercise his individuality but not for a woman? Even as trends of today have changed, this factor, to a large degree, remains unchanged.

As cultural change occurs, personal viewpoints and positions are to change as well. All of the old simply do not fit with the new. Matter of fact, for a woman, much of the old didn't even fit with the old. Now, as cultural changes take place, the way of doing things must change to meet current times. Adjustments have to be made in order for things to fit their best for all. Woman however, was more accepting of yesterday's terms even though there were disgruntlements, daily living was simpler. Today, with all other involvements, it's almost impossible to operate on yesterday's terms. Now, a woman's approach must shift and reposition for her betterment.

Such needed change can be compared to that of having purchased a dress years earlier, which at the time, it fitted perfectly; loving how it looked and how attractive it made you feel. It was special. Years later, that same dress, having been kept in the closet unworn, waiting for that special event, you go to the closet, pull it out and try it on. What has happened? Even though you may not have gained a pound, it simply does not fit the same. Why? It's because your foundation changed. Certain features changed and shifted as well as the trend in fashion. Now that same dress fits totally different and doesn't have the same appeal. In order to recapture a similar fit and feel, the dress has to be altered. The old will have to be modified to fit the current. It's the same dress, but it needs alteration to fit your current body and adjust to current need and trend. So, it is in the life of today's woman; there are times when we must alter and reshape.

As you go through your own altering and reshaping process, remember there's always the element of choice. The factor of choice in many regards is easily ignored, being overshadowed by the perception of what is believed to be required of the "role" as a "responsible woman". Choice is overlooked as being a viable option and becomes hidden in the course of daily operations.

Remember, choice is always present. The sooner this factor is understood and released into the equation of your life, the sooner you are on a path which leads to becoming a more content individual. Also remember the only one who constrains your element of choice - you. You really don't have to operate in the realm of expectation as predetermined.

As I began to better exercise the element of choice, I accepted I could not and would not continue the predetermined model; solely accepting the predetermined mode and code of conduct. These factors didn't solely determine my individuality. I released myself of certain expected mandates. It became no longer a matter of holding true to the model, but more so a matter of holding true to self.

It wasn't a single act or happening that brought me to this point of breakthrough, it had been a combination of acts and happenings propelling from point to point, finally arriving at a point of understanding. Initially, I had to allow myself to explore my thoughts, feelings, and circumstances, and from that point to gain an understanding of how I wanted to proceed. I had to make some choices to go forward differently. Not to forsake family or other involvements, not to stop doing the things

I was accustomed to doing, but to simply modify my way of doing; to make the necessary changes to meet current times, current circumstances, and current desires.

It requires courage to make forward steps when you are so programmed to stepping sideways. I knew I wanted to establish a lifestyle where I was evident in my own life in a manner satisfying to my spirit; no longer stepping sideways but forward. I had to recapture the joy and inner-harmony I once possessed and even greater. I had never been taught and guided to seek out self. My quest became to come out from hiding and retrieve what made me unique as me; to journey my way back to home in self.

Keep in mind, hiding is a state that develops over time, stemming from different circumstances and originating at different points. Its evidence varies from one woman to another. Remember, it isn't an intended happening; it simply evolves. My hiding journey began early on, starting with training and influences of my upbringing. The era of my upbringing was a key component. It was a time when a child, especially a girl child, was continuously told what to do and how to do, and personal opinion was rarely invited or considered.

As you examine your own situation, you too may find your journey into hiding began as a child as well. For someone else, the starting point might have been during early adulthood, filtering through life, but was influenced to go opposite the desired way. For another, perhaps it began during the course of marriage, while establishing a family, where dreams and goals became misplaced. It could have been a matter of serving as a long-term caregiver for an ailing or dependent family member, and it was perceived necessary to place personal desires and needs on hold. Even though the hiding start point may vary; the resulting effect however, is very similar.

Young or older, married or single, conventional or modern-day, whatever the particular situation may be and regardless of the initiation point, if you are one on the "hiding" path, there are commonalities among those experiencing it; feelings, interests, aspirations and voice are sacrificed and concealed as the inner-self goes into a form of hiding. All the time perceiving you are doing what is required and expected. I guess to some, "hiding" is looked upon as a form of character weakness, but now, looking back on it, it is actually a strand of character strength.

Although a woman in hiding can be a very influential force, a tower of strength, a weak point is that she doesn't feed into self to sustain her overall well-being. She finds herself running on exhaustion - mentally, physically, and emotionally. Still, she continues on this path considering it important to maintain the status quo within the family.

Adversely however, as she continues this path of self-neglect, and this pathway into hiding, she eventually corners herself into an unhealthy position. And sooner or later, she begins to experience inner-warring, her actual performance conflicts with what is actually desired. At a point, the force of this tug becomes one of much turbulence, as the inner-self struggles to force its way out from under the restraints and pressure.

This woman in "hiding" believes all is required of her and believes she's woman enough to do it all. Not only does she feel she's woman enough to do it all, she also believes she's supposed to do it all. It is perceived that once she establishes a family, she is to transform into this other character as if her own characterizing distinctiveness is supposed to simply go away, or be placed on the shelf for future use; a future use that may never come about.

Those who are in such a position can clearly understand and identify with what I am putting into words. For those experiencing "hiding", and in the midst of inner-warring, what I am describing is crystal clear. Isn't it?

Not to minimize any cause or effect, but it's important to understand as you journey out from hiding, you are not to dwell on the whys, but rather understand your position in the whys. Dwelling on the whys will bring about a whole other set of issues. Rather, what is most important for this particular quest and journey is that you first acknowledge the facts you uncover, then after acknowledging, go forth to put something in place to turn it around. Acknowledgement and owning-up gives a certain freedom; to admit what actually pushes us to look at truth. Truth in many regards is freedom.

You are not to focus on assigning blame to yourself or others. That is not the direction to take either. To delve into blaming can become very exhausting and depressing. Blame-dwelling can hamper the progress of going forward and will keep you stuck. Besides, it is you you're trying to figure out. Figuring out you is enough. Don't invest your time and effort in trying to figure out the whys of someone else.

I do acknowledge though, past experiences influence and shape behavior, and we somewhat become a product of our experiences. So, I do not wish to diminish any impacting results of past experiences, or any unfortunate acts inflicted upon you. Still, to focus on who's the blame for your circumstance is not an essential element in finding the path that will lead to your healing. For your own well-being, shake it all off and start anew. It may not be an easy thing to do, but it important to release and let go. Don't allow someone else's actions to hold you captive.

Regardless of the whys, even when valid, even when painful, it is not the past where we should wish to dwell, but rather the present and future. Neither should we wish to dwell in the misery of blame. We may not be able to change history, but we most definitely can influence the present which leads to the future. We can decide to remain as is, dwelling on what has been, doing as always has been done, and ultimately receiving the same. Or we can decide to change - our thoughts and actions; therefore, changing our direction and outcomes. You must ask yourself, "Do I want to remain as is or do I desire change? If you desire change, then find the needed courage to begin your journey to renewal. Don't continue to hide self within. Take the needed steps and make the needed changes to restore self to self.

Am I advocating self-centered indulgences? No, I'm not. Am I advocating uncharacteristic behavior? No, I'm not. Am I advocating neglecting responsibilities for selfish gain? No, I'm not. Am I advocating forsaking traditions and roles? No, I'm not. Am I advocating neglecting your family, leaving them to fend for themselves; absolutely, not. But I am an advocator, advocating and encouraging you to live a lifestyle which promotes and exudes a healthy, mind, body, soul and spirit. I am advocating living life in a manner that contours to one's individual personality, talents, and interests. I am advocating promoting a lifestyle that fulfills the inner-person and the nature of one's innateness. I am advocating establishing self-liberation to pursue the path for which one has been designed. In summary, I am advocating re-establishing YOU as a distinct individual.

I advocate bringing awareness to the fact that this woman in "hiding" exists. My intent is to give her a voice. My endeavor is to redirect her from the course to hiding and to encourage and motivate, enabling her to establish a renewed spirit; empowering to maximize the fullest potential of self.

I most sincerely desire to impress upon this woman that it is okay to engage one's true self, and to consider it a sense of duty to become the best you can possibly be. And for those that may be headed in the direction of "hiding", I endeavor to discourage you from further traveling in this direction by sharing empowering information.

If you are one who is living a lifestyle where the characteristic of "hiding" is all too familiar, and you feel I have described your existence, then you must begin to put in motion the necessary actions to redirect your path, begin the journey to recovery and declare a renewed you.

During the process of the journey, you will begin to revive and restore passions that lie deep within as you restore the joy that once captured your being. If such joy has never captured your being, then you most definitely need to redirect your path, guiding you to discover the true you.

You will begin to view life from different lenses, and to consider yourself as a priority in your life. You will come out from a cloud of dimness into a ray of sunshine. You will begin to enjoy your moments, not merely, busily, coast within them. You will realize, not only will you remain loyal to responsibilities and obligations; you will gain a better understanding of how to be true to self as you integrate self into your daily operations. You will find yourself awakening prior interests, dreams, desires, and at the same time, strengthening your self-determination, and most importantly, strengthening your spirituality. You will transform into a joyful, well-rounded, well-seasoned, self-accepting person. You will begin to evolve into wholeness; the wholeness your soul craves.

Be advised, healing and recovery is not instantaneous; it is a step-by-step progression. But once achieved, you will walk in newness, experiencing a lighter, healthier atmosphere. At a point, as it all begins to make sense to you, you may need to share with your family your feelings and the purpose of your quest. Along the way, as they begin to notice your differences, they will need a measure of understanding and patience. Remember, they were used to you as you were, and perhaps appreciated you just as you were. They didn't see the need for you to change what was working well for them. But likely, they didn't realize the depth of your inner-strife. And although they may have noticed your moods, frustrations, and discontentment, they didn't have an understanding. If you think about it, in many regards, neither did you.

If your family allow themselves to accept that which you express to them, they will gain an understanding of your needs, or at least be open-minded to accept your undertaking. But, if your family is not willing to accept the renewing you, it will make your journey a lot more challenging for it may appear you are on opposing sides. But, if they understand it is not to be taken as an attack against them, or taken personally, and it's not about what they haven't done for you, but rather, what you neglected to do for yourself, then they may be more willing to support and promote you with understanding. So, it's important to include them on this journey. Hopefully, they will be willing to ride with you. But if not, I believe it's a journey you must take, even if journeying alone.

Although these pages have been written especially for women, but not exclusively, men may also receive a blessing by taking time to read the message it contains. While it may not be a message they particularly want to hear or accept, I wish for them to pay attention; after all, they have mothers, wives, daughters, sisters, and friends experiencing the same situation. For man to realize the signs and symptoms of a woman in "hiding" may be of great benefit to him as well as woman. Men may not agree or understand this "phenomenon" as I refer to it, but it most definitely exists. With understanding, maybe they can offer support to the women in their lives. And better still, may help prevent it from happening.

It would be most valuable for man to become aware of the silent struggles facing many of the women he loves and with whom he associates. Understanding and support go a long way and are much appreciated when demonstrated. Also, men may need to realize, intentional or not, they in part attribute to this situation, even though there are many contributing factors.

Each of us however, is responsible for our own outcomes, regardless of past history and experiences. We don't have to become the sum product of those experiences and influences. How we allow those experiences and influences to define and control our livelihood is a personal call. In the end, what truly matters and makes the definitive difference, is the responsibility, accountability and ownership we accept for ourselves; therefore, empowering us to assume control, move forward, establish peace, become successful in self, and migrate toward wholeness. "Hiding" hinders progress and success.

I agree with the words of wisdom once spoken by a brave and noble man:

One day we will learn that the heart can never be totally right if the head is totally wrong. Only through the bringing together of head and heart – intelligence and goodness – shall man rise to a fulfillment of his true nature.

Reverend Dr. Martin Luther King, Jr.

I personally believe power and courage lies within each of us to bring together head and the heart into wholeness. It is this fulfillment of the true nature that each of us seeks. God has placed within each of us this great power to birth that oneness of head and heart; soul and spirit.

Once this alignment has taken place, you can actually look to the future and take advantage of the great and honorable opportunities that will come your way. The greatness God has placed inside you needs to come forth. You need not hide that greatness.

"He who has begun a good work in you will complete it."

Philippians 1:6 KJV

Chapter Six
Elements of the Why

Once an older friend and I were engaged in conversation, and she shared a childhood experience. She talked of times when her family, immediate and extended, would come together for Sunday dinners. She pointed out that during these events, the men would gather on the porch or another area of the home to engage in conversation and joyful activities while the boys gathered outdoors to engage in play. The women and girls on the other hand, were busy in the kitchen preparing the meal. Once everything was prepared, the men and boys were called to dinner.

In her reflection, she expressed appreciation in regard to her family get-togethers, but she wasn't as positive in regard to her assigned role as kitchen helper. Nearly forty years later, it was obvious as my friend related her story, negative impressions and resentment remained. Resentful of the fact the men and boys were carefree while the women and girls were busy at work in the kitchen. With disgust, she expressed that following the meal while the men resumed their leisure socialization and the boys resumed their enjoyable play, the girls without choice in the matter, were faced with the clean-up.

Although my friend understood the general practice of her era, that women generally served and men waited to be served, she still thought it was an unfair practice. The female's role to serve was based solely on gender and tradition. She further expressed it had not been the actual work which most disturbed her, but the matter of fact attitude the men and boys had about it all. They viewed the female's serving position as common practice, as if the women and girls were dutifully performing as expected. She also felt that although the men may have applauded the tastiness of the meal, they didn't applaud the lady's efforts for the service rendered to them.

Years later in relating her story, and after having established her own family, what she found most surprising and somewhat paradoxical is that she continued many of the same practices which she earlier considered unfair. Still resentful, yet continued the same pattern which she had been trained as a girl growing up. She felt she had not been granted the opportunity of expression as a young girl, only later to discover as an adult she had again denied herself in the same manner. As an adult she simply followed suit and performed as she perceived was expected of a traditional woman's role; whether she agreed or not.

Having listened to my friend's account of this situation, her feelings, thoughts and ideas, it clearly supports my own views that girls then and now, are often trained to perform in ways opposite of their actual desires, which in turn conditions them to disguise their true feelings. Girls may desire to go in one direction, but time and again are coached to go in another. Their desired direction may be perceived as impractical, and/or unconventional. As a result, actual interests are denied; therefore, not given the needed attention to develop.

More often than not, girls are encouraged to become domestically savvy, whether they are interested or not. It's viewed as her responsibility to develop domestic skills. To take it a step further, she is expected to master an art in which she may not have an interest. How well a young woman performs in this area, supposedly indicates her status as a "bona fide woman". She is actually critiqued on such matters, and such skills may even be considered a prerequisite to marriage. She is often posed the "can you cook" question. And when such a question is posed by man to woman, do you suppose he has her best interest in mind? Or is it more of a selfish thought on his part; a cook for his benefit and pleasure.

When a woman accepts these traditional and cultural demands, she may even tend to think herself as inadequate when she's not gifted with these skills. In reality however, she may not desire to become skillful in this manner; knowledgeable perhaps, but not necessarily masterful. Often times, during the process of developmental training, her mind is conditioned to accept that a primary focus is to be one of pleasing others with her domestic craftiness. She is trained to believe that this skillset is later used to measure her worth as a "total" woman. She tends to feel threatened of being stamped as substandard if she is not successful in this area.

Being female shouldn't necessarily dictate she become a master homemaker. Should it? She may desire to be an out-of-doors type of girl; a different type of hands-on girl; perhaps being more interested in working alongside her dad, instead of being in the house with her mom. If that is the case, should it be frowned upon? Does it make her less feminine or does it simply make her a happy girl engaging in the interests of her choice?

Another aspect to take note of is, as a young girl is trained to please with domestic skillfulness, and as a young boy looks upon her in this regard, he too is conditioned to expect such performance from her. His perception becomes the better her domestic savvy, the better his benefit. He becomes conditioned in thinking her primary focus should be one of servicing others, particularly him. As if a girl learns these skills primarily to benefit and satisfy the male species. Otherwise, later as an adult, why would man feel privileged and entitled to voice disapproval when a woman's performance in this area is not to his liking? As if how and what he likes supersedes other considerations, including hers. Where did this view come from, and why has woman felt directed to meet this approval? It is not my intent to imply that domestic skillfulness is not a virtue nor of great value, quite the contrary. I feel domestic skillfulness renders great benefit. I personally take pride in my own skillfulness in this area. But females and males alike should develop enough domestic skills to become self-sufficient and productive individuals. If you think about it, why would anyone want to be tasked with the primary responsibility of cooking meals, cleaning a home, and maintaining operations of a household when it's a shared household? Why would one individual want such a task? And why should one who shares the household expect such of another? If one chooses to accept such responsibilities, it certainly should be appreciated and respected by the receivers; to be looked upon as an honor granted them, not as a service expected.

It may appear I'm attacking traditional practices, again, quite the contrary. It's absolutely okay for a woman to express pride in domestic skillfulness, and to feel a sense of satisfaction in demonstrating her soulfulness in this manner. It's all about choice. But even when a woman makes this her personal choice, those receiving should remain cognizant of the fact that it is by her choice, and it should be honored.

I know there are two sides to every coin. And I know man too, is expected to adhere to certain cultural traditions. There are certain stereotypes for him as well. He is expected to perform certain tasks typically perceived as "man's work" just as woman is expected to perform "woman's work". I'm sure males, similar to females receive training in their rearing in ways that hinge solely on gender. Both have gender stipulations. But, of this particular two-sided coin, I find there to be one huge distinction which I believe requires noting.

Although both man and woman may be comparably diligent in doing whatever is needed to get matters completed; what I find to be a distinct disparity which makes a world of difference is that, a man generally completes tasks on his own terms and timetable; whereas a woman tends to feel the need and is somewhat programmed to operate within a sense of urgency. In many ways she may apply this urgency upon herself, feeling - I've got to get it all done, I need to do it now, and, it's expected now. As a result, her timetable becomes immediate while his timetable becomes whenever I manage to get to it. A most strange thing is she is expected to accept his timetable of handling matters.

As she takes herself through mental and emotional changes of applying urgency, mental and emotional stresses results. Where man's attitude of - I'll get to it eventually, conveying the task will still be there whenever I manage and decide to do it, the element of urgency for him is not the same as it is for her; therefore, he's more apt to escape such mental and emotional stresses. Where he may decide to take a break from the task and do something totally different; something more relaxing and satisfying, she on the other hand, remains on task and festers in frustration. She's stressed and he's relaxed.

Oddly though, while man doesn't generally operate within the same realm of urgency for himself, he does however, apply a sense of urgency to woman as he makes his requests known to her. He likes her to take care of his needs and requests instantly. For her to strongly suggest to him when and how he should do things, even if her points are valid, doesn't seem to set well with him at all. It appears he receives it as "telling him what to do". When she's insistent, he then labels her behavior as "nagging"; which incidentally, seems to be a term used by man chiefly to apply to woman.

Somehow, a woman has accepted the idea that her insistence is to be regarded as nagging. She even tells herself, "I don't want to nag". Therefore, she extends her expressions only to a point, and then curbs her actions so as not to fall into the category of "nagging". In doing so, it quiets her voice and the real reason for insisting in the first place is muted. When she's quieted, man is satisfied, but woman, on the other hand, is frustrated. What she actually needed is lost in the midst. The act of quieting her becomes familiar as she develops and matures.

We know traditionally a male child is allowed more freedom to self-express than a female child. Boys are directed toward their natural flow of expressions, while girls are deterred from that same kind of freedom. Traditionally, males have been encouraged to "sow wild oats"- go out there and seek adventure, express self, and experience life, as if this adventure is to solidify his development and maturation. After he does, he's given a pat on the back for certain achievements. The female child, on the other hand, generally is not encouraged in this manner. While he's out sowing wild oats, the female child is at home practicing how she is to perform for future use; preparing to meet future expectations. So, for her to go out and pursue her interests and seek adventure is not as accepted. Her pursuit becomes more guarded and directed.

Since a sense of freedom is not encouraged for a developing young girl, her mindset doesn't freely move toward the natural flow of her personality and interests, but rather is shaped and guided to agree with that of the family structure, family demands and social expectations. Even in contemporary times, although different than yesterday, when a woman takes it upon herself to seek adventure or pursue nonconventional interests, there is still somewhat of a negative overtone which follows her. Still to a degree, she is disapprovingly labeled. So, in order to avert such labeling, a woman may restrict her actions and adhere to the traditions expected of her.

As she continues to develop, she follows through with this mind-conditioning behavior. Her natural flow of desires, interests and talents are gradually transferred over to a flow of adaptive and compliant behavior as bits of true self become hidden within.

She begins to adapt to ignoring her true feelings, and to quieting her voice, while the maturing male is encouraged to openly assert his voice. As he develops a sense of entitlement to express self, a female develops a sense of compliancy to do what is expected.

I believe this contrast in mindset, greatly attributes to a major controversy existing between male and female, and often intrudes upon their relationship. His thinking appears to be that a woman is to be dutifully submissive, giving, composed and pleasing, while he on the other hand is to be natural, outspoken and receiving. And when she becomes resistant to his ideal model, and acts differently, it results in an emotional battle between them. She battles to be different than his model, and he battles to keep her conformed to the model.

To keep the peace however, the woman is more likely to conform to tradition more so than he is to conform to non-tradition. But, as she continues to conform and shifts away from what is personally needed and desired, and instead yields to her largely expected role, day by day, she becomes more and more acclimated to ignoring self, and therefore, begins to bottle-up her inner-most wishes.

Bottling or repressing feelings, over time, can become like that of a pressure cooker. Bottled pressure builds up as time progresses. If not attended to, and as the pressure mounts, vulnerabilities set in. As in any case, as pressure intensifies, and if not properly channeled, it will explode. At the point of exploding, you cannot pinpoint the direction of the impact, the extent of the impact, or the damaging affect that will follow.

I believe this is a danger many women face as feelings and desires are kept inside and ignored. Bottling is not a healthy way to exist. Suppressing feelings, thoughts and desires eventually wreaks havoc on mental, emotional and physical well-being. To avoid such pitfalls, however, I believe women in general must do things a bit differently than yesterday's model. Today, there are too many other variables to take into account.

I acknowledge all women aren't alike, nor do all face the same issues and struggles. I don't want to paint a picture which indicates it's the same for everyone, or that every woman falls within the category of "hiding". That is not the case. But I do believe there's a common thread for many; and many perform within this common thread; traditional or otherwise.

To speak on the other end of the spectrum however, and to compare to the traditional conformist, there is a type of woman that views things differently. She's a type of woman which has a self-focus. Contrary to the traditionalist, she's not as locked into the conventional ways, and tends to grasp the ability and courage to express the nature of inner-self earlier in life. She doesn't entirely ignore traditional and conventional ways, but she understands how to coexist with certain traditions and expectations, selecting the ones which are in accordance with her desired lifestyle. She is more apt to exercise personal choice in a manner in which the traditional-minded woman is reluctant. She exercises the freedom to demonstrate assertiveness in drawing the line as to how far she is willing to extend herself to others, regardless of what is expected. She, unlike the "true traditionalist", is able to extend herself to others without routinely sacrificing self, setting limitations and enforcing those limitations.

This particular insightful woman doesn't allow the scrutiny of a role to overshadow that of her own personal expectations. She tends to expect just as much of others as they expect of her; and she lets it be known. She seems to recognize and accept the importance of revealing and expressing ownership of self. This type of woman categorizes life in a more integrated perspective, with self being a priority.

Whereas the traditional conformist, the one more likely to migrates toward hiding, feeling everything needs her hands-on touch, the self-focused one performs from a different viewpoint. To her, a personal hands-on touch is not as important; anyone's hand that can successfully get the job done is just fine. And if for reasons the job doesn't get done right away, she's okay with that too; she feels it will eventually get done, regardless of whom does it.

This self-focused woman is more apt to pursue personal interests and goals, even if it may upset the family routine for a time span. She expects them to respect her wishes. The family will just have to make the needed adjustments for the time required. The traditionalist instead, tends to make the necessary sacrifices herself and does not demand as much compromise from the family unit. Her stance is to first assist the family to achieve their wishes, and is more apt to put her own on hold.

The self-focused one may often be viewed as selfish, but is she really? Or, is she simply one to acknowledge her freewill, and view herself as an equal priority? It's not that she doesn't put equal effort into those she cares for, but she doesn't negate herself because of it. Therefore, she's not as vulnerable to travel toward a path to hiding. Women of a traditional mindset don't tend to grasp this sense of freewill and to make that separation as easily. Her mindset is fixed on the expected role.

Many women, as I once did, feels an obliging urge to comply with the established conventional model, as if somewhere it's recorded as standard performance. A woman doesn't necessarily view herself as being controlled by the role, but rather, led by the roll. She sees strength in being able to accomplish the things she achieves and in the manner in which she achieves them.

As a matter of fact, she is so fixated on the "model", she allows herself to be compared to other women – how she looks, how she cooks, how she keeps her house, how she takes care of her man, how she engages her children, on and on. While she's chasing the infinite mold, she sees herself from a standpoint outside of self, and her sense of distinctiveness dwindles as she resolutely chases that mold.

Later on, though, as time passes, a woman in this position begins to question her circumstance. She somehow becomes awaken. She begins to question her viewpoints and current standing. More than likely, she comes to a place where she is tired and weary; and perhaps feeling a bit under appreciated. She begins to see many of the things she perceived as necessary, actually weren't necessary; efforts were applied in areas that needed not have been applied; dreams and desires delayed which needed not have been delayed, and much remained unspoken, which actually needed to have been said - all being done in the name of the perceived best.

It takes time and a kind of wear and tear before a woman comes to this point of realization. It also takes a great measure of courage to accept. Sooner or later though, she's likely to get there, eventually to feel sacrificed and compromised one time too many.

Her family on the other hand relies on her to remain just as she is, since it has been an established pattern. The family is accustomed to it and wants things to remain the same. If she doesn't have a made-up mind to do things differently, chances are, she will continue to accommodate her family in the same manner, even though the heart desires differently.

Make no mistake, when it comes to this woman in "hiding", understand she loves her family and respects her obligations. That's why she does as she does. She makes sure to the best of her ability family needs are met. She is a solid rock for her family. She gives a lot of self to every aspect of her life, but simply doesn't give the same to self.

Those that depend on her, those near and dear, don't really focus to see if her needs are met. They are busy with their own personal agendas and eliciting her assistance. It doesn't occur to them she's without an agenda of her very own; an agenda that requires their equal support. They actually view their personal agenda and her agenda to be one in the same. They are so accustomed to getting her attention and assistance; she's instrumental to them. So, as she surrenders her own desired agenda, directing her attention toward theirs, her core needs go unnoticed; thereby remain unfulfilled.

Women in general, but especially those in hiding, must learn to blend responsibilities, and obligations while engaging personal needs and desires in a manner which grants a lifestyle affording a satisfying balance. For if the inner-self does not receive a sustaining degree of inner-satisfaction as a way of life, there will be an inner-void. And if this void remains unfulfilled, it can linger on for years. Perhaps not understanding its nature perhaps, but surely aware that something is seriously missing.

In an attempt to soothe what is needed to fill the void, a woman may very well pacify herself with acts; work, family, church, employment, community, and other involvements. She does more and more of the very type of things which attributed to her weariness in the first place. Since these acts are important to those receiving, and she feels a sense of gratification in performing them, it gives a false sense of fulfillment. So, she continues down the same path, as these acts only serve as a cover-up, just covering the surface of the injury. Still, she doesn't listen to the warning whisper from within.

This void however, cannot continue on indefinitely without consequence. In her mind, she rationalizes that all

is well, but in her heart, she knows it's not. As she continues toward the path of hiding; she continues an emotional war. Even so, her mind is on the "model" so she forges ahead in silent weariness; holding true to that model. Again, in an attempt to fill the void, she may venture in other directions attempting to explore, pursuing what the inner-person craves.

When going through such a turbulent time of search and uncertainty, if she is not careful and insightful at this point, her judgment may be clouded. Decisions made while in this vulnerable state could end up becoming self-defeating. This is a most critical point in decision-making. Wishes and expectations get tangled. At this critical point one must go forth with caution. An already unfavorable situation can easily be made worse if wise decisions aren't made. At this point in a time of uncertainty, don't become hasty in trying to find the fix. Be patient, think things through and pray!

As you go forth on your journey, at some point you will meet challenges. You may feel it is easier to accept matters as they are, and perhaps want to give up the pursuit. It may feel easier to simply resign. But if you don't do different, you won't receive different and unfortunately, the heart and head will remain separate.

You may ask yourself what I am actually recovering. Basically, it is to re-discover self as an independent person and to engage that independent person. Realizing and accepting the core of what you need as a distinct person is essential. As you seek to recover self, and find inner-peace, you will not forsake family. You will still want to continue to serve them well and be proficient in your daily performance. But the biggest difference is, you will do things differently, and begin to see self as a priority in daily operations.

No one is to blame as to why you have accepted the position of self-surrender. There are many elements of the why. Circumstances may have contributed, and prior training has taken root, but it has been more of a mental resignation on your part to follow a particular path; perceiving certain actions as required and needed.

I believe though, a woman can and should have it both ways. I believe she can be supporting, nurturing, and serving others, and at the same time, capture contentment and joyfulness in self; respecting self and commanding that same respect from others.

In my associations, I haven't witnessed many women who actually are living a lifestyle of balance. It is as if in their realm of thinking, they're not to have the full rights to joyfulness, as if they have to be either or. But you don't have to be either or; you can be both in balance.

A woman is God's design, created uniquely and to engage that uniqueness. Each is endowed with special gifts and talents and those gifts and talents should be used and appreciated in a manner that is fulfilling; purposefully. Our special design defines character, and for that reason we should utilize them and permit them to blossom.

Although a woman is known to be a natural nurturer, it doesn't mean she doesn't require nurturing. Not just pecuniary and physical support, but also emotional and mental support. And when it comes to the man in her life, it is most important for him to demonstrate she's appreciated, and respected. She may be different than he; she still wants the same liberties as he wants for himself. There's a saying "men are men"; as if that in itself permits him certain privileges and freedoms, and certain behavior is simply to

be accepted. Well– "women are women", simply different, but core needs are so similar.

To live a lifestyle in balance, where self is considered an important entity, doesn't take away from family and relationships. A relationship becomes more enriched when each person involved experiences a level of self-fulfillment. This is a point I think escapes many men when it comes to the woman in their life. He needs and expects so much from her that his perception of what she needs is distorted by his view of his own needs. In some cases, he sees it as a threat when she directs her interest to areas other than the ones concerning him, as if her interest elsewhere takes something away from him. He has narrow-vision in this regard, for he's busy seeing her as that constant source of help, a means to obtain and achieve that which he needs and desires. I don't believe his actions are intentionally selfish, and he's not totally to blame for operating within such a viewpoint. She too has been trained and conditioned in this manner as well. But just because something has been done a certain way, doesn't mean it has to remain that way – does it?

A husband, and rightly so, should look to his wife to be his helper. She should be that constant support. But he must understand that, she would like him to invest in her the same kind of support, nurturing, availability, understanding and sacrifice that he expects of her; whether she voices it or not. It's a no-brainer. Why not return that which you expect to receive?

Generally, men don't appear to give much thought to the daily weight applied to a woman being a wife, mother, manager of the household, cook, cleaner, errand runner, and however, she may be needed. Man, generally expects a tremendous amount from the woman in his life as if she has

a bottomless, untiring pit of doing and giving. This fact doesn't only relate to married couples; it tends to be the trend in relationships across the board. Man tends to expect woman to be consistently upbeat, serving his needs, maintaining the status quo, nurturing, accepting, and attractive for him at all times. How is all that possible? Does he expect the same of himself for her? Why is it he applies such weight on her and thinks it okay? But more importantly, why is she accepting of the weights he applies?

What she desires is not a mystery. She's usually expresses it. If a man really wants to bring out her best for the relationship, he would pay attention to what she says. He should sincerely listen, observe, and respond. He should not close his ear to the facts and overlook the reality. She needs him to know the status of how she is doing, not simply assume. But more importantly, she needs him to want to know.

Man, often pats himself on the back when he assumes he is doing well for the woman in his life, often working from his own perspective and presumptions. He does deeds; supposedly on her behalf, which he perceives as something good, but often without having a clear understanding of how she feels about what it is he is doing.

For instance, he might forever bring her flowers, bringing daisies when in fact she loves yellow roses. The deed is good, but he should know her heart well enough to know that she loves yellow roses. She in return may honor and value the actual deed out of respect and appreciation. But has it actually touched her heart? For him to show that he knows her desires, and she feels he has not given her

earnest consideration, it touches her heart. She would be more honored and pleased with what he has done.

At times when he sees himself as doing "good", he will often toot his own horn, because in his opinion he has done a great job. He brags to others about the things he does, as if his lady should be elated simply because he has done something that is, in his opinion, a good deed. But, in tooting his own horn, he appraises his performance by his own merit without a true understanding of her point of view. The very sound his horn toots may not be the music her heart desires to hear. It isn't that she doesn't appreciate his good deeds, she actually does, but she also wants him to have an understanding of who she is, what she likes, and how she likes it.

If he would simply take the time to listen to her words, gain an understanding of what it is she expresses, honor her wishes and incorporate those facets into the whole scheme of things, he would not have to be concerned about tooting his own horn. She would be in such awe and appreciation of his actions; she would toot his horn for him, loud and clear. And speaking of servicing him, she will service until his heart is content and a few other parts are content as well. Because she would then feel assured of his compassion and affection toward her, and she would feel he allowed himself to gain an understanding of not only who she is and what she needs, and that he's willing to honor it. Therefore, she will honor him beyond measure. But it seems to me, man wants to be honored without the work and effort to gain her honor. I may be wrong in this assumption, and I apologize if I am, but this is how it seems to me.

Women acts of caring aren't to be taken for granted simply because they love doing what they do for their love ones. Everyone deserves and wants to know they are appreciated for what they do. A sincere "thank you" goes a long way.

There are many elements of the why factor which determines a woman's path. I've simply pointed out a few. Regardless of the whys of the past, for the future, engage all aspects of self and achieve a balance that renders joyfulness and inner-peace. And, require that you are respected as sincerely as you are willing to respect.

Chapter Seven
Time for an Honest Self-Check

After all that has been stated, you may still be self-assessing to determine your position, or you may now recognize you are indeed a woman in "hiding". If you are one in hiding, be assured you are not an island – you are not alone to this experience. There are countless women just like you walking around. Some have become masters of disguise, fooling others and even self. Some are in denial, portraying all is well, but deep down there are signals that it's not. Others have just given in to circumstances and have accepted a lifestyle of surrender. And now I ask – which are you?

As I have grown older in years, wiser in experience, and am one to have traveled this path, I've developed a discerning spirit in identifying the "hiding" persona in others. I can recognize its appearance, and too, there's a certain look in the eyes. Regardless of all pretenses, it is obvious in the eyes. No matter how well a woman performs, or how well she succeeds, or how well she dresses it up, or how well she disguises it, the eyes are always the give-away. When there's an opportunity for me to take a closer look, to go even beyond the surface glance, I can see other recognizable traces – traces of disillusionment, weariness, pain, anger and longing; all deep-rooted in the eyes.

A woman in hiding has learned to mask in many ways. Maybe consciously, but I believe somewhat subconsciously as well. The face may wear one expression; the masked one; the one for show, but the eyes reveal the unmasked. Yet she flows in dignity and productivity. She's generally buried so deeply in daily operations, daily functioning becomes methodical, and in some cases – frozen. Others may not differentiate the masked person from the real one. Sometimes it is difficult for her as well.

Are you one who has become so crafty in disguise that the authentic you is hidden somewhere deep within? And if that is the case, don't you feel it's time for the real YOU, the natural YOU, to come forth?

You may be thinking you've functioned in this manner for a long time, or you are up in years, so why is it important the real YOU surface at this point in your life; why not just leave things as they are? Why disturb matters now? You may feel that circumstances are basically stable, and you've made the necessary adjustments, so why change?

I would not encourage you to change anything you don't desire to. You can remain as you are and go forth as usual. But if you want to change and your heart desires something different, then why not now? It need be now if you desire to attain different. If you don't allow yourself to make the necessary changes and opt to leave circumstances status quo, you may never gain the level of self-contentment your heart desires. If you continue as is, you will continue to receive as is. Is that what you want? I don't know your circumstances and specificities, you do. I don't know your heart, you do. But if you are relating to what I am saying, and the words are like a dagger in your heart, slicing it to pieces, then, I'm talking to you. And more than likely, your heart requires change and healing.

Over a period of time from all the nurturing, servicing, sacrificing, and minimizing your voice, aren't you tremendously drained - emotionally, mentally, physically; and perhaps spiritually? You may try to convince yourself and say such things as, "Well, it could be worse", "Others are not as well off as I am", "I love caring for my family", "They need me as I am" or even "What's wrong with me, why do I feel this way?" How is that rationalization working for you? As you continue in self-talk, you'll come to realize all of your rationalization efforts will not suffice the yearnings and void you possess inside.

If you would just begin to shed some weights, and peel off those layers one-by-one, you'll begin to feel much lighter and daily living will begin to look much brighter. Not that you will eliminate what is, but you will enhance what is. As you shed those weights, and open yourself to other ways of thinking, and other ways of doing, you will begin to notice that empty void will begin to fill itself with joys.

For years, I invested time and energy in observing the expressions and demeanor of women. Primarily, at a time when I was trying to gain a handle on what was going on within me. Something about women and their relationships was particularly captivating. Of the things I could personally identify, I began to recognize similar traits in others, and began to study them.

As I began to take particular notice, I paid attention to actions, expressions and mannerism. I particularly observed couples in restaurants; restaurants being a common place where people of all kind come together. Without even knowing anything about these couples, there were certain things that were just obvious to me. Before even noticing if they wore wedding rings, I could almost always pick out those that were in long-term relationships. There was something about their body language. Age wasn't really a factor.

I was both fascinated and troubled by what I observed. As couples dined, there were some good impressions, some appeared comfortable and fluent in communication, but there were countless others that didn't appear the same. Although I observed both, the good and what I perceived as the not-so-good, my primary focus was on the latter, and they became my subjects of study; particularly the women. I wanted to better understand the common in their actions, expressions and mannerism. There were elements of commonalities which spoke volume of one in hiding or of one headed in that direction.

As my husband and I dined, I would often draw him into my acts of observations, and unknowingly, he became my collaborative partner. He and I have had many, many discussions about our finds, some jokingly and others serious. But as we sat and observed couples, much was revealed and I have based certain conclusions on my observations.

Sadly, in these cases, I found many of their faces to be absent of pleasantry; just somewhat bland. On occasions when I take an in-depth look at the women, I observed many had somewhat of a gaze; sort of an indifferent expression, actually not particularly focused on anything except their thoughts; some an expression of distant thoughts as if they were mentally somewhere else. The men generally appeared to better enjoy their food, and were focused on what they were eating. But the women didn't appear to have the same experience of enjoyment in eating. I also often noticed many couples didn't engage in chatter. Instead, there was an occasional glance at each other and few exchanges of words. Of course, laughter didn't exist among these couples. When children were present, it kind of softened the atmosphere, as the adults interacted more with the children, which in turn would pull the parents in to conversation.

One thing I know about a woman, we immensely enjoy good conversation and laughter, especially with that special person in your life. More than likely with the couples I observed, these enjoyable traits once existed among them. Where did they go after a while? What happened? What went off track and why? And what was behind the weary expression so many of the women wore? At what point did it begin?

Even when driving, I've taken time to notice a woman in the opposite car while paused at a traffic light. I've noticed so many of them wear that same weary look; a look of stress, tiredness, and especially one of preoccupation as if to be weighted down with thoughts. I see them stroking their temple as if they have a headache. Why? In similar instances, when I observe the men, I don't notice that same kind of look on their faces. I see them in their cars bopping to music, waving to everyone, smiling, and looking around taking in the scenery. Why do the men seem so much more relaxed; not appearing as stressed and preoccupied as the women? What is the difference?

What was going on in the lives of these women that their facial expressions reaped stress and disconnect. In varied places and circumstances, I saw too many wear a sad look, worn look, bored look, over-worked look, aggravated look, I'm tired of this look, and the I want to be anywhere else but here look. Not only did I observe it, but also, as I talked with women, and I heard countless expressions of the same sentiments. No doubt, and by in large women love their family life and are not seeking to shun responsibilities.

But I think they find themselves increasingly overwhelmed by the demands of it all. And she becomes some accustomed to denying herself of those things which she needs in its midst.

She even feels guilty when she doesn't put love ones first at all times, and family members contribute to applying this guilt, especially if they are feeling neglected. But, should she feel guilty at times when she wants to take time for self to enjoy personal interests and pleasures? Or even, moments to be alone; personal private time. In fact, it would only make her a more improved and content person for her love ones. She would be more calmed and pleasant to be around.

When I think of the women, I've had the privilege to associate with, most are productive, hardworking, and caring individuals. Too many though, just seem so overwhelmed with matters and so disconnected with what it is they need personally. I bet, if they took a moment, each one could remember when it wasn't that way. I bet each one could remember when times were more self-fulfilling. So, in traveling through life, when and how did it derail from the original course? What happened?

Unfortunately, in the news today we hear unbelievable stories about things happening in the lives of women; stories we didn't used to hear so frequently. Have you noticed more and more women are dealing with addictions - whether it's food, drugs, gambling, shopping, sex, and even crime?

We are hearing today about run-a-way wives and mothers. Why are there more and more women neglecting and abusing their young children? Why are there increasing numbers of women with suicidal tendencies? What is missing in the lives of these women? What are they seeking? What is it they need in their lives? Are they turning to outside sources and means to compensate for what is missing within? Women of all walks of life are experiencing these happenings; it touches all sectors, to include those of the religious faith.

Through my associations, I've listened to women talk and express feelings. I hear about their hurts, regrets, and disappointments. Many feel as if they are vanishing in a lifestyle, having lost life's sweetness and sense of self. They silently long for release, but continue to contain all within; hesitant to share their innermost feelings; hiding. Many I believe keep quiet because they are afraid it may appear as claining. Some are too prideful to speak out to disclose the secret of contradiction-appearing okay but not okay; pride stands in the way. And there are others who are just too fearful to allow the truth to be unveiled and be forced to deal with the raw facts. Then too, there are those who are confused about it all and simply don't see any resolution in sight; resignation is their answer.

If you determine you are a woman in "hiding" and you want to avoid traveling further into the tunnel of hiding, then accept you must make immediate change; to transform the present negative restraining forces and actions into ones that are positive driving forces and actions. You will need to adjust your mindset followed by different actions. But before any change, it is crucial to do an honest self-check. Examine yourself first. Ouch!

It is the innermost YOU, where you start. Your goal is to produce an overall healthy and content self; the type of contentment that only you know when it has been achieved. You are dealing with self, not all the other that surrounds you. All of that will become the focus at a later point. Allow you to speak to you honestly and earnestly.

Allow yourself to remember the individual you were prior to getting off course, regardless of what got you off course. Discern what it is you need that will enable you to get back on track. Recall previous interests, goals, dreams and aspirations. Remember your joys, and by all means, remember your voice.

What do you imagine when you are alone in thought? What are your daydreams? Daydreams speak truth. What is it that actually makes you tick? What are your passions? What do you really want, and more importantly, what do you need? Dig deep! You can do it! The answers lie within. Only you have the answers to these questions. Allow the real you to come forward. You can actually be responsible to others, meet responsibilities by, and yet be true to self. You must bring the head and the heart together in oneness. What is it that allows you to feel satisfied in self?

Forget for a moment all the things others expect of you. Forget for a moment those things you are doing simply because you have been conditioned to do, because seemingly, those things have been the right and proper things. Instead, think of the things which actually personify you, those are the things which will transform you into who you wish to be, or perhaps, who you were once upon a time when your head and heart better synchronized. What were your thoughts at that time? What were your aims? And at what point did you give up YOU? Think! Feel! Be honest!

It is your responsibility to become an overall healthy and content individual. Not only will you benefit, but also you will serve as a model for your daughters and other young women observing and following your lead; demonstrating that healthy mind and spirit are main ingredients in establishing success in self. You will demonstrate that women are not just one dimensional, but of many facets; facets to be utilized, appreciated and celebrated. And they will witness appropriate assertiveness as you take control of self.

Women need to witness other women who are comfortable in body, mind and their life. This message is not exclusively for traditional-minded females, but for contemporary minds as well. Modern-day woman is still faced with certain stresses and disparities. I believe, in ways, they allow peer pressures and the need for acceptance to steer them in the misguided directions. Acceptance-seeking is not new of course, but today, it has a more in-depth spin on it. It appears many of today's girl's sense of self-esteem and self-worth is at risk. They seem to feel a strong need to be validated by others, especially by the opposite sex, placing them in compromising positions; compromising values, morals and good judgment, while basically seeking approval. Validation should come from within, not from without. But today, many seek validation from without. Seemingly, there's a void within, and they seek from without to fill it.

Seasoned women must set the example for their daughters, nieces and others. We must train them to grow in the direction to achieve a strong sense of self; not be self-absorbed, but to know, appreciate and to assert self; therefore, apt to become strong-minded and focused young women. This sense of self doesn't come automatically; although it does come easier for some than for others. but it comes by training and example. Strong-mindedness doesn't necessarily mean a take-charge, authoritarian attitude. But it is to be authoritative when needed; having a strong sense of who you are, demonstrating confidence, and knowing what you're willing to accept, or not.

What lifestyle are you perpetuating? Remember, your daughter, niece and others are sure to mirror what they see you illustrate. If they are to become what they see in you, what kind of woman will they become?

From what I see, there are numerous women out there that are seeking direction and counsel, young and older. Many are confused about what it is that is actually happening in their lives, and even more confused about how to rectify the situation. Women are turning to all kinds of outward measures merely seeking - going in unwise directions - just seeking, having never learned to capture and achieve what is desired for self; having never established autonomy in self to release the courage to enjoy daily living in a personally satisfying, healthy manner. In many cases, in reference to a relationship, women may just accept what's available, having a mindset that to have something is better than having nothing, and to have someone is better than no one; even though the "something" may not be a "good" something. This is such an unfortunate way to think, because it devalues relationships and it devalues self.

Now, if you have not yet admitted to yourself you are a woman in "hiding", and the jury is still out, then allow me to nudge you a bit more and give you a more thorough look into other signs and symptoms. Allow me to pose a few classifying questions to help you do an honest self-check. Questions that hopefully you're in a position to answer in a positive way, but if not – oh well – hiding.

There are many aspects to consider, but let's take a look at a few questions just for your pondering:

- Are you pleased with your inner-joy, not works, but self?
- Do you have peace within (not with achievements, but as a distinct being)?
- When you take a look in the mirror. Do you see a well-adjusted, satisfied person looking back at you, or do you see a wounded individual; wounded from all the woes that have infiltrated your life?
- When you reflect on inner-most dreams, are those dreams a part of your reality?
- Better still, what are your dreams? Are they in action?
- Are you walking in the shadow of a significant other to a point you are actually a SHADOW?

117

- Does anyone, anywhere know and accept the true essence of your spirit?
- Are your wishes and aspirations supported as you do for others?
- Do those close to you know what makes you truly content, and do they aid in that attainment, simply because they want what's best for you - aside from their own wants?
- When did you last have a real gut-wrenching laugh-even at yourself? Or do you even laugh?
- How often do you have quality time where you take time to do exactly what you want without feeling guilty about neglecting something or someone else?
- How often do you do something you truly enjoy, not appreciate, but actually fill you with joy? Or, do you even know what those things are anymore?
- Do you have hobbies? Or are you one to ask, "Who has time for a hobby?"
- As you help others to steer their life's course, is yours being steered in the direction you desire to go?
- Do you have a passion for anything that is healthy and nourishing, just for you, something which breathes life into your being?
- In your most intimate relationship, are you performing as the person you desire to be when you are with that person? Or has your voice been softened, and your desired actions mutilated.
- When it all boils down - are you performing one way - but inwardly and secretly desiring another?

Now, having honestly self-assessed, what is the conclusion? If your answers to these questions are positive, then you just might be that well-balanced and joy-filled woman many women wish to be - and you are to be applauded. Congratulations! You are a testament to women. But, if you answers rendered a negative conclusion, then you just might have discovered you are a woman in "hiding", living lifestyle, of neglecting self. And you are the one to whom I appeal. You are the one I wish to awaken the fibers of your innermost being so as you to recapture the authentic one who resides within - that person that desires release.

Be informed though, journeying out of hiding can be challenging. I encourage as you travel this path, remain steadfast to your goal, anchored in strength and faith. Otherwise, I don't foresee you having the courage to successfully complete the journey; breaking habits and coming out of what is familiar and complacent is not at all an easy task. But if life is to be sweet and enjoyed; self must be on the frontline, even as you devote yourself to others. This is not a selfish act.

It has been my sound spiritual faith-base that has been my saving grace. I am grateful to God for the magnificent happenings I have experienced during this journey. On the

way, my walk with Him has magnified a hundredfold. It is through Him; I have found the courage and direction to do what was desperately needed to revive **me.** I have kept His Word by my side and in my heart as it has given me strength, spiritual wisdom, knowledge and understanding of the direction needed to gain my fresh wind and fresh fire. I have always kept prayer on my tongue through which God has directed my path. And through it all, He has directed me to a renewed sweet savor in life, as an individual.

As you go forth on your own journey, be true to your feelings. Distinguish the genuine feelings from that of the conditioned feelings. Allow yourself to get to know you again. Don't permit guilt to claim control as you work to recapture your thoughts, feelings and desires, deceiving you to believe that your responsibilities and obligations will be neglected. They won't. You are committed to them. You will continue to have good judgment and meet those responsibilities – but they will be rearranged and perceived differently, incorporating you into your daily actions in a different manner. You are now grooming yourself to become a priority to yourself.

I urge you to begin this process today; begin this journey to renewal. It's going to be a wonderful journey getting to know you again. It will be exciting getting back in touch with the essence of your soul, the essence that you have long laid aside. It is like becoming reacquainted with an old and dear friend you have longed to see and spend time with. Be aware though, at times in the beginning, this journey may be a bit scary, uncomfortable, and sometimes

downright difficult. You must realize, you are being rewired, straightening out faulty and crossed wire lines. The laboring can be discouraging if you allow it. Many of

your thought processes, inclinations, practices, habits, tendencies and comforts, are being jarred and challenged. It will feel strange for a while, but stay on course.

Think of the process similarly to times when you look forward to a most relaxing and satisfying tub of bath water after a long hard day of activities. When taking a hot bath, many times when you first stick your toes into the water, you find it a bit too hot. You're looking forward to the soothing bath but the water feels too hot, so you withdraw - it's uncomfortable. But you don't give up on the bath – right. You simply wait and try again or add cold water to make it more comfortable. The next try, you'll find the water a bit more comfortable, your body becomes more acclimated to the temperature change, so you slowly submerge limb by limb into the tub of water - subsequently, achieving a feeling of calm and comfort, a feel-good sensation. Finally, you'll begin to enjoy this relaxing, soothing water. The next thing you know, your full body is so comfortably submerged and relaxed; hat uncomfortable feeling forgotten.

That's the comfortable soothing feeling your inner-self desires to experience in your life. After adjustments, some temperature acclimations, you should feel so good that you're awesomely comfortable in yourself. That's the renewed and revived feeling you're going to restore to your life if you remain steadfast to this blossoming out from hiding journey.

Can you just imagine such a renewed feeling? You will see you are going to establish a certain sense of joy and autonomy in self, a kind of freedom long forgotten, or

maybe, a feeling never before possessed. The TRUE YOU who is going to emerge will be astounding. You are so going to like the new you. And what is even more astounding, those around you will like you better too, once they adjust and learn to appreciate your newness; and even more so if they allow themselves to understand your position.

Regardless of the obstacles that may surface, and they will, just keep forging ahead. The outcome is so worth it. Keep in mind the analogy of the bathtub of hot water. Eventually, just like that tub of hot water, you will come to the point that you will begin to feel comfortable and relaxed. It is the same with journeying out of hiding; you will come to a point of self-contentment. The renewed you will begin to feel so comfortable in your own skin.

Get going – now! I wish you well! Create balance in your life. Balance! Balance! Balance! Joy! Joy! Joy! God wants you content, balanced and joyous!

A false balance is abomination to the Lord: but
a just weight is his delight.

Proverbs 11:1

Chapter Eight
A Bit of Selfishness is Healthy

As you continue to journey, remain mindful that it is a process. I can personally attest to the fact that deliverance out from hiding doesn't occur all at once. It is to be an unhurried; constantly evolving process. So, understand it isn't simply a matter of having a made-up mind to make changes, but to allow this development to run its course. Your "hiding" status didn't occur all at once, and the deliverance phase will not occur all at once either. Both are a process.

In retrospect, as I traveled the path of "hiding", part of that time I didn't realize what was happening. I unknowingly headed in that direction. Another part of the time, I did realize it, but did not know exactly what to do about it to make a difference, or even if I should do anything for that matter. Basically, my environment was stable, my economic status was comfortable, my family was healthy, my employment productive, and I had those around me who genuinely loved and cared for me. So, what in the world could have been wrong? But inwardly, there was something wrong.

I felt buried in the midst of things, all kinds of activities and commitments; just robotically going; somewhat programmed. Many of the activities I was involved in weren't ones I would have chosen for myself. They weren't really the activities that provided me personal satisfaction. But because of feelings of obligation, I just did; I was accommodating. So, I had pieces of me distributed everywhere. Everyone and everything had a piece of me.

And somewhere in the fog of it all, I couldn't see me. Eventually I arrived at a point, feeling if I didn't uncover me as an individual, I would eventually disappear.

I had somehow lost the power of control to experience wh I was as desired. For whatever reasons, I had voluntarily relinquished that power, not to anyone or any force specifically, just a subconscious resignation to a lifestyle and mindset; a true traditional-bred girl. But I knew I needed to recover distinctive entities which formed my individuality; intricate entities of self which I had allowed to become inactive.

Not that I wasn't grateful for what I had, I was. Not that I wasn't enjoying and appreciating aspects of my life, I was. But amid it all, I had allowed the other to greatly overshadow that of self. I knew if I continued to travel this same path, I could foresee myself becoming an old woman, with thoughts of "I wish I had", "I should have", and "why didn't I". I no longer wanted to simply wish, I wanted to make my wishes a reality.

To do so, I had to figure out who I really was at that very point in time, what I really wanted, what I really needed, and how to fulfill those wants and needs in a manner true to my character. More importantly, how was I to accomplish this feat in a way that would build around my family and existing lifestyle. I didn't want to abandon anything; I just wanted to place it all in a personally satisfying order; to come out of the shadows of husband and children – being known distinctively as theirs. I would still belong to them, still love and care for them, but I would become mine. I believe it is okay to belong to you.

What I also realized was I would have to be self-reliant. I was the only one aware of what I truly needed. I had to go deep within myself, and pull "me" out again, do some mental rearranging. I had to make some decisions. I had to decide which practices to keep, which to let go, which routines to keep, which to let go, which involvements to keep, which to let go, which activities to keep, which to let go, which relationships to build on, which ones to modify, and further, which ones to lay aside. I had to step back, take a look at my life, take an in-depth look at who I had become and actualize how I now wanted to go forth.

I had to become like a stranger to myself as I reacquainted me with me. I was the only one who knew about my particular inner-desires, and the only one to understand my dilemma. I had to silently rekindle and locate me as if I were my very own private investigator. Even more so, initially I had to do it as I continued in my daily routine. I think of it as an outer-body experience.

It's not an easy task to find yourself when you're not certain where you are in the first place, and when no one else knows you are missing. After having traveled the opposite of my fundamental nature for such a long time, to try and figure out how to realign everything was rather mind-boggling at first, and in some cases agonizing. But I had to figure it out; otherwise, my status would remain the same.

Determined, I worked undercover. I had to work alone to accomplish this endeavor. Besides, those close to me would not have understood how to assist me, nor would they have understood why it was all necessary at that point in time. Also initially, I didn't know what assistance to ask of them. What's more, because my outward appearance projected differently than my inner feelings, to them, everything seemed okay just as it was.

Another thing to consider is I had pride. After all, I was portraying an individual that others admired, a picture of a solid rock, and one to be patterned after. So, I felt I needed to continue that outward portrayal of a traditional strong superwoman. But, in the midst of my renewal journey, I came to understand such a portrayal wasn't necessary at all. It wasn't required. Why do we women think such an image is even necessary anyway? I believe now, first and foremost, you are to be true to self.

Pride can become your own worst enemy if you allow it; it covers up truths. I had to become goal-focused, and pride couldn't stand in the way of good judgment. I knew I had to pursue my renewal with vigor, but most importantly, with a clear understanding of truth, of myself, my surroundings and of others involved. Pride, if I allowed it, would hamper my progress.

We know however, as we focus on any goal, and as we make one successful step forward, something occurs that makes it seem we are going two steps backward. This forward-backward process can occur repeatedly until solid footing and understanding are established. So, as I began my journey, certain aspects of my life began to go haywire. There was so much to figure out and so much to confront.

To others, at times, I probably appeared angry, indifferent, or oppositional, but I simply had to test my feelings, and I had to grasp an understanding of how I regarded certain matters. I didn't want to simply react, or do the expected, as I was programmed and accustomed to doing. I needed to actually feel and respond to what was truth and fact, as I desired. It didn't mean I would selfishly have my way, but I needed to at least acknowledge what was my way, and then exercise freedom of choice. Prior to this point, I had lost a sense of balance in choice. so often I went in directions I perceived to be expected and required.

As I continued to further self-examine, I privately and silently forged my path through re-discovery. I discovered there were a few emotional doors that had to be unlocked, and unfortunately, but fortunately, a few doors that even had to be locked. I had to discover my own space and my own peace within my environment, inclusive of family, work, other obligations and involvements, and then realign it all.

I had to learn how to grab hold of and bring back to life my true spirit once again; perhaps in a manner never experienced before. I had negated my heart feelings for years, and I realized it hadn't been necessary at all. Who had asked that of me anyway? Why had I assumed such a sacrificial role? Why had I let go of me? Why had I let go of inner-peace?

However, I was bound and determined to recapture my soul essence. Through soul searching, meditation, trial and error, I realized one cannot truly experience peace without, short of capturing and experiencing peace from within.

The heart and head must come together and establish a oneness.

Again, I began to focus in fervent prayer, ushering God's presence to discern my new path. It was at this time; I began to look even deeper inside. I didn't want an egotistical, self-righteous person to emerge; I simply wanted who I was naturally – my improved and true-self renewed. I wanted the real me to resurface and as I continued, God began to reveal things within my spirit. It was through prayer revelation I gained the courage, boldness, and most of all direction that led to my deliverance.

I learned how to prayerfully become my own mentor as I coached myself into accepting the freedom to experience my own feelings - freedom in a manner that brought me self-fulfillment as I coexisted with those I loved, and coexisted amongst that which they loved. But, most importantly in the process, I had to be utterly true to self about my innermost thoughts and feelings. Most often it's not that which is outward that needs to change, but from within. It doesn't mean that outward circumstance won't require change, but for newness to occur, the depth of the change will come from within self.

My self-liberating journey wasn't always comfortable for me, nor at times, was it comfortable for my household. They were accustomed to the way of the old familiar me. They knew how to relate to that person. So, at times, I imagine, my actions, or lack thereof, raised a few eyebrows. More than likely, at times, they didn't appreciate the newness that was coming forth. And too, during this phase of the process, it wouldn't have been of any benefit to try to explain my actions. Much talk had already taken place earlier when I was seeking and soliciting a listening ear, and simply talking hadn't afforded me satisfactory results. So, I was beyond the point of talk. I was at a point of action.

People generally don't understand change when their lives are being affected. They don't consider it to be better for them. To break patterns and practices can be rough for all involved. Not only was I rearranging things for me, I was rearranging in ways that would extend to others as well. Not radically, but yet changes. Nevertheless, it was crucial I continue my journey, because on the other side of the journey, I knew all would benefit.

Thinking back, you too probably can remember yourself as a young developing girl, exuding energy, enthusiasm, drive, and passion, and then as a young woman having all kinds of plans and ambitions for the future; anxiously anticipating living life in a manner defining to true character? Can you remember the feel of it? You possessed a bit of selfishness, focusing on the things that interest and excited you. Those selfish identifying traits put you in touch with your heart wishes. Why then, once married and with children, responsibilities and obligations, those very elements which identified you were allowed to be hidden? Wasn't it that self-interest component that captured your heart core?

So now, at this point in life, allow yourself to recapture the feeling of youthful anticipation and the remembrance of being in tuned to self. You've become programmed to think that self-centeredness is taboo? But if you think about it, a bit of selfishness is healthy. Within that bit of selfishness is where one focuses on personal interests that identify the very things that fulfill the heart and gives joy.

To illustrate that point - observe a child at play and pay attention to how that child selfishly expresses what it is he or she wants. Observe how instinctively that child engages in what is of personal interest and importance, and how innocently the child displays natural talents; engaging just an innocent bit of selfishness.

From childhood we mature into adulthood, and although we may express things differently, instinctive interests continue as we grow up. Natural interests remain a part of our character, we don't lose it. We should allow those interests and talents to blossom, not forsake them. In a sense, we should remain child-like in that regard; experiencing joy in those particular areas which bring us delight. Joyful children are healthy-minded beings. Joyful adults are healthy minded beings.

Another aspect for a woman to take a look at is how a man can often engage in enjoyable activities, such as spending a day at the golf course, spending hours away from home with his friends, going fishing, or being involved in a cause of interest. At times, a woman may look at his conduct as being selfish, particularly if she doesn't allow herself such privileges, and thinking he needs to be home doing some of the things which need to be done. In her mind – how dare he be frivolous when she is busy with their affairs at home?

But now having a renewed mindset, I'm thinking, maybe women need to rethink the matter and perhaps not waste aggravation on it. Thinking, when he does spend time away from family enjoying something of interest, maybe it is simply his way of expressing self. Perhaps, it is his way of expressing there are interests and passions in his life other than ones centered on family, work and responsibilities. Perhaps, he doesn't view it as neglecting family, work and responsibilities, instead sees it as healthy enjoyment; a needed get-away.

Men appear to recognize their needs and follow through to satisfy them. It doesn't mean they don't hold their relationships in highest regard or that they put other activities ahead of family and love ones - but just maybe they are simply conveying the need to enjoy something else in addition to the relationship, and aside from their responsibilities; to engage other areas that feed into their soul. So, they go for it. And from what I see, they will defend it to the end, even when there's opposition.

Woman on the other hand, often feels when she makes a request to her man: he should forsake all other, especially for the sake of her and family. Women expect it of them and feel men are supposed to do exactly the same. When they don't, women generally perceive their actions as callous. When it comes to the man in her life, a woman has been known to perceive the time he gives her synonymous to caring. Men obviously view it differently, and appears to place each – time and caring on different and separate tracks as if one doesn't have anything to do with the other; two important factors, but on totally different tracks.

Where women will forsake their interests, men tend to migrate toward theirs. They tend to engage their interests despite woman's complaint. They will often pursue things of interests with or without her blessing; not that they wouldn't desire her blessing, but even if the blessing is not given to him, they continue on. They don't appear to see a reason as to why they shouldn't. A man pursues his interests, a woman forsakes her interests. Why is there such a difference?

Man seems to have more zeal to engage in diverse activity outside home. Women no doubt have a desire for activity diversity, but don't as often seize the opportunity to engage. A woman's perspective in general, is to forsake many things of interest for what she perceives as the betterment of the whole. And because of this point of view, she takes it upon herself to be the sacrificial one and neglects herself while she assents to him doing as he wishes. She'll stay around home, while he takes liberties away from home. And as a woman continues this sacrificial way of life, after a while, man begins to expect it of her. It becomes routine. By her doing so, she actually frees him up to do precisely what it is she doesn't want him to do in the first place. It is a little tricky twist on his part, isn't it? Win—win for him, lose—lose for her.

Think about it, a man may leave work, stop on the way home and spend time with the guys, engage in conversation and laughter, play a game of golf, a game of basketball, or simply engage in activity that provides him relaxation and satisfaction; doing that which he feels he needs to do for himself at that point in time. The tricky twist is, woman accepts his actions thinking he deserves and needs these moments to himself. Even if she doesn't agree, she goes along with it, considering he works hard, and for him to have his time will help him better cope with everything else; he's a man; he needs "man time".

Facing her at the end of her work day are many other responsibilities centered on family and home which she considers priority over "me time." There are tasks to be done, children to be cared for, dinner to be prepared, and clothes to be washed and so on. She doesn't grant herself the same considerations. She feels it is neglectful if she stops off on the way home to indulge in joyful activities and spend time relaxing doing something totally for her enjoyment while everybody and everything else at home is put on hold. She becomes stressed over all that's awaiting her at home.

You don't often see a man stressed out about having to cook dinner, wash clothes, clean house, or any other routine household chore. At least it hasn't been my experience to witness such. Not to say he doesn't perform these tasks, but to be stressed regarding them is not a part of his mindset. Men know how to exhale; come right in from work and go straight to the couch as if all that other doesn't even exist at the moment.

Frankly speaking, I don't think man would be as accepting toward woman if she performed in the same fashion as he. And I don't feel he would like it much if he was expected to go home and immediately begin chores. Or, if she was the one to come in from work and go straight to the couch and relaxingly waited for him to prepare dinner. I don't know if he would willingly accept her actions. And if he did accept it, I believe he would do so with ATTITUDE. Why do you think he feels it's okay for her but unacceptable for him?

In view of it all however, just maybe women have been misreading the situation and need to take a second glance at the matter of man's performance. Perhaps, as he communicates and demonstrates in ways - I love you, and appreciate you, he also communicates - I love and appreciate other aspects of life as well, not more important than you, but vitally important to my well-being. Conveying since it is important to his well-being, he sees nothing wrong in partaking in it. So just maybe, a woman needs to adjust her perspective, take notes from him, do similarly, and require him to be accepting of her actions as well - without attitude.

A woman needs to regularly engage in healthy activities that afford enjoyment, fellowship, and relaxation, similar to that which a man does. Not retaliate because he does, but to convey she too needs comparable time for her own mental and emotional well-being. So, it's important for them both. Of course, we must use common sense in the matter, plan mutually and establish respect between the two.

Within my newfound perception, and on behalf of the integrity of man, I now believe his follow-through of personal interests, in general, is a healthy endeavor. I now think his view is really not a bad idea after all. Instead of bashing the men for their conduct in this particular instance, I believe women need to take note. Take note of their hardy laughter, child-like playfulness; their practice of engaging in enjoyable activities, their taking time for relaxation, and doing things just because it is what I desire to do at the moment. We women need to do similarly and the men in our lives need to accept and appreciate it. As a matter of fact, they need to promote it.

Women, of course we love our families, whether single parent homes, married couples or whatever the case may be, and we place them first over self. That's who we are; we are natural nurturers; it is God's design. That's just the way it is. But we can love them, honor them, serve them, and just as well, respect and love ourselves.

As you realign and redirect, take time to pamper yourself, and engage in activities that give you delight. Adjust to the fact that, you can't do every work task perfectly every day. Some things have to be postponed, even important things. Prioritize! And remember your own voice. I can't express this point enough. Not only express it, but make certain it is heard. Then, not only heard, but respected.

Go back and grab hold of childhood memories. Remember those daydreams. Take time and put forth the effort to develop and appreciate those parts of your character which God has placed within you. Then, put some things into action. You need and deserve it. Your well-being hinges on it.

Why not indulge and enjoy your interests and gifts! Why not engage yourself in your own life? I have learned and decided to do just that. So can you. Adjust mindset and perceptions as needed to allow you the freedom and courage to experience YOU. I have learned to accept that a bit of selfishness is okay.

"God, draw me close to your heart and renew my vision. You are the Lord of my life, and the One I trust with all that I am and all I have yet to become".

Chapter Nine
Framed by Beginnings

I've talked much about mindset, perceptions and other attributing factors which may lead to a state of "hiding", However, there's a major element worth delving into; an element which molds and programs us; that is our upbringing. Our upbringing becomes the framework for the future. Each of us is encased by the entities of our upbringing - our training, values, and ways and means, become a picture by which we are each framed. These frames come in different sizes, shapes, forms, structure and quality. The frame can enhance the picture, distract from it, and in some cases, simply blend – just ordinary.

I think it's beneficial if we take a close look at our beginning. I believe it would grant insight into many of the whys we ask ourselves. I believe a look into the beginning will serve in understanding the factors surrounding many of the whys. That which has been placed in us accounts for much. Some things become a part of us before we even realize it, and we respond accordingly.

We often beat ourselves up over decisions we make, especially if they lead to negative results. Even with the best of plans, we cannot minimize the fact that the framework, our beginning, largely dictates how we will later conduct ourselves. We transfer developmental and circumstantial precepts into the experiences of life. Allowing ourselves to take a deeper look into the beginning framework, will perhaps provide a better understanding of some of the choices we actually make.

Then just maybe, we wouldn't be so harsh and critical on ourselves.

Understanding self is a powerful force, and in many regards, it is freeing.

Having been framed by the particulars of our upbringing, certain thought patterns, mannerisms, and idiosyncrasies just remain with us. It's our internal framework of reference. Later in life, we reveal indications of this framing, its structure and quality. As our framed picture is viewed by others, visual resemblance of our mental images is revealed. We show evidence of whether the structure of the frame compliments the picture, providing a supportive and strong character, being a framework of advantage; or does the framework simply blend, neither particularly adding nor distracting, but still affording adequate support. And in other cases, the framework may be unflattering and structurally weak, showing evidence of a frame which requires restructuring and possibly reframing.

With a framework of advantage, some pursue a preferred direction without great struggle, having been equipped early on to know what is desired in life. They are the ones who have been afforded frames to complement their picture and provide solid framing. They are likely to become self-directed to achieve. Their frame advantage offers them greater opportunity to establish a solid footing in life's direction to achieve identified goals; recognizing inner desires and achieving a better understanding of self. They are less likely to follow a path of hiding. Their training and established mindset guides them to see self as a priority in their life.

Others however, lacking in frame advantage, may be latent in such realization because the frame structuring is not as solid when it comes to similar matters. These persons may experience more of a struggle to identify and achieve an understanding of self because it has not been engrained in them. They think outward more so than inward, as if to think of pleasing self is wrong; selfish thinking. They may wander from point to point, perhaps taking years, and for some, many, many years to reach that exact point of discovery, simply because of a frame disadvantage. To succeed in self as an individual and to be content in self as an individual may be more of a challenge.

As life would have it, children are born into all kinds of situations; advantaged, disadvantaged and somewhere in between. Not all have the same framing structure. It's not so much based on material and monetary factors; although those things could be most helpful, for it could possibly broaden horizons, exposing to diversity for which one can make choices. I guess in a way as far as framing, you could say some of us are born to a silver spoon, others a silver-plated spoon, and still others, simply a spoon.

It is fortunate though, for those who have parents and guardians who are focused on providing insightful leadership; depositing sound principles for future guidance and decision making. Silver spoon or not, if parents were insightful and in tuned to what defines a particular child, and to help and assist in activating it, it could spark certain elements in that child; elements inspiring uniqueness, true character, and interests; sketching a blueprint outlining a pathway to attain self-fulfillment. The goal for parents is to promote an overall healthy-minded child, one that will later develop into an overall healthy adult which is content in self and productive in society.

Good or not so good, advantaged or disadvantaged, it is that beginning that sketches a rough draft of our framed portrait. Established perceptions which follow that beginning framework greatly influence how we function in any given situation; it has a direct bearing on our choices and actions. Even at those times when we don't clearly understand our actions.

Another dynamic force is to recognize and accept that perceptions and actions may need to be modified in order to achieve what is desired. Poorly structured frames can be refurbished and enhanced, weaken or damaged frames can be repaired and strengthen, and in some cases, replaced if necessary. And that is quite okay. We can actually rebuild our frames into a custom design one. Not so good can actually be transformed into good; what is hidden can actually be uncovered.

Unquestionably, home preparation, solid frame building, can jump-start one to become established within self, society and profession. One of the greatest of gifts parents could ever bestow upon a child is to instill a sound sense of stability, self-worth, confidence, and most definitely, a sense of direction into life's journey. For parents to invest time and effort in getting to know the child as an individual, be knowledgeable and nurture the child's heart desires, talents and special gifts - will definitely be valuable for the child's future success in; possibly minimizing struggles and time wasted.

For parents to have conveyed to the child that he or she is indeed loved, should be loved, should love self, and to respect and value self-opinions, can be viewed as a picture solidly and uniquely framed. If this message is not instilled from within the family structure, then how does a young person move confidently out into the world of adventure? How does one actually avoid a path to hiding self?

I am sure parents could appreciate a guidebook containing instructions on how to become the perfect parent. Then, they could just follow the instructions contained in the book and all would be well. But such a book doesn't exist. Generally, parents simply do the best they can, drawing from their own sources, values, traditions and framing. But even with all their good intentions, things don't always go as planned, nor as wished. But, if the frame is built solidly, rebound comes more naturally. And without a doubt, let's not overlook the wisest and most helpful tool of guidance of all, the authoritative source of instructions which provides essential directives and principles unfailingly; the Holy Bible. Its instruction, coupled with invested time, efforts, and interest is surely to increase the odds of a child's success in self; confidence and assurance which can be extended to others.

With our girls, even more special considerations have to be applied. There are certain aspects of life in which females are more vulnerable. And if they don't receive fundamentally sound training, guidance and role modeling from within the family structure to safeguard them from such vulnerabilities, then from where ,whom and when are they to receive that model? Furthermore, how would they otherwise have obtained the ability to set needed standards for which they seek? It is within the family structure the frame is crafted and artistically designed to equip them for entering into life's adventure.

I have seen evidence however, that many young girls and young women misguidedly go from point to point, accepting whatever comes that appears good, falling short of having the sound judgement with which to seek and select what is actually genuine and best. Many seek a male to determine their identity and worth; such worth which needed to have been formed and framed from within - prior to allowing him to enter her life. If solidly equipped prior, young girls and women would find themselves better positioned to make sound choices, being assured in self; therefore, in a better position to recognize quality and genuineness when it approaches, and will possess stamina to reject those things (and people) which are not suited for them.

Even though yesterday presented particular challenges, today there are situational happenings different than ever before. Women face uncertainties which women of yesterday didn't have to face. Modern-day woman has more liberties, and is not faced with the rigid structures of yesterday's woman. Yet today, in many cases, there appears to be increased numbers dealing with mental and emotional entanglements. Down through the ages, women most definitely have had to deal with issues of disparity among males and females, and the issues of the to-do verses the not-to-do. Still not the types of issues which face women of today. On one hand, modern-day woman has so many more advantages, personally and professionally, but on the other hand, she faces significant struggles. And I believe, more severe.

Although they have proven to be more unconventional, and have overcome many of the traditional demands, but actually in my opinion, in some ways, they are more captured. Whereas yesterday's woman accepted an ownership of a role, it was clearly defined. She maneuvered around it when necessary. Today, traditional roles have been loosed, and male and female roles are intertwined. Stemming from the change, woman's "role" has magnified ten-fold. She has taken on a contemporary mindset, but yet holds onto much of yesterday. Actually, her role has become enlarged with increased responsibilities and stresses.

I believe, in her pursuit to change from that of old, somewhere along the journey of the shift, respect has been compromised. Somehow resulting, is a new spirit wave to reveal all - revealing that which should be private, and being casual about those things which should be cherished. This mindset to reveal all didn't exist so much in that of old. Today's woman seems to have to prove more - but to whom? Yesterday's woman sought self. Today's woman has all the advantages in achieving self, yet she feels the need to prove self. Why?

Today's woman is less likely to accept the separation of male and female roles, projecting a sense to be equal. If man can, woman can as well, and if man has the right, so should woman, and if man is not to be ostracized for his actions, nor should woman. I believe these actions are done in an attempt to reverse the paradigm of the old double standard; liberating from what held yesterday's woman in a rigid form. However, this conduct, in my opinion, appears to be a mode of operation which further entangles rather than frees, granting a false sense of liberation. We as women don't need to compare our actions to man, but to be the best you that you can be – for you. In order to find true liberation in self, we only compare self to self, not to another. We should seek what we personally want and need. It is not to be contingent on what someone else has or does.

In the realm of all the improved newness for woman, isn't it strange though that we now hear far, far more cases of troubling issues concerning women. Why? Is it a matter of unpreparedness and framework disadvantage? Or, is it a matter of escape? If escape, then escape from what? I believe women of yesterday were more protected by the of the times; extended family, more watchful eyes and defined structures which safeguarded them from certain vulnerabilities. The defined structure in and of itself wasn't a bad thing. However, women of yesterday didn't appreciate being pigeonholed, viewed primarily as a domestic being. Much of their discontentment lied in the fact they were stuck in a pigeonhole. Being pigeonholed didn't allow opportunity to explore self. But for the most part, they were safeguarded in ways which women of today appear not to be.

As I have observed, even with all the advantages today's woman has, a clear sense of identity still appears at risk. Roles are tangled, liberties are tangled, and the old and new is all wound up. She has advantage of liberation, but I'm not certain she has allowed herself to be. She's still focusing on much outside of self instead of fulfilling what truly lies within to connect head and heart.

Definitely, we cannot overlook the fact that things have changed from old to modern-day, things that I believe to be of great benefit, and others I think not so much. A woman must deal with the changes, and all that comes along with it. But within the changes, her essence remains constant.

We cannot send our girls out into the world with false beliefs; believing that woman's nature has changed. It hasn't. Yes, there are many more opportunities awaiting her, and yes, she has the freedom to do basically whatever she chooses to do, but without a sound sense of self, where is she going once out there're out in the world? We cannot risk their being ill-prepared; otherwise, they may very well become consumed by the ills of modern-day society, in the midst of liberation.

Parents generally do the best they can in most situations to prevent their child's struggle. But struggles are sure to come in one fashion or another. We must realize it is the

beginning that anchors, and provides the groundwork that sculpts each individual framing to face what lies ahead. It doesn't prevent struggles, but it most definitely armors to minimize them. Again, if parents don't provide a solid foundation for our girls, then from where are they to receive it? Better still, who will they depend on to guide them? Most importantly, where will they place their trust?

A mother should want to be the most important person in the life of her daughter and invest what is needed to be so. Mothers, don't allow it to be a wedge between you where she goes elsewhere to seek that which she needs from her you. We mothers should capture our daughters love, trust and confidence. We should position ourselves to guide them where they desire to go and where they need to be. Let's take more control of their framing to ensure better output of a picture uniquely and artistically designed; one granting her self-assurance and peace in self.

I believe if each young girl's framework is designed to exemplify her awesome uniqueness and supports are in place enabling her to grow to be well-rounded and balanced; to engage interests and talents, to ambitiously strive to achieve personal goals, and to know and acknowledge self, she's more apt to develop into a woman of strong character; one which is confident in self, content in self, and has peace within; manifesting a healthy mind, body and soul; thereby warding-off a path to hiding.

We must spend much time guiding and supporting them as they try to find their way. We must become a most important entity in their day-to-day functioning, establishing between the two a trust and secure bond. So, when times are confusing for them, they will feel confident and at ease to come to us for advice and guidance. No doubt, fathers should have their rock-solid place in their

lives as well. Who else can best teach a daughter about a man better than another man? Fathers are the ones to teach a daughter how she ought to be treated by another man. So, man must also have their act together in order to be the best example for a child which he fathers. Therefore, women be mindful of who you choose to father your children.

Mothers, grandmothers and aunties, we must learn to listen to our daughters, granddaughters and nieces, and be mindful not to attack them simply because we do not understand or agree with their choices. Rather, we are to offer and guide them to see other options, as appropriate. Sometimes however, we must accept their ideas even when we don't agree, and even at times when we absolutely know their choice is not in their best interest. Of course, we are to let them know our views and concerns, but if they don't accept the advice, we are to assure them we will be there for them regardless of the outcome; having allowed a bit of leverage for them to feel comfortable in the exchange. As a result, they may feel more at ease to allow us into their space, thoughts and feelings. Then hopefully, they will learn to trust our advice without feeling judged, and will know their views are respected as well.

We want our young ladies to become assertive enough to hold true to their views and standards as they extend themselves to the world, respectfully, but assertively. Hopefully, through lessons learned and engrained, and having had a picture solidly framed picture, they will become equipped to make informed choices which best suit their unique needs.

Chapter Ten
My Personal Framework ~ As I Now See It

When I think of my personal framing and reflect on my own beginning- my training and developmental precepts, I understand now that my actual entry onto the pathway to hiding began when I was very young, considering my family structure, partly in light of the era, but mostly, because of the particularities of my family dynamics. As I think back, I clearly can see the structuring of my personal frame. I can understandably see how I formed certain mindsets; ones which later followed me into adulthood; certain mindsets which I now feel were more of a disadvantage than an advantage to aid in seeking and securing self. I can clearly see elements of how my picture was framed.

During my time of upbringing and considering my family's socio-economic environment, a family's primary focus was to establish and maintain an honest survival. Parents were simply busy making a living for the family. Overall, children were cared for, housed, fed and clothed; basic needs were met with a few personal wants thrown in occasionally. Parents taught their children to become hard working individuals; productive citizens, and to earn a living rather than focus on personal interests. And if children were fortunate to receive a higher education, most times, the area of study pursued was likely to be one which parents selected.

For in many cases, parents had to work hard to afford it, and compromises and sacrifices were made on that behalf. But as good of intent as this gesture was, most times the

child's personal interest didn't carry much weight.

It wasn't the general practice for parents to encourage their children to express and pursue personal interests, or even more so, to direct their children to discover what those interests actually were. Particularly the girls and especially when they expressed interests contrary to popular belief and stereotypes. And too, girls were steered in a direction to one day find a husband to support her. That pursuit became a main focus. So, these factors overruled seeking personal interests.

I can remember as a girl I spent much time with playmates playing house – basically the dad, mom, and child pretense. Rarely did girls venture play acting beyond family and housekeeping. We girls cooked mud pies, cleaned our fantasy house, and dressed and combed our baby doll's hair. Our imagination basically remained in that realm. We didn't often imagine ourselves in professional roles. And even when we would venture beyond those common play roles, we limited the venture. We pretended to be a nurse, but, not a doctor, or a teacher, but not the principal, or a secretary, but not the office boss. We contained our thoughts, imagination and vision. When parents observed our play, rarely did they encourage any differently for girls. So, we did not expand the horizon of our possibilities even in our playful minds. Now, I can see how such a mindset could transfer over as we matured. And if there weren't influences to show and steer us differently, then our mindset would remain limited to the future opportunities.

Also, when I think back and remember times when my sisters and I were busy doing house work, I simply don't remember my brothers being tasked with similar chores. I

have vague memory of times when they washed dishes -very vague in fact. And, yard work was limited, since our yard was more sand than grass, so they weren't that busy grooming the yard either. I do however, remember my brothers bringing in firewood. But I also remember the girls doing so as well. So actually, what were my brothers busy doing around the house?

As well as the girls being busy with the housework, we had to learn how to cook. That was a huge deal in our home. Not only were we taught this skill, but we were tasked with cooking meals daily. Along with that, we were trained to prepare dishes to the liking of others, and particularly to the liking of my dad.

I don't think my dad saw anything wrong with this point of view as conveyed to his daughters. I believe his view was, he provided for and took care of us, so he was lord of his little castle. Therefore, we learned to satisfy his taste and style. But now as I look back, what kind of message was being conveyed to his daughters? And what message was being established in our minds to later transfer into adulthood; especially in regard to our husband and sons?

Speaking of a husband, there was always the echo of a young woman needing to know how to cook before she gets married, as if knowing how to cook makes her more marketable in securing a husband; holding true to the old adage, the way to a man's heart is through his stomach.

What does that really mean? Surely a man can appreciate a woman's cooking, and surely a woman can appreciate preparing a meal for him, but is she to be taught such a chauvinistic view, really? Why not be taught the art of cooking for the reason that it's a worthwhile art to know. And how, for whom, and if she's to use this skill is totally her choice.

To cook for another adult should not be considered a requirement or stipulation of worth unless it's your employment. Otherwise, a woman doesn't owe another a good tasty meal; it's a privilege to be received. It should be respected by the receiver as such. A woman may accept the responsibility to prepare meals for her family; however, it shouldn't be a task considered her job.

When a dad teaches a maturing boy to repair a car, is he conveying the message it is a marital prerequisite, and that he is to learn this skill primarily to one day be prepared to repair his wife's car. Is he conveyed the message that his value and worth hinges upon his ability to fix a car? Or, is he simply taught this skill because it is a worthwhile for him to know.

No doubt there's a mix-message in what is conveyed to girls and boys. Boys are conveyed messages of entitlement, and girls are conveyed the opposite message. Females give, males receive; females do, males watch her do; and females decrease, and males increase. And these messages and practices become normal. Wow!

My upbringing followed suit with these practices. My dad most definitely presented and exercised an in-charge approach. What he liked was how it was, rarely any deviation. What he said was the way and only way, no ifs, ands, or buts about it. He presented himself as a strong force that commanded respect, and as a force not to be ignored. He worked hard and he provided – end of story.

He was a man with many skills and trades; carpentry, electrician, painter, builder, mechanic, gardener and business man and well-versed in many subjects. He was simply a jack of many trades, and I believe him to have

been an actual mastermind of his time. He expected his boys to mirror his works, and for the girls, it was a matter of doing as a girl is "supposed" to do.

My mother was also a strong-willed person, but different than my dad. She like my dad, performed well in so many areas – an excellent cook, baker, seamstress, and she had a flare for style and beauty. Even though strong-willed, she had more of a quiet strength, and often yielded to my dad's wishes as his demeanor overshadowed hers.

Although she portrayed somewhat of a meek spirit within the home environment, even as a child, I knew her true personality wasn't meek at all. I recognized within was another dimension of her character. Others evidently saw this side of her as well, as they gravitated to her charm, strength, wit and counsel. But in the home, she was reserved, and the inmost-woman, the other dimension which I believed was a part of her, remained reserved. As with my dad, I can clearly see the message she conveyed to her daughters, and the message her sons would take note.

Aside from the home environment, my parents were entrepreneurs. They owned and operated a café in the local downtown area. The business being the family's primary source of income; all family members were required to work at some point in time. For the children, whether or not to participate, how long you participated, and when you participated was rarely an option.

At that time, to own and operate your own business was quite an achievement for the average family and, an endeavor which required hard and long hours of work. It was primarily the family that worked it, my parents, siblings and I, with a few others hired as needed. However, as we children matured, the few others hired came to a halt. Therefore, as working teenagers, there was little time for a social life. While we watched our peers enjoying social activities, we were busy at work. Not that our peers didn't have responsibilities of their own, they did, but they weren't stuck the way we felt we were.

As early as the age of ten, I was on my way to becoming busgirl, waitress, cook, sales person, and young entrepreneur. When I was sixteen, my older siblings, grown and gone, I found myself operating and managing an independent business; a spin-off of the café business; a sandwich and ice cream parlor. Although it was an esteem-building endeavor for a teenager, it most certainly was not what I really wanted to do, but rather what my father directed me to do. So, I lived it.

Eventually however, out of high school and a couple of years into adulthood, I grew tired of working the business and felt a need to go in a different direction. But I didn't know what I wanted to do, or where was I to go? I wanted newness- but what? Not having a clue of what direction to take, I once again followed my dad's direction. Needless to say, again, it was an area for which I had no particular interest.

It was suggested I enroll in the school of cosmetology. Since my primary objective was to establish a new direction, and to leave home as many of my peers had already done, I agreed. At least it would take me into a different environment and a different vocation. Yet it wasn't my heart direction. Nevertheless, off to school I went, establishing residence in a nearby city for a full year to receive training in cosmetology.

Shortly into my training, even though I had a great instructor, I knew cosmetology was not my calling and most definitely would not be my preferred vocation. It was evident my heart wasn't involved although my actions were

thoroughly engaged. Remember, I'd been trained to satisfy, so, I did well. With money and time invested, well is what was expected, and well is how I performed.

I completed the course, passed the state board exam, and followed through by obtaining a position in a local beauty shop in my hometown. Even with an honest effort, almost immediately, I knew cosmetology would remain my field of work. I endured that path for a while since I felt obligated for time and money invested, but cosmetology just wasn't it. I know it's a gratifying vocation for many, and can be very profitable, but it simply wasn't for me, although I greatly appreciated the experience, and friendships established. Thinking back on it, I don't even know how the thought of my becoming a cosmetologist ever surfaced. I don't ever remember expressing any interest in that field to my parents. As a matter of fact, I know I didn't. And how I actually ended up there - to this day, I don't really know.

However, there I was, twenty years old and still feeling somewhat without a desire vocational direction; an experienced food service entrepreneur and a licensed cosmetologist, and I weren't truly interested in either. I tried working a few other type jobs, but none provided vocational satisfaction. Although I personally thrived in each and grew in life experience, I desired something else. I wasn't certain what direction to take; my true interests and talents had not yet been unveiled. To readily identify what my talents and interests were had not been a part of my picture framing. My framing had not allowed such an advantage. I had developed skills, but my interests yet remained hidden.

Fortunately, and I can't recall how it particularly came about, but I remembered a high school class I really enjoyed; one I found intriguing; the study of psychology. I received excellent grades in this study and was given compliments by my teacher. I really liked its study. It hadn't registered in my mind to pursue furthering my education in this area. The study of psychology simply wasn't a common area of study to those I knew. Personally, I hadn't known anyone who had gone to college to study psychology. But I felt I wanted to give it a try.

I didn't know how to explain the study of psychology to my parents though, because neither one would have understood how it would benefit my future employment, and most definitely would not have encouraged me to go in an area in which they knew nothing about. So, I didn't try. Still, I felt a desire to pursue my own interest. They agreed for me to attend college, and with their support off to college I went. A few years late, yet it was a decision I made for myself based on my own interest.

I was excited about my new adventure, but was soon to encounter cultural shocks. I soon found out I wasn't really prepared for what was ahead to experience college dormitory life with freshman girls. At first it was a bit unnerving. The feel of this new setting didn't come natural to me. While my adolescent and teenage years had been spent working and growing in business, my peer socialization aspect had suffered. Outside of having my at-school friendships, attending a few school social functions, participating in church related activities, and a few other events, which were all structured, I hadn't experienced a social life. My social life up to this point, in large, had been experienced inside of the work place. Socialization actually came in to me instead of my going out to it; business interactions and business friendships. I was exposed to people of all walks, all interests, and all ages. I had received training in a fashion far beyond my youthful years.

At college I was living amongst a community of youths. I didn't know how to live simply as a youngster. I had existed in an adult-like world at home and in the work place. The school of cosmetology had offered a similar world. Those that attended were of varied ages and stages of life. My framework simply had not been inclusive of what I needed to equip me for this new environment; it simply had not prepared me for the social life of college. Initially, it was like living among foreigners.

I found my freshman roommates to be girlish; such girlish playfulness was no longer a part of my make-up. My three roommates and I operated in different zones. I wasn't much interested in their activities and conversations, nor were they in mine. But they were the ones who were on track in their actions. I was the one off track. I didn't realize that fact going in. I soon realized I was indifferent to the lifestyle and would actually have to adapt to the social culture of a youth. Those that know-know that the first year or so of college life, outside of managing to absorb a bit of learning, can be a big social event in itself.

Whatever social deficit I was experiencing however, it wasn't about to be rectified at that point. Whatever hadn't been developed, and should have been, would now have to remain undeveloped. I could not turn back the clock and experience the youthfulness I had lost. At one point I tried, but it didn't work. I realized my phase for certain kinds of experiences and preparations had passed, my picture in that regard had been framed. I would have to move on to the next phase.

All in all, my choice to attend and complete college indeed had been the best choice and it had been my own decision. The outcome of that choice opened doors to areas of personal interest, and subsequently, positioned me to

choose vocational positions and to establish vocational parameters for which I have found to be gratifying. The decision to enter college and study the science of psychology charted the course of my career path, and vocationally shaped who I was later to become.

I could have continued in restaurant business and followed the path of my family's business, or I could have continued as a cosmetologist. I feel I would have done well in either, but, I would have been doing so without real passion. Neither would have granted me a sense of vocational satisfaction as I later found. Although, I cannot deny the knowledge and skills I gained from both, and I refused to look at any of it as time wasted. I believe we gain from each experience. However, I do whole-heartedly believe to engage in interests of the heart breeds passion and life into the soul, which strengthens the fibers of your being. And one should pursue a vocation of interest and passion. It will seem less like a "job".

Among all the wonderful qualities instilled by my parents, and there were many, to train to develop interests and follow dreams and desires were not among the lot. Matter of fact, I'm almost certain my parents never realized what my actual dreams were. Not that they taught their children to settle for less, and not that they didn't encourage them to succeed, they did. But they didn't encourage them to tap into self and to pursue dreams. Our pictures simply were not framed in that manner. My siblings and I were taught to work hard and be productive in life. But I must say they are skills and values which have served me well indeed.

Ready or not, life brings about many challenges. How we initially approach and deal with those challenges largely depend on how our picture has been framed; prior

157

preparation. However, even when dealt a frame which is of disadvantage, we can take the negatives and convert them to positives and refurbish the frame – if at all possible, and in most situations it is. After all, challenges and adversities can build strong character if we so allow.

I don't hold my parents responsible for what I view as a framing shortfall. I now know they did what they knew to do, and in many cases, the best they could. After all, they had been reared in an era where they faced fewer options and greater limitations. My parents, like many others, had so many boundaries set by the culture of their time, they didn't have much opportunity to explore their own interests and unveil their own talents; so it was unlikely they would pass those traits on to their children. Survival and family wellness were the main focuses. They merely trained their children similar to how they had been trained themselves. Along with that, they had their own inner-issues to deal with and most often those issues of concern were ignored. So, I am sure my parents felt, in many ways, they did a whole lot better for their children than what had been done for them.

The fact remains, however, each of us needs to be guided to determine who we are as an individual. Our framing needs to be inclusive of such input. If not, we are likely to be faced with certain struggles trying to figure things out. This input can be received either by means of parental and family training, or it will be received by means of life's experiences and perhaps the school of hard knocks.

Much can be minimized in the struggles of life only if we are trained from the beginning to know self, to explore self and to assert self.

Unfortunately, if the family is dealing with particular issues, which many are, and mine most definitely was, it creates even more challenges and struggles to work through

as you seek to find your comfort zone in life; facing struggles which you need not have faced, wasting time which you need not have wasted, and making choices which were best not to have been made. Our initial framing accounts for much and parents need to pay close attention to how they frame the picture of their children. Their future hinges on the frame.

Even though I wish my parents would have been more insightful about this matter, I still give tribute to them for all that they did for me. I know they dealt with their own shortfalls, insecurities, and personal issues. My dad, even with his strictness and tunnel-view regarding a woman's place, still was the best teacher ever of life skills; such training proving instrumental in my life. My mom with her beauty and charm taught the most valuable lessons in the art of being a lady, and an example of possessing inner-strength, for which I can now identify. Even though neither of my parents is with us today, their lessons live on. For that, I am immensely grateful. Their lessons have served me well and I delight in passing them on to others.

My portrait looks a bit differently these days, and I'm totally pleased with my frame. I found a way to express my uniqueness and innateness in a manner I feel proud of.

I utilized my home training, life lessons, mixed with personal interests and desires, and found a way to alter and enhance my frame to be one which is custom designed for me.

I hope your beginning framing has been one of advantage, but if not, you really can change your frame design. Regardless of how your beginning frame was structured, and even if it has been one of disadvantage, you possess the power to rebuild that frame. Claim that power. Don't allow opportunity to pass you by. Act now! Explore your uniqueness, your talents, interests and desires. They are God's gift to you. If necessary, rebuild your frame. Let all you have experienced work together into wonderfulness.

> *"And we know that all things work together for good to them that love God, to them who are called according to his purpose..."*

Roman 8:28 KJV

Chapter Eleven
The Woman in Mom

The most influential aspect of a female's life, one which has its own special place for discussion, one which is most crucial to her framing, is the woman factor which exists within her mother. Even though this aspect has already been mentioned, it's such an important entity in a girl's life that it requires further noting, Not only is she mother, she is woman as well, with all the feelings, traits, desires and nuisances which involve being woman. So, at this point, let's take a closer look at this intricate as well as delicate aspect which greatly influences and contributes to the character of a developing girl and who she is to become.

Whether it's mother naturally, by adoption or as surrogate – it doesn't matter as much as does the lasting impression and influence which she deposits into a girl's development. Very early in life a girl begins to pattern after her mother – her ways, actions, thought patterns, etc. She is encircled by her mother's presence - positive, negative or indifferent. Whether she gives voice to it or not, a young girl wants to please mom and be accepted by her. It is vitally important to her, and basically, this is the way it is for the daughter throughout development and lasting even longer; perhaps, forever.

Later on, as a girl becomes a young woman, and as the mother/daughter relationship advances toward a more mature one, their positions transitions, and a different kind of relationship forms between them. To the mother however, although she sees a girl physically changing into a woman, but in many regards, in her eyes the daughter remains a child. But to the daughter, it's quite different. She views herself as an adult, like the mother. To the daughter it becomes woman to woman.

The mother may not easily relinquish her close parenting ties, and may try to hang on to what has been. The daughter on the other hand, may tug for her independence, even though she still relies on mother for many things. It is at this point of transitioning the mother needs to guard and direct her daughter into womanhood more so than clinging to the child. This is a critical point in the daughter's life as well with their relationship. It is at this point where their future relationship as two adults is seeded. It is at this point where the daughter is establishing herself as woman.

This relationship forming between them can be one of smooth sailing, or not. Hopefully, smooth sailing because in the heart of each mother, she desires a beautiful relationship with her daughter and future grandchildren. A mother wants to be a central part of her daughter's life. The daughter, whether she knows it at that point or not, will most definitely need the support and advice of her mother, and a good relationship will serve her well.

As the daughter steps out on her own into life, she takes with her all the facets and messages which she has acquired from her mom, the intentional, unintentional and subliminally transmitted. Those facets are now a part of her. She hasn't yet learned to master being one in her own. So, she actually walks into life being a mirror image of her mom, at least the attributes which mom has allowed the daughter to see. However, there are some things which mom needs to reveal, but she doesn't disclose. She mostly allows the daughter to see mom, but not so much the woman in mom.

If mom would allow the woman aspects to be seen – such fears, hurts, and disappointments; to be more transparent to the daughter, it would place the daughter so much further ahead in self. As her daughter steps out into the world, she will carry with her a better understanding as she transitions from girl to woman. She will already have an inside-view of what to expect, and an inside prospective of how to handle what is most definitely to surface. She will be less blind-sighted in what she is to experience. The woman who lives within mom is a person daughter needs to know. Mothers should not conceal self from their daughters.

I was attending college at the time of my mother/daughter relationship transition. As I experienced newness in my independence away at college, I also was experiencing newness in becoming woman. It was a new adventure, new feelings, and overall, a different world from what I had experienced previously. I needed mom's wisdom and embrace.

Most definitely, as a young woman goes out on her own into the world, one person she is going to need is her mother. And the bond between the two needs to be relaxed that the mom is comfortable to give her advice and support, and the daughter would want to elicit her mother's advice and support.

Going forth in my newfound relationship with my mother, I was so ready to absorb all of the advice and wisdom I believed she could impart; wisdom she had gained from her own life experiences; wisdom to aid me in becoming woman. In addition, I wanted and needed to know my mom differently. I needed to know her as woman.

Somehow as a child, I had established more of an attachment to my dad, as girls often do. But then, as I was becoming woman, I wanted a more affable relationship with my mom; the woman which through birth which I was more adjoined to than any other in all of earth. I needed this particular woman to guide me through this particular gateway. I wanted that connectivity specifically.

As my mom and I entered this gateway, and as we were establishing a more woman-to-woman relationship, I began to see her in ways other than being just a mom. A lot she and I had not discussed prior to this point, we then began to touch upon. I began to better understand the essence of the woman I had lived with all those years. I began to realize we were more similar than not, which was a bit surprising. I began to gain a better understanding of many of the whys; the whys of certain stances she had taken and the whys of many of her choices. I was beginning to view her through a different set of lenses. I was seeing her as a woman with her own desires, interests, feelings and rights.

For a daughter to understand her mom as woman, and to understand her essence and character as a woman is a huge element which she needs to grasp. It is this element that helps a daughter with answers to her own questionable whys about herself. This is an element that needs not be taken lightly because a daughter will surely see her mother within self-face-to-face as she grows into her own womanhood and develops her own relationships. To understand mom will help daughter to understand self, for in part she is the same.

My belief is that, the relational temperament a girl establishes with her mother, or surrogate, is likely to be the same approach she will emulate in other relationships; female to female, and female to male. If daughter is comfortable laughing and talking with mom, she will transfer those traits over to other female relationships. If daughter and mom are reserved in their communication, she will more likely mirror that behavior as well. If mom is one to work and serve the needs of others, daughter will more than likely be similar in one fashion or another. If mom is comfortable and confident in self, daughter is more apt to be the same, and if mom is reserved in mannerism, daughter is more likely is too. Not that their personality will be identical, but many of their traits will be the same.

A daughter becomes her mother in disguise. And, she will likely remain like her mother until she recognizes a need to change. Otherwise, she behaves similar even in ways she hadn't previously agreed with or liked.

A physician once expressed to me, even though he was speaking of a physical aspect, but I think it extends to other things - and I paraphrase his words is in saying - we are what we are. Whatever your make up is, whatever your predispositions are, will eventually surface if we're not proactive in doing something to either delay or prevent the likely inevitable. So, I'm thinking, whatever tendencies are inside us; whatever our structural make-up, it will eventually surface; like mom, like daughter.

As my mom and were transitioning to an adult-to adult relationship, at that same time my mom was experiencing her own life changes. I began to notice things about her that had not been evident prior to this point. I witnessed her change into a different kind of woman. Newness was surfacing as she began to engage a kind of liberty within self different than I had ever seen. Whatever her personal reasons were, and whatever excited her personal blossoming phase, I noticed a change was taking place from the inside out. I observed a woman having spent nearly forty years married and with children, one which had traveled a common path nearly all that time, decide to make change; to actually transform into newness - self, relationship and environment.

I don't know to this day what gave my mom that surge of energy and strength to make her own life-altering changes at that point in time in life. She apparently had had enough of the old and wanted newness. I suspect she needed a fresh wind and fresh fire. I suspect she needed to live out the woman that had been contained inside. I suspect she wanted to blossom out from hiding. And I suspect, she didn't see herself too old, or think too much time had passed to make the needed change.

She and I never got an opportunity to have that particular heart-to-heart talk of disclosure, since she passed away suddenly not many years following. But eventually as I experienced some things in life, I now understand her decisions and I applaud her actions.

In a way, I wish the newness I watched emerge, had been the demeanor which had been evident all along - that it had been the unmasked, assertive woman from which I

166

would have received my earlier impressions; my earlier framing. I believe the qualities of that renewed spirit would have left different lasting impressions upon me to carry over into adulthood. For at her renewed point, I saw her composed, yet bold; more outspoken, self-determined and adventurous woman. A spirit no doubt which had been in hiding for years.

In a strange way though, in my naiveté, initially I didn't especially appreciate her change at first for it was different than what I was used to; a different persona than the woman which had raised me. And at the time, I viewed her actions as being a bit selfish. I had no real understanding of her inner needs and heart desires. After all, she was mom, placed on this earth to provide her service. At least that was my perception at that point in time.

As time progressed however, I could see the newness was very refreshing and gratifying to her. What I was seeing then, was a woman that was putting self into the equation of her life; a woman that decidedly acted upon her own needs and desires to a greater degree; a woman that stepped out of the expected mold, the mandates - spoken and unspoken, and decidedly acted upon what she expected and desired of self. I was able to observe my mom experience a more diverse lifestyle - in friendships, in travel, and in fun; somewhat a total character make-over. I could see that her perceptions and mindset had shifted. I witnessed her regain authority of life's adventure. She reframed her picture right before my eyes.

Yet, I don't know if she ever verbally expressed to anyone what it was, she wanted out of life for herself; or even knew how to express it. Although I could discern, she was a lady of adventure, with many special gifts and talents, possibly any interests. But early on, she had surrendered to a lifestyle and had permitted her voice to become softened. And now I ask, for the sake of what? But she as so many others of her era had preconceived ideas of how a traditional wife and mother should perform, and probably felt it dutiful to do things as were done; submissive, sacrificial and self-hidden.

Prior to that however, it wasn't that my mom lived a life in total submission. She didn't. Or that she didn't do things on her want-list. She did. But she lived as many women did, and as many still do. They follow a path of expectations and pre-determined traditions. But with my mom, through it all she made a determination to make change. And if she hadn't, I believe she would have continued in a lifestyle weary, worn and unfulfilled.

Mom, however, didn't share her personal thoughts and feelings. Then, parents didn't involve children in their personal affairs. Even so, children were able to feel the mood of the environment. So, when mom began to make a change, although I didn't want it, I somehow accepted it and, in a way, understood it.

Now with much respect, I appreciate the strength my mom had all along, and I especially appreciate the strength she possessed which fortified her "to blossom out from hiding" It was her inner-strength she tapped into which made it all possible.

Unfortunately, our mother/daughter, woman-to-woman transitional relationship never achieved its fullness due to her untimely death. Many of the anticipated experiences I presumed we would share also died. We never experienced the fullness of sharing many things a young maturing daughter looks to share with her mom.

As I traveled life's journey, experiencing my life's struggles and even the joys, I missed my mom. I desired the woman-to-woman talks and times we could have spent. For many years, I felt robbed, even envious of other mother/daughter relationships; especially when observing them spending time together-talking, laughing, shopping, and just sharing. I wanted my own mother/ daughter relationship. I needed my mom to help me better understand my feelings, and needs, and to give direction. I needed her guidance as I became a wife and mother. There were many a time I simply needed to rest my head on her shoulder and to have her listening ear and an arm of support.

A young budding woman needs the strength and support of a caring mother or mother figure; such care and support to become her anchor. Without that anchor, a young woman often finds herself somewhat at a loss in many regards in matters pertaining to womanhood. A mother's presence should be a place you can rest and totally be self. Who else knows and will accept you like mom. And if that is taken away, who else will ever know and accept you in that same unique way; probably, no one.

I know losing my mother at my very point of need, in part, attributed to my "hiding" state. There were certain traits that weren't developed because that particular aspect of training and influence had been removed. I simply cannot explain the depth of such a loss to a daughter, especially when you're young, and not yet secured in self as a woman.

Your mother is your hero, confidante, teacher and role model. There is where a daughter goes in times of needed motherly advice? What happens when she doesn't have that mother/daughter dialogue she needs to help her along the way? What happens when mom; the woman that symbolizes the daughter's own being, becomes absent forever?

There are phases of growth in a young woman's life. And when she's in a particular phase, and needs to share with mom, but mom isn't there, it can result in despair. This despair can manifest itself in varied ways. The daughter may try figuring things out on her own, but may make so many mistakes and unwise decisions in the process, simply because that guiding force is missing; that force and source which serves as her extended anchor.

Oftentimes, I hear daughters say, "I don't know what I would do without my mother." They express it would be so unsettling to be without her help, guidance and support. Unfortunately, many are without, and do experience such unsettling affect. I recognize it's not always death that separates mothers and daughters. There are all kinds of situations of separation – but the result is the same, and the lasting affect can be disabling. And for many, they never get beyond the lingering disconnect of being without mother. We learn however, to compensate for whatever is lacking, or at least we try, and we develop ways to move forward in spite. But to find a trusting surrogate to fill some of the gap can be most beneficial.

My advice to any daughter fortunate to have a caring and nurturing mother is to appreciate and celebrate her presence in your life. She is truly a gift to you from God. Love and cherish the gift that has been granted you. And my advice to mothers is to cherish and support your daughters. Be the anchor of positive influence in her life.

I have tried to be such an anchor to my own daughter and build a relationship we could openly share self with each other. I feel I have succeeded in many regards. And I'm so thankful for that. But I am my mother's daughter. And when my daughter was born, I was yet operating in the mindset of tradition and expectation. So, I tried to contour and frame my daughter similarly to how I had been framed during my upbringing.

Blessedly, my daughter, being the individual she is, and has always been, would not succumb no matter how much I tried to forge it. She was determined to be whom and how she is, even amid special needs challenges. Even though I operated out of a mindset of tradition, I did have the open- mindedness to expose her to diversity. My daughter received such advantages and built upon them, allowing her to blossom in her own special way. And she remained steadfast, unmovable to change her innate character. She remained true to self. And sometimes in my attempt to persuade her otherwise, I could detect her having a smirk, suggesting – it's not happening mom.

If my mom was in our lives today, she would most definitely appreciate her granddaughter, Tammi. For she has been able to figure out some things that took my mom and me quite some time to figure out; how to be uniquely comfortable in self; to portray that inward individual representing the essence of self. Tammi has never been one to accept limitations of expressing who she is as a unique individual; a trait I now affectionately admire, and I know my mom would as well.

I don't know from where my daughter received such self-assuredness and at such a young age. She has never allowed herself to be pigeonholed-even though there have been many times I've tried, thinking it was best. There were times when I tried nudging her to conform to what I thought she should be; that which I felt fit the viewed "norm". But insistently, she refuses to portray herself any differently than who she is. And who she is, is this dynamic attracting force to which others are drawn.

I now realize, if I had been successful in altering my daughter's personality, that very uniqueness would have been hidden, and her true spirit broken. Wouldn't that have been so unfortunate, for she is the most original person I know, and have ever known? Even though she is faced with many challenges, she has never viewed herself as limited or disabled. And because of her point of view of self, others don't focus on her limitations either. They simply see her personality - the bold, joyous, witty, smart, expressive individual she is. She actually epitomizes the very platform I now promote - to be joy-filled in self; to be who you are, to live out who you are, appreciate and use the gifts and talents God has given you, and to enjoy the adventure of life. And in this case, my daughter has become the teacher.

There were times however, when my daughter was much younger, I allowed her special circumstance to create barriers for her and me. She didn't see limitations,

172

but I did. And I operated within that view. I allowed her special needs to narrow both of our worlds of venture and activity. While there were definite parameters to acknowledge, I however, allowed those constraints to impact greater than

Often, we don't maximize what can be achieved in spite of limitations. Rather, we minimize because of perceived limitations. My daughter refused to confine her uniqueness. She held true to her individuality. This is what we ought to do, hold true to individuality.

I am most grateful for the spirit my daughter possesses, and that she's one who exemplifies that one should exert one's own uniqueness, even when there are special circumstances. Isn't that what we all want, to be seen first for whom we are, then all other can follow.

Command your strongholds to be released and allow contentment to surge your soul. It can be done. And for a girl, a mother is such a dynamic tool to aid in this process and progress. But a mother has to allow her daughter to see her as woman as well as her mom.

As I think back on the memory of my mom, I acknowledge she left with me meaningful lasting impressions; ones of courage, strength and determination. However, there was a time, I didn't understand nor appreciate her actions; but I have reconciled my feelings and changed my view, realizing that foremost, mom was a woman, one with her own desires, needs and interests. I am so appreciative that I had the opportunity to witness her blossoming out from hiding journey, leaving with me memories which I sincerely cherish.

Little did I know that one day I too would be faced with a similar journey. My mom, unfortunately, wasn't with me to guide me through. But she left with me the assurance that if such a need should arise; it's okay to act upon it. It doesn't matter how old you are, or how long you've traveled a path, what's most important is that you realize the error of your ways. Then, take stock in courage and determination and move forward to make the desired changes.

As I see it, many women today are in hiding, simply feeling the need to do what is perceived as best for the circumstances. But we owe as much to ourselves as we feel we owe to others. We don't have to perform a certain way, when in fact it's not the way we need things to be. It not okay that you neglect self.

Mothers, teach your daughters how to become content in self by embracing their individuality. Embrace your own as their role model. They will become a by-product of you; your perceptions and your actions. They might have different interests, goals, and drive, but the inner-woman will be so much like you. I cannot express enough how crucial it is that a positive relationship between mother and daughter is established, and a true line of communication always remains open. And by all means, allow them to see the woman in mom.

Women, we must receive it as a serious matter to train our daughters in a manner that will equip them to become successful in self and content with who they are. We don't want to raise selfish and arrogant young women, but we must empower our daughters to feel confident in self to a being soundly grounded so they don't feel it necessary to compromise their integrity, character and self.

We must train and instill in our daughters to feel that they are a jewel, a true gift to be offered. To understand they are not one dimensional, but many dimensions. And, if others do not appreciate their individuality and uniqueness, then they are to surround themselves with others that do. The best way to instill such qualities in our daughters is to first instill them in ourselves. In that light, a daughter is able to see a living example.

I give tribute to my mom Reba, for the example she modeled. Her spirit lives on because as I look in the mirror, I see traits of her face and am reminded of her presence. I feel she would be proud of the fact I too recognized the need to do things differently, and that I took action to blossom out from hiding; a lesson well taken mom.

We don't have to be cornered into being something or someone we're really not. We don't have to become a one-size-fits-all type of woman. We are all different, and that difference should be embraced and executed.

My mom's strength and actions allowed me to know it was okay to change. This is the message she left with me, a message I shall continue to share with others. I trust others who are in need will receive it as an awakening.

I am so glad I got a chance to see a glimpse of the woman who lived in mom.

Thank you, mom!

Chapter Twelve
"I Do"

There's yet another important aspect of a woman's life; one which is imperative to look at; one which greatly influences her presence; one which becomes the center focus in her life, one which impinges on her judgment; and one which can either build her up or plunge her further onto a path of "hiding".

To marry becomes a primary focus in most girls' lives. Girls prepare themselves for this happening. They are groomed as little girls to one day find that person who will provide love, support and happiness. From a little girl to teenager to young adult, the thought of marriage, the "I Do", lingers in her mind. When a woman feels she has found him, that special one, and their commitment made, vows are said and married life begins.

Hopefully, prior to "I Do", both would have had good examples of how a couple is to conduct themselves in the union of marriage. Both are bringing with them their preconceived models; their influences from upbringing, training, prototypes, and personal experiences.

A woman, over time has had tendency to lean toward the ways and means of her husband. She receives him as her guide. Hopefully, he takes his lead seriously and has her best interest at heart, for after the "I Do', she on her way to follow him however he may lead her.

A new bride – especially one whose belief is that her husband is considered head of household – takes on many of her husband's stances, and he, in many ways, becomes her prime influence. She loves him, so she believes in him and trusts him in this role. She places her well-being in his

hands and has faith he will be the defender of her body and heart.

When the two joined at the altar to profess their "I Do", they openly expressed their love and intent to live a joyous and dedicated life together. They made vows in front of God, family and friends; sincere intents. But, hidden in the midst, along with the explicit vows, were concealed ones – the unspoken ones which will later forge their way into the relationship. Each of them brought undisclosed agendas and expectations regarding the other to the altar, stemming from their individual programmed precepts; ones which the other was not aware of at that moment of "I Do".

A woman however, as she stands at the altar with eyes of awe, makes vows to her intended husband – to be to him what he desires of her and what she perceives is her required role as his wife. She has plans to deliver all the role implies. As she admiringly stands by his side and makes her explicit vows of love, faithfulness, and commitment, she also accepts the hidden ones. The traditional practices and mores that are brought to the altar which typecasts her in a role simply because of gender. Initially, neither he nor she may realize what is actually happening, but it surfaces shortly after the "I Do".

Initially however, being oblivious to the unspoken ones, she accepts and vows …

Today, as I become wife – I vow to surrender my surname of heritage as my identity and to accept yours as my own – forsaking my own as whom I am. As your wife, I do vow to leave my surroundings of familiarity and follow you to yours, forsaking mine. I do vow to walk devotedly in your shadow as I postpone my dreams, goals and desires and

work beside you to first achieve yours. I do vow to understand that I must accept certain actions from you for reason simply because – you are man. I do vow to accept daily household tasks as woman's responsibility, and to appear grateful at times when your assistance is provided. I do vow to accept responsibility to prepare meals for you, and will take lightly your criticism of my efforts at times when the preparation and/or taste are not to your liking. I do vow to accept that I am to work diligently to maintain my personal appearance, to look nice and desirable for you even though you neglect to do the same for me. I do vow to pretend not to notice your lack of discretion at times when you find it necessary to take curious, admiring glances at another woman in my presence, even if it offends me. I do vow to refrain from causing a quarrel by expressing my opinions during those times when our views conflict, rather in honor of peace, I will reserve my expressions for those times of mutual accord. I do vow to understand that I shall not, in your opinion, become a nagging wife – even when I view my requests as important and necessary. I do vow to understand that I am not

178

to be too pushy toward you for tasks completion, but to be patient and realize that all tasks asked of you will be completed – eventually. I do vow to be supportive in all endeavors that are dear to you, but will understand your lack of effort, time and interest to promote the same for me. I do vow to make our home a comfortable environment, investing time to ensure that family needs are met, even when my own needs may be overlooked. I do vow to understand that over time, my generosity and service is to be taken for granted as I aim to live up to the role of woman as nurturer, supporter and servicer. And, I most solemnly vow to understand that, in the midst of it, as I grow old and weary, and likely have suppressed many of my feelings, thoughts and hopes – I am to find comfort in the fact that – I have served well.

Unspoken, I Do Vow…

Perhaps this "I Do Vow" scenario is somewhat exaggerated and boldly stated, but not totally unmerited – because within it rests truths. And many women live out much of these truths. Although there are many variations of such a scenario, relationships and mannerisms differ, yet within it contain similarities where portions of it hit home to many wives in a manner that is disturbing to her.

Most certainly and especially for the traditional-minded, it's a happening that takes place in lives as they accept the position of wife. And, in a husband's eye a wife becomes the expected service provider, as he steps into position to become recipient of those expected services. Not that he consciously approaches the altar with a list in mind, but within his being – whether he admits it or not, he certainly expects her services and compromises and may even feel entitled once they wed.

I don't think a husband really views his wife as being in a position of compromise and sacrifice. I don't even think he thinks he takes advantage of her willingness, or that he imposes his beliefs or role expectations onto her. I believe he just sees a wife from his own lens of precepts. He has a version of her role in his mind and he expects her to perform to its gender prejudices.

Further, within this mindset of gender prejudices and double standards, I believe a husband expects from his wife certain allowances beyond which he is willing to give of himself; in the like manner he expects of her. He expects her to be okay with his unwillingness; and generally, she accepts these conditions. How she feels about this

arrangement and how it affects her doesn't appear to matter much to him; because she is woman and that's how certain matters are generally handled. But if she doesn't perform as he thinks his wife is supposed to, then to him, it matters – a lot. So, to avoid the uncomforting feelings about the whole matter, a wife often obliges, and man is okay with her resignation. To operate within this realm of double-standard is simply a part of his psyche. Traditional practices, even if unfair, have allowed him this vantage point.

It's not my intent by any mean to debase man's character, his good intent, or his good will, for woman is not blameless in this matter as to how he regards her. She marries with intent and conveys to her husband that she is willing to be his all – all that he desires. In part because of her love for him and in part due to her view of what the social order expects of her role as wife. Since she's willing to give her all, he's willing to accept it.

This may be an altruistic gesture on her part, but not totally realistic. A wife cannot be a husband's all-in-all without compromising self. As wife, she should be willing to give of self to him generously and willingly, but not to give up self for him; and he shouldn't want her to. When she gives up self, she will find over time she loses the very uniqueness that first attracted him to her, and that very uniqueness that once defined her individuality to him. It's kind of a catch-22, isn't it? What initially attracted him, she loses. And what she initially took pride in, she forsakes.

No doubt within a marriage, each will need to make certain compromises, over and over again in fact, but not to the point of surrendering self as routine practice. Neither should. But a wife is more likely to be the one, if any, to become cornered in such a position. Unfortunately, if this assumed position of sacrifice continues unending, over time, she becomes an over-worked and distressed woman.

To be fair about the matter though, there are unrealistic expectations woman brings to the altar regarding man as well; precepts that have been planted in her mind regarding a husband's role. Other than the apparent ones centered on provision, a woman brings certain other expectations to the table. To her, he is to be the main provider of all her needs – tangible and intangible. Unknowingly, he too accepts unspoken vows; ones which she believes and is depending on him to deliver.

At a point, he too will face the reality of the unspoken vows he has unwarily accepted – ones which are sure to surface as time progresses. Maybe not the hands-on servicing types which are expected of his wife, but still yet, gender typecasting ones. He will begin to comprehend that in her mind, as he stood at the altar for the "I Do", he agreed...

Today as I become husband –as proof of my love: I do vow to accept the obligation to complete you. I do vow to accept the responsibility to be in charge of our family, and to pilot us to the road of success, conquering all hindrances and obstacles – at all times. I do vow to work hard to provide finances to take care of all needs and many wants. I do vow to be insightful to your personal needs and to provide understanding and the cure for all your distresses. I do vow to love you unconditionally, demonstrating understanding of all your mood variations, insecurities and etc. I do vow to become a mind-reader and to know and understand what distresses you even when you do not openly express it. I do vow to accept responsibility to make you feel beautiful and desirable. I do vow to put you first above all, at all times- regardless of any circumstance requiring attention. I do vow to keep you feeling secure and content at all times. I do vow to understand that you will expect me to be the fixer of everything, whether I'm knowledgeable to do so or not. I do vow to accept that you may rely and rely and rely

and rely and rely on me to make it right –
whatever the situation may be…
Unspoken, I Do Vow

Well, to be honest, this view is also unfair for a wife to have regarding her husband, isn't it? And although this is an exaggerated scenario as well, again not totally unmerited for much truth lies within. Even so, it is unrealistic for a wife to expect her husband to be this Omni-powerful person. But wives actually expect it, and furthermore, have been conditioned to think in this manner.

Initially, the husband is not aware of all the expectations she has in store for him. He may have been given clues of what she expects, but still not a clear understanding of her conditioned mindset. Women however, have a better understanding of what a husband expects of her. She knows she's expected to be the nurturer, servicer and supporter, and anticipates delivering it. So, she's not quite as blind-sided by circumstance as it unfolds. But what she doesn't grasp, which later becomes her downfall is its ill-effect in the long-run; the emotional and physical wear. But, how can either possibly understand unspoken vows when in fact they are not communicated? They are simply expected and implied.

For man however, if he actually realized how emotionally needy a woman is trained to be, he probably would be too afraid to accept her terms; afraid of failure and afraid of becoming burdened. My belief, woman wouldn't be as emotionally clingy if she was trained to be more independent, self-developed and self-focused prior to "I Do". Then, she wouldn't expect her husband to be the panacea for all her wants and ills. But girls are groomed to accept the idea of the mystical "knight in shining armor", a knight who has all solutions - the fairytale; find that knight and all will be well.

Maybe without such a fairytale perception entrenched in the mind, maturing young ladies would possibly achieve a greater level of self-reliance. Not that a woman should become so independent that she wouldn't feel the need to depend on man, rather she would gain control within self-strengthening individuality prior to that point; therefore, being more self-reliant in a relationship; choosing someone to bring into her life who appreciates and admires her strength rather than feel threatened by it. And it would be that same strength that will aid and support him.

Years ago, when I approached the altar, I too came with preconceived notions and expectations, some valid; some not. I didn't gain a thorough understanding of what I was committing to although I knew it was definitely a lifelong commitment. Marriage and family were what I desired. But I wasn't aware of all the unspoken vows I would be accepting. Those aspects weren't clearly understood. I didn't have clear vision of my new role as wife according to my husband's expectations. Nor did I clearly define to him how I wanted to be perceived as his wife. We didn't invest efforts to clearly understand our future goals as a new couple, with merging aspirations and goals. We simply never had discussions to outline what we desired and needed of each other in our new relationship; to establish an understanding that would carry us through the long haul.

So, as many other couples do, we became vulnerable to the unspoken vows.

Although, collectively we would bring to our union life experiences, education and trained skills, and those aspects would prove to be of great benefit. But we failed to bring clarity of expectations and a viable plan as a new couple. Courting compared to marriage are totally different worlds. Together you become somewhat different people than when you were before marriage.

With us, it seemed we just wanted to get on with life together as a family. I believe we were both functioning on a premise of expectations and anticipation. We had a history as childhood friends, so we had many common memories to share and much to talk about. We felt we knew as much about each other as we needed to now. We didn't talk much of our expectation for each other as a spouse, or as a parent for that matter, especially since we were establishing a blended family; a gross error.

I think we simply felt our history of knowing each other, our feelings for each other, and a shared hope for the best future was well enough. But actually, each was bringing to the marriage preconceived ideas of how we wanted the other to behave – many of which we failed to mention. How the other was supposed to act was simply a given in our own minds. But had the unspoken became spoken, we would have experienced fewer unwanted surprises, fewer trials and errors, and fewer tug-of-wars; minimizing wasted time and efforts, all which would have placed us much further ahead in the process of where and how we desired to be as a couple and family.

However, the model of our parents' marriage would follow us into our marriage. In ways, we would try to intertwine aspects of both as if we were them. But we were not our parents, neither were we of their time.

Since we had not determined our own perceived model through discussion and planning, we simply followed suit with the examples we best knew. I suspect in my husband's mind I was to be similar to his mother, and in my mind, he was to be similar to my father. But I wasn't his mother nor was he, my father.

Generally, people are drawn to traits they recognize, and often seek what is familiar. My husband and I undoubtedly, recognized similar traits of our parents in each other, and possibly the recognition of such traits was somewhat of a comfort zone and drawing force. Let it be known though, just because it's familiar, doesn't mean it's an ideal fit. To know what fits, you must first know self, and too, discuss what you expect and need. And hold true to it. Otherwise, you're just guessing and blindly hoping.

During the course of a courtship, there needs to be heart-to heart, honest communication between man and woman regarding what is expected and desired; bold discussions. Each needs to be honest in conveying to the other what is personally needed to maintain well-being within the relationship – for both. Not only do you want what best suits you, you want what best suits the other person as well. It's a combined relationship, and you want it to be a flourishing one.

Each needs to be honest regarding his or her willingness to deliver what is being requested by the other.

Don't just say what the other person wants to hear. Speak in truth. Each deserves the privilege of knowing what is being required and to what they are committing. Then each has an opportunity to agree or not, and the freewill to

accept or not. At least going in, one becomes more knowledgeable about what is expected.

The aim of course is to have a compatible relationship where both involved are content, in self and with each other. Think about it; how can one truly commit to the reality of a situation without having a clear understanding of the situation. If you plunge into a relationship without an understanding of the expectations and mindset of the other, then to what in fact are you committing? To have an understanding of the mindset of the person you're about to commit to is crucial for the success of the relationship, and crucial to one's contentment within it.

We can't simply hope for the best, we need some indication or evidence that it is the best. Of course, there's never absolute assurance, but sharing honest and open communication unveils information to better make informed decisions; as a result, lessening the odds for ill-perceptions; thereby, increasing the chance of having a lasting and satisfying married relationship. If an understanding is not established prior, why is it believed that by chance, all will fall into place following marriage?

Even when there are initial red flags, so many women forge ahead anyway, and go into marriage feeling a change will come later, feeling assured of possessing power to change her man after he becomes husband. Too many women put the cart before the horse. Let's secure the man first, and work out problem spots later. This is in reverse order, isn't it? It should be at the start of the relationship when particular needs are expressed, concerns are dealt with, and viewpoints are compared. Chances are if it doesn't feel right in the beginning, it won't feel right later on either.

Prior to "I Do" is where you want to work out certain kinks. And some personality kinks may not be worked out for you. But many settle anyway, knowing certain things are not agreeable. Why settle for less than what is required for self? More so, why settle for one that offers less than what it is you need and desire. It's not a judgment call and may not even be about the person. It's about what matches well with you. What's great for one may not be so good for another, and what's not so good for one may be absolutely what's good for another. But, it's about what personally fits you to bring about the best in you and the best in the other. Otherwise, what is the purpose of coming together in the first place?

To secure what is personally needed is not a selfish act; it's an insightful act. To receive what one needs is important for content living. What you need is the make-up of what represents you. We are talking about a lifetime commitment, not a mere episode. So, to feed into self is crucial.

A point which cannot be minimized, and warrants reemphasizing is that, prior to coming together in a marriage, time needs to have been invested in self to understand self - who you actually are – considering all aspect. It will place you in a better position to approach the relationship as a more composed and wholesome person.

188

It grounds you to know what it is you want, need, desire and most importantly, what you will accept.

If maturing girls are trained to recognize these factors along the way, they will be better equipped to make relative and wise choices. Again, it doesn't necessarily assure the best choices will be made each time, but it does afford better grounding to do so.

Women are often led by emotion. Truly, emotion should not be the most decisive guiding force. Too often though, emotion becomes the primary guiding force. A course

should not be plotted based primarily on emotion. Much more is needed. Love and attraction are great, and are essential and endearing keys. But love and attraction coupled with awareness and understanding is greater. The mixture of all can be dynamic.

We cannot down play the foundation needing to be in place prior to committing to "I Do". To have acquired a sense of your fundamental nature, values, and standards, and to have a handle on the direction which you desire to go in life – along with having education, exposure to diversity, travel adventure, desired goals in focus and partially achieved, and rooted in spiritual faith; are all important entities in a young woman's development and stability. They most certainly will serve to heighten overall awareness and broaden choices. Together they give power; power in self and power in prospective.

If a woman gains in these areas prior to the point of "I Do", there will be less need to compromise self; certain blinders will be removed and certain personal requirements will be commanded. She will not desire someone else to complete her, rather to grow alongside beside her. The other person enriches, not completes.

What is confusing is, women are often ambiguous in expressing their thoughts and feelings to men, especially in their communications while dating. But clarity in self must be attained in order to be in position to effectively express and articulate it to another. We cannot navigate in confusion and obscurity on one hand and at the same time be viewed as one in clarity on the other hand. Failing to clearly express what is expected, desired, or acceptable, inevitably sabotages what is required for future well-being. We cannot expect a boyfriend or husband to provide answers to what we don't know and understand ourselves. Clearly, time must be invested in self to clearly know these things.

I read in "Think like a Man, Act like a Woman" –a man's point of view – women often are too vague in expressing what it is they expect from man in a relationship. His sentiment to paraphrase – women don't hold true to their "standards and requirements". He suggested that a woman often fails to voice what she needs of a boyfriend or husband; therefore, she compromises what she actually needs and desires. She settles for less, and often settles for what she doesn't even want.

In this case, I'm thinking, the field is left wide open to man for other possibilities and actions; and likely possibilities and actions opposite of what a woman actually wants. She inadvertently conveys she's willing to tolerate such conduct by accepting it. Then, as a man realizes his behavior is acceptable, these actions are put into practice and subsequently become his routine. Her accepting disposition gives him assent to continue the very actions she dislikes.

While she's thinking these little kinks and situations will eventually work themselves out, he's establishing a pattern that's viable for him. So why would he see a need to change later? It works for him. His actions have become his norm. He may listen to her "nag" about it, but his actions remain the same because the pattern has been established.

She has set a standard of accepting other than what she desires and needs. And in doing so, her level of frustration goes up, but he is content in his actions. So, what happens is, she gives up how and what she wants and accepts what she doesn't; and the cycle continues.

I don't think his action serves as a measurement of his love, but I do feel it infringes on his respect level for the relationship as a couple. I don't know what's in a man's mind, but it appears he is willing to accept what a woman is willing to tolerate. If she accepts it, then it means I can do it. Maybe, man sees her accepting disposition as a form of passivity – I don't know. But I do know if a woman doesn't hold true to what she needs and requires of him, likely neither will he.

A pattern is to be workable for both. One shouldn't have the upper hand. A relationship is to be a mutual partnership and mutual consideration has to be given. Respect should be full-circle. Considerations should be full-circle. But one must respect self first. Treat yourself as you would like others to treat you.

As woman, you reserve the right to command what is reasonably needed within a relationship. It doesn't mean you will possess a dominate persona; it simply means you're taking charge of self. Commanding what is needed doesn't have to be done in a rough, tough, aggressive manner. But, most definitely it is to be articulated in a manner that exemplifies seriousness about what is being requested and seriousness about what will be tolerated. Again, why settle for less. What would be the purpose?

Women, we shouldn't become so emotionally needy and so hurried to get into a relationship that values, requirements and standards become compromised; or to a point we think we must conduct ourselves in a particular manner for the sake of "that's just the way it has been done". You must personify strength and certainty in self.

I believe marriage, as God designed, should be one of the most fulfilling and exhilarating experiences of life's journey. But it definitely depends on the two people

involved. Often, it is inferred that married life is to be a struggle. I don't agree with that opinion. Challenges at times; some more difficult than others, but a struggle? Now days, it appears common place to expect the struggle, and somewhat to expect to fail. As if to succeed in a marriage is almost impossible.

Surely, marriage is an effort of dedication requiring patience and endurance. But should it be such a struggle to share your life with someone you love, respect and are passionate about? Not to insinuate that married life will be void of difficult and trying times. There most certainly will be demands and trying times, but this is true for life itself. There will also be times when there are lower periods of affection and intimacy shown. Still, I don't believe two people committed to the relationship having sincere love, appreciation and respect for one another have to struggle to maintain a loving relationship. I don't believe that's God's design. But if a struggle is constantly necessary, what does that say about the relationship?

Outside the relationship is where struggles are expected, the day-to-day adventures of life. But, inside the relationship is where you should expect to find rest and solace; two people having opportunity to share the most intimate dynamics of life, supposedly with the one you love and trust while maintaining the other's best interest at heart; two people working together as a team, sharing, sharing and sharing. Isn't that awesome? Of course you are going to get mad, disappointed, disillusioned at times, and maybe even bored at some point. And at a point, may not even like the other one. But if the relationship has been solidly built in the first place; love, respect, honesty, and priorities are in order, you'll find a way to work through those down times. But, if within the relationship there's

presence of dishonesty; breeding distrust; the presence of self-indulgence causing hardship upon the other; lack of effective communication breeding misunderstandings; and slackness in supporting and promoting the other's personal growth and happiness – then, there most assuredly will be struggle.

If such conditions persist, then you wonder if real love and commitment actually abound. And if not, why marry? Why would two people want to entrust their lives to each other to endure struggle? And why would one want to selfishly impose struggle upon the other? Also, why would God ordain marriage and offer such a special gift for us to struggle through it?

Now, I am not so naïve to think it does not take constant concerted efforts, and a display of heartfelt commitment in order to make marriage a beautiful dwelling. Nor am I so naïve to think marriage is a land of constant euphoria. But I believe it can work very well and be fulfilling to both.

Does it mean you must constantly wear blinders and be inattentive to other people who surround you? Or, that you have to live a life of recluse separating yourself from others to avoid temptation? I think that is almost impossible. We are going to notice other people. And we are going to be somewhat attracted to other people for whatever that reason may be. I think that is especially true for man since he is more visual. But still, you don't cross lines. You make known your position of marriage and respect it, and always protect the heart of your spouse. If you want marriage, then you must act like you want it.

Within the confines of morality and character boundaries, both parties involved in the relationship can experience true essence of self within the partnership. Each

however, must be open-minded regarding the other as an individual, to accept differences whether in agreement or not, invest time in each other's needs, interests, and goals and be the most proactive cheerleader and encourager for the other.

It should not be a competition between husband and wife. It should be a partnership growing together. I desire for you what I desire for myself, and I will do everything in my power to help you achieve. No one has to be the sacrificial partner; yet, no one can be self-absorbed either and expect the other to be okay with it. It cannot be a one-sided relationship and expect it to work well for both.

Generally speaking, a man doesn't put forth intensity to become familiar with his wife's needs and desires as he expects of her for himself. His concentration is demonstrated more in his own interests. And as he engages those interests, he expects his wife's allegiance and assent.

A great portion of man's time and energy is used outside of home while a woman is busy taking care of matters in the home, keeping home operating smoothly. He can rest in the fact she's at home. And while she's home, it allows him liberty to do those things he views as important outside of home; often matters which don't have anything to do with the functions of home and family. He operates as though his conduct is justifiable; wife is home, children are fine, home is good, bills are paid, so all is well. But is it all well with his wife?

Many men seem to think their provision for the household and family should be sufficient. But to a woman, it's not. And now that women are a definite part of the workforce, they can financially provide for themselves if they so choose. No longer is it all about his provision, although it's still very much appreciated and respected.

What she desires of him equally as his provision, is quality time and considerations.

Anyways, who makes the assignment that husband goes out-and-about and wife stays home to do what is needed? The house, the family and their operations belong to them both – mutually. A wife doesn't consciously agree to these terms; it becomes an element of the unspoken expectation. A husband brings this viewpoint to the relationship and acts upon it without any real dialogue with his wife. As he expends so much of his time and energy outside of home and family, even if his involvements are productive and worthwhile, the fact is, it takes him away from home and causes separation between him and family. Yet, when he returns home tired and indulges in rest, relaxation and sleep, it again removes him from family interactions, and household tasks. And if his wife voices complaint regarding his conduct, "nagging", it only causes further dissention between them. So, she leaves it alone. Then, while he's unwinding from his busy day, the wife is riled up in frustration.

Actually, her gripe isn't about his busyness in itself, rather her feeling that his choice of busyness overrides consideration of her and home. That if the tables were turned and she did likewise, placing her focus on matters outside the home to a similar degree, what would his thoughts and feelings be when all of a sudden he noticed the dirty clothes hamper was running over, dirty dishes were piled up in the sink, home cooked meals became take-outs, appointments were overlooked, home management gone haywire, children managing themselves, and all other routine tasks went undone simply because his wife was too busy with matters outside of home and family? Would he be as accepting and assenting? What would he think of her outlook on priorities? And would he be calm and collected as he expects of her?

A woman has been groomed to accept certain terms from man simply because he's man – that's fact. To accept that if husband is content, then wife is to feel content as well, as if his contentment, pleasure and liberties are supposed to satisfy her. That's not quite the way it should be – is it? But, if she appears tolerant of his actions, then he views all as well. To him, things are flowing along just fine and dandy.

On the other hand, if she doesn't fall short on all that she is expected to do, and it works without conflict of his schedule and plans, then he is open-minded to his wife spending time employing other activities and interests. But, if her desired direction conflicts with the steady flow of home and family and interrupts his personal flow, then she is looked upon as the one needing to make concessions. She's looked upon as the one who's disturbing the congruency of their daily living. Then, not only does he expect such concessions, she expects it of herself as well; traditionally speaking.

I must acknowledge however, that many of the contemporary-minded men view things a bit differently than that of man of traditional mindset. At least their actions are different. Many modern-day men appear to take more of an active role in the overall picture of family and household. Still, even in modern day, many hold many of the conventional thoughts even if their actions are otherwise. I believe at heart, many still hold true to tradition, but are willing to let go for the sake of modern day. But even with them, you still hear an expression such as "women aren't like they use to be", seemingly conveying, in my heart - I wish they were.

Seeing a change in trend, I recognize, some of the traditional-minded men are trying to get on board and become more active in household tasks. But from personal experience, these men will allow themselves to go only so far in doing these tasks. For rooted in their minds is still the notion that housework is "woman's work". This viewpoint is confirmed at times when they say things such as, "I help my wife in the house". When a husband calls himself "helping" is he not mentally assigning the responsibility of these tasks to his wife? Is he in essence saying, "I am helping you to do your work"?

So, while the modern-day man is feeling a responsibility to be different, the true traditionalist tries to convey a contemporary attitude to match the newness of the times - conveying I ought to be doing things differently. He feels somewhat pressured to do differently. He puts effort in the appearance of being contemporary-minded; but really, the traditionalists are simply old-school spirits masked in a contemporary face.

While he's willing to "help", his wife, he wants her to praise him for his part in "helping". He expects his wife to notice and show appreciation and praise for his efforts of "help". By the same token however, when his wife routinely performs these same tasks, time after time; day after day, shouldn't he notice and express to her similar praise and appreciation? Should her service be taken for granted while his "help" is given praise?

There's even another little twist to the matter which requires noting. When a wife doesn't applaud her husband's efforts and instead challenges his, "I help my wife", perspective, he has a way of turning the whole situation around to his advantage. It's done quite cleverly too. Astutely, he expresses that what he actually does isn't appreciated by her, as if he's a victim in the situation; that her focus is placed on the negative of what she feels he doesn't do rather than the positive for what he has done. He insinuates the fact that he is participating should be appreciated, so why dwell on his word "help". His sentiment is – I contributed, so show some appreciation.

Then, by hook and crook, the wife begins to feel guilty, while simply trying to engage more participation. Now she allows herself to feel guilty for not appearing more appreciative of his efforts. Then, she begins to question her own stance, the switch is flipped. Now, to avoid being a nagging wife, she again accepts his actions. Not only has she not gotten the results she wanted, she finds herself applauding him for his "help". That tactic is rather clever of him, isn't it? But it has been working. When he does little, it's applauded, when she does much it's unnoticed.

Eventually, after such an exchange over and over again, and to avoid further exchanges, wives just simply do the work. They want tasks completed as soon as it can be. She doesn't want to listen to her husband's complaint as to why it cannot be done, nor does she want to put up with his procrastination, so she simply does it herself.

Disturbed and frustrated, yet she does the work. And while she does the work, guess what, her husband engages in some activity of his choice or simply relaxes in front of the television while looking at his wife engaged in work. She has defeated her own argument – and assumed an "I will do it myself" attitude – which actually aids and abets the continuance of the very thing she dislikes. She does the work which is expected of her, and at the same time releases her husband of responsibility just as he wants; to be released from "woman's work".

Man knows our culture places housekeeping responsibility primarily on woman. He also knows our culture somewhat thinks unfavorably of a woman when her home is not maintained in a particular order. And, even though a husband may not verbally recognize his wife's efforts, he desires a well-kept home; even when he doesn't put forth any effort to maintain it that way. And really, a wife wants her husband to notice and appreciate her skills in maintaining a well-kept house as she accepts responsibility for its upkeep. But when her efforts are not appreciated and are taken for granted, it robs her of feeling appreciated.

All that said however, I do accept the fact there are defined roles within a home and family. But roles shouldn't be imposed simply because of gender. Outside of birthing and nursing babies, there shouldn't be ironclad roles. A couple can define and agree upon what works best for their particular household and relationship. It doesn't have to be based on what has always been done.

We cannot typecast every household and expect it to work the same for the sake of tradition. And, we cannot typecast each other, wanting the other to act in a certain manner for ones' own self-centeredness, failing to consider the ill-affects upon the other.

When both husband and wife hold employment outside of the home, why should a wife be mostly responsible for household tasks? Why would a caring husband want her to be, and why should a wife expect it of herself?

The goal is to produce an environment that is healthy and content for all involved. We cannot expect negative aspects to produce positive results. We cannot mismatch electrical wires, placing negative ones with positive ones; it short circuits and possibly explodes because the wires are not compatible. Well, it is the same in a relationship, the two must know if they are compatible. When two beings connect with each other, for best results, we want to connect positive to positive. Otherwise, there's danger of short-circuiting, and in some cases, possibly exploding. A couple must figure out what it takes to produce the positives ongoing for both.

I know marriage can be challenging for both because you have two different people coming together striving to establish common grounds. Both must make sure priorities are in place. And each is to feel secured in their rightful place as a spouse.

When a woman is seriously committed and weds, she expects to hold first place in her husband's life. She expects his love, covering, protection, and provision. She doesn't want to compete with any other woman, any other cause, any other involvement, or anything else for that matter. She simply expects to be first in his life regardless of what else he's involved in and regardless of whomever else is a part of his life. She simply expects to have first place. For her husband to hold her in first place in his heart and first place on his list of priorities, to her, it demonstrates his love and adoration.

Generally speaking, man doesn't grasp this point. Man seems to put what is important to him in a single category; grouping things he considers most important together. But a wife doesn't want to be grouped. She wants to be singled out. She wants her own special place in her husband's life. Aside from the spiritual realm, which is to be topmost, a wife sees only one first place and that place belongs to her. Any other she considers competition.

I don't know what's in man's mind when he does this grouping. Or if he's even aware this is what he does. But I

do know how a woman perceives this action, and that she doesn't agree with it. As a matter of fact, she abhors it. When a wife feels her husband has placed her other than first, she feels she has to compete for what she considers her natural and rightful place anyway, it puts her in a place of strife; a place where no woman wants to be in regard to her husband. A wife's desire is to be first and above all to her husband – his mother, children, employment, friends, hobbies, any other cause and any other thing. Anything other than first is disconcerting to a wife.

If she considers herself first, she will work beside him to ensure all other in his life has its proper place and proper considerations for she trusts in him and knows her place in his heart. But if she feels forged in a position where she has to compete for his affection and focus, then she will not feel at liberty to give of self fully to him. Nor, will she feel secure in his loyalty. She will feel that he feels other people and things are more important to him than she.

It doesn't mean she thinks others should not be cherished or that other endeavors are not important – rather, she feels she must be the most cherished amongst those things which are cherished. This is an emotional need women have in regard to the man whom she has committed and given herself. She doesn't want to be lumped in a group. In her mind, first place ranks in order of importance. And, there can be only one first place.

This place of importance is an emotional need that must be met if her husband is to receive her love and efforts without limits. As a woman opens herself to her husband - literally so – she needs to feel secure in his love, trust and devotion. Otherwise, she cannot relax her mind, body and soul to give unconditionally with sincere liberty. If she feels secure in his heart and loyalty, she will extend to him her love, body and service immeasurably. She trusts her place in his heart.

I admit men and women are wired differently and approach situations differently. A man wants an immediate fix to a situation. Let's get it out of the way; solved or not, and let's go on. But a woman wants to talk it out. He seems to cringe when his wife says to him "let's talk". But a woman wants discussion and understanding; resolution to the problem so it doesn't keep resurfacing. It may be uncomfortable, but to her, at least it gets dealt with. When it doesn't get dealt with, it creates even more of a disturbance, and even more with which she has to contend.

If a husband wants to successfully relate to his wife, he must be willing to talk when she brings up concerns, assure her she's actually heard, expressing his understanding and compassion. And by all means he needs to respond. When he relates in this manner, he invests in his wife's emotional well-being. It gives her a feeling of being heard.

A wife who receives well-rounded support from her husband can be a most amazing and powerful force for the family. It feeds into her strength and a sense of balance which she then feeds back into her family – all benefit.

In general, a woman really doesn't ask for much from her family. She accepts being the doer, nurturer and supporter; it's engrained. Other than that, what she mostly wants from her children is respect and caring, and from her husband, his ear to listen when she speaks and his heart to receive once she has spoken.

For a husband to fix the situation is not always the issue. Rather, a wife wants his genuine attention when she expresses concerns and issues, and a genuine response. This will please her. But if he doesn't listen and responds caringly, and this nonchalant conduct becomes his general practice, then she may become hesitant in bringing such matters to him.

In turn, this places a wedge in their communication. If her husband remains inattentive, she withdraws from trying to communicate her needs. Her demeanor in regard to him will eventually change for she feels what's important to her is not important to him.

Once he notices a change in her demeanor, he wonders what in the h____ is going on. To him, circumstances are the same, and he's the same, so what reason is there for her to change? He may even become suspicious of her actions since he's not accepting responsibility for matters being as they are. So, to him, it's a sudden change, but to her the change has been an oncoming process. She's tried to get him to do things differently time after time after time. Now she feels, why discuss it if circumstances remain unchanged. Their communication suffers. Yet, she hides within and continues on anyway.

Initially at the time of "I Do", when a woman has in her mind to become superwoman for her family, she has no way of knowing what lies ahead; the tumultuous road she may encounter in trying to be a superwoman. She starts out thinking she can be the perfect antidote for all her family ills, failing to realize the magnitude of the undertaking and its wear and tear in the long haul.

While she performs as this superwoman year after year, she becomes tired out and fed up with practically everything. As wife and mother, she has tried to do it all and be it all. So, when she arrives at a point of feeling she no longer can perform the same, or no longer wants to be this super person, at that point, she questions her stance. The need to reclaim begins to surface.

Eventually, signs of what she's feeling begin to surface and her family may begin to notice. They will begin to see changes in her conduct, and perhaps signs of growing discontentment. It's unlikely though they will understand what is happening, and likely they will not like the changes which are taking place. They are accustomed to her superwoman performance, and don't want it different. It works for them; she is a great commodity.

With unrest brewing inside, when she approaches her husband with her dilemma, attempting to make sense of it all, she doesn't necessarily expect him to understand what she feels, but she most assuredly needs him to acknowledge her feelings and accept it requires attention. His initial handling or the situation is crucial. His attentiveness and compassion make a world of difference to her. If he handles the situation as she needs him to, its sooths what ails her. Then, she will feel comfort in the fact that she can go to her husband; feeling he's giving a listening ear and has a compassionate heart; that he has her back, and they possibly can work through the quandary together.

If, however, he fails to listen to her plea and her heart, she is likely to feel let down and isolated. If her feelings are intense and she feels the need to unload the weight, she may well seek other avenues, searching for a listening ear. Because she feels frustrated and wants to soothe what troubles her, she seeks answers, direction and comfort.

She still wants to be the all for her family, but doesn't want to continue sacrificing self in the manner in which she has been doing. To her, it's actually okay that they depend on her because she is the woman of the house. But not to that her role as server takes precedence. Server is not to define her for it devalues her true worth as an individual.

Even with traditional strongholds, today's wife focus is more diverse. With the usual household responsibilities, a woman's work now extends to the exterior as well – gardening, mowing, raking, even repairs, and the list continues. This is quite a load. Then, you must consider full-time employment and all other activities in which she engages. How can one person possibly be such a super person without hindering self? How is a wife/mother supposed to do it all? How can she not be overwhelmed? And why does she agree to burden herself with such an endeavor?

We must ask, what picture are we presenting for our daughters to see? How do we want to frame their minds in regard to relationships? A wife/mother must maintain overall wellness in order for a daughter to see in her mother what the mother desires to one day see in her daughter; a content person in a relationship and marriage.

We want them to know what it is they desire from a relationship, and equally important, who it is they desire to be with in the relationship. We don't want them to settle for something or someone that is not going to promote them to be their best self.

If a maturing girl can see a well-adjusted wife, then she is more apt to become the same; generations perpetuated. Therefore, when she stands at the altar, to vow "I Do", there will stand a balanced young woman; personally focused, self-motivated, and less likely to be surprised by the unspoken vows.

Mothers are not only a model for their daughters, but also for their sons. For when their sons choose a life mate, they too will have witnessed a model of a woman exemplifying signs and traits of self-contentment. And they will be better prepared to recognize when they see it.

I have placed much focus on a wife and mother of traditional practices, but as I've previously alluded, the contemporary-minded wife still struggles with issues of self-identity.

Although many modern-day women don't want to identify with traditional practices, yet, don't want to throw away all traditional comforts and niceties. They seek a comfortable place betwixt and between that of yesterday and today. Exactly what they want to hold on to of yesterday still hangs in deliberation. As if you have to be one way or the other. But really, you don't.

One thing contemporaries do know is they don't want the label of "traditional" hanging over their heads. They don't share the same propensity as tradition has it, to serve and cater to husband and children. They don't see themselves becoming servant to a domestic lifestyle. I imagine after years of observing mothers and grandmothers demonstrating such a lifestyle, somewhere along the way they decided they wanted different; a new and different era of conduct. Family to them may remain in high regard, but viewed from a different angle. And although a husband may still be viewed as the household leader, his position as leader is viewed from a different angle.

Yet, when she stands at the altar, though her position is not as rigid as yesterday, she stands betwixt and between that of yesterday and modern day. Her position is not yet clearly defined. Being betwixt and between, she still seeks to secure her rightful place amid it all. She knows man, in many ways, man still expects tradition regardless if his words express otherwise. Double standards, male chauvinism and dominance, to a degree, still prevail. This contemporary minded woman may tell herself she's in a better position than that of yesterday, but considering all that is involved nowadays, I'm not certain she is.

Old or new, traditional or non-traditional, certain elements of a woman's place haven't changed a great deal from generation to generation. Circumstances have changed greatly, but her position hasn't changed to measure up; issues are merely compounded. She has one foot in tradition and the other in modern-day while trying to find that common balance. She continues to add more onto an already full plate; seeking balance in her rightful, and comfortable place.

Yet, an attempt to find this new-day balance in a relationship, I've noticed the emergence of different strands of attitudes and viewpoints. One is that, a sector of young women who simply refuse to operate within any form of a premise of "submission" to a husband. Within her relationship, she and her partner operate more on the basis equals. This wife doesn't necessarily desire to be as her husband, but neither does she consent to what she views as subordinate to his lead. She doesn't place herself in a position to be role-typecast. In her view, traditional practices as wife have no place in their relationship.

Regardless of this shift in mindset or achieved strides, she too seems to want to hang onto certain components of traditional traits; ones which appeal to her. She wants it both ways, but she wants to pick and choose on her terms.

She views herself as independent and capable of providing for herself. She makes her own money and can make her own way if need be. She expresses she doesn't desire to be taken care of by man – yet, in many regards she wants his care. She wants her husband to operate as an in-charge person, yet she doesn't want him in charge. But, when he's not in charge and fails to take care of matters, she holds it against him. It's kind of confusing, isn't it? And I wonder how confused he must be.

For this role-equal woman, surprisingly, her husband may take on a traditional wife-like persona himself as he performs many of the duties previously viewed as woman's work. He tries to appease and perhaps please his non-traditional-minded wife. It's not clear to me whether he what his actually agrees with this perspective or he is simply willing to accept it because it is his wife's stance. I do believe, from what I can assess, in his heart, he wants tradition, for he continues to compare present-day wife to that of yesterday; and seemingly in favor of yesterday.

In my opinion, a downside for the role-equal type woman is, her husband adjusts his mindset that they are to be equal across board. Appearing, if they are going to be equal in household tasks and childcare, then he expects her to contribute equally to the financial provisions. He also accepts that she will do some of the things that he would have traditionally done. After all they're operating as equals.

My question is - is this really what his wife wants. Or, is she simply trying to denote that she is not to be regarded as a traditional –viewed wife. When in fact, all she is striving for is to be content in the relationship, with all the rights and privileges to be a content wife. I don't believe it is equality which her heart seeks.

To delve further into the matter of a role-equal family lifestyle, I've observed the parenting model in this household also demonstrates one of equality. Children go to their fathers for nurturing and personal assistance as much as they go to their mothers. These fathers provide childcare needs to their young children in a manner I have never before witnessed; much unlike that of the traditional

families where the moms are the primary childcare provider and the fathers do more looking on. But in this role-equal's relationship, the man not only meets the woman halfway, but in some cases surpasses her in nurturing the children-while the mother looks on. I don't see anything wrong with fathers serving as nurturers. It's quite commendable actually. But, do these mothers really want to be replaced by the fathers in this area?

It stands to reason, and it is evident that the role-equal husband doesn't clearly understand how to relate to his wife's position. Seemingly, her ruling changes from moment to moment while her thoughts of what she wants from him changes from instance to instance, even when it's a similar instance. I think this wife is so consumed with the fact of not wanting to become a submissive partner, and traditional role wife. While she's is trying to figure out what she really wants from him, she's sending mixed-messages. And, since he's regularly experiencing her rule change for him, he may become confused and perhaps indifferent. She's trying to demand her rightful place, and he's trying to keep up.

Now on the other hand, in contrast to the non-submissive, role-equal type of woman, I've noticed there's one who lies on the other end of that spectrum; a segment of young women who are passive in their relationships; and in some ways, more "submissive" than that of the traditional-minded woman. She's more emotionally dependent on her mate.

With this particular woman, she seems to operate on the premise of – I'll be whatever you want me to be for the sake of sustaining the relationship. In some instances, her partner may even be considered a "kept man" in her attempt to keep the relationship as what she perceives is intact. She's willing to work and provide for him. Or on other hand, she may be the "kept" one, in his attempt to constrict her activities and maintain control. She's willing to accept this condition in order to keep what she views as a must-have relation; she feels she "needs" him. For him to be present in her life is critical. Emotionally, she's sold out to him and what he requires of her.

This "passive-dependent" woman appears to deal more with self-esteem and insecurity issues. She relinquishes her authority and places it in the hands of her partner. She, in an odd sense, perhaps is actually selfish in her attempt to maintain the relationship, for she has become dependent on him – emotionally and provisionally. She is willing to retain it at a high cost - even at the cost of self value.

Unlike the role-equal kind of woman, who demonstrates independence and determination to receive what she perceives is rightfully due, and unlike the traditional woman who demonstrates self-sacrifice as an attempt to do what she perceives is best for the whole, the

212

passive-dependent woman demonstrates neediness. She conveys to the man he is the definer of the relationship. She is driven by his desires. She receives validation through his eyes. Her emotions are completely wrapped up in what he desires, and how he desires it. Even at times when he means well by her, it doesn't render wellness.

This "passive dependent" woman is truly in a state of "hiding" because she hides behind someone else as well as hiding within self. She is more identity masked than both the "old school – traditionalist" and the non-submissive role-equal.

One thing about the old school – traditional couple, each individual had an understanding of their expected roles. The man was responsible for family provision and

the woman was responsible for care of the house and children. Although the traditional woman may have expressed a desire to extend self beyond home, she accepted her expected role. She was woman of the house and in many regards, that was okay. And he accepted his role of provision as well. There was role clarity among the two.

For me, I cannot deny that a traditional-type relationship brings along some most positive attributes. I must give credit where credit is due. Traditional-minded men, as household leader, generally assume responsibility to work however needed to provide for the family and take care of household maintenance. These are very admirable attributes in a traditional woman's view. In the past, women have looked to men for such provisions. Women didn't place much thought on certain matters. Women just looked to man to take care of a particular aspect of home and were satisfied with it. It gave woman a feeling of being cared for, and responsible men accepted that role. They were the provider, the fixer, and the overseer; and for a traditional woman that is A-Okay.

Both my husband and I have been scholars of old-school and have lived our married life much to this regard. At the beginning of our marriage, I assumed the position of traditional housewife. I believed that was my role and my husband followed suit and demonstrated the true spirit of a traditional husband. Within this mindset, he, as most old-school traditional men do, viewed the wife as the homemaker. The wife is to assume primary charge of the home and children – whether she works a full-time job or not. That is just an unspoken vow that was expected. But as mentioned, overtime, a woman can become very tired performing as super woman.

Over the years my husband attempted to convince me he was more of a liberal thinker-but he's not. He simply puts forth the effort to keep me hushed of complaint – nagging. But he's just an "old school" guy at the root – deep root. This simply has been his upbringing and established perception. Regardless of what his words express, his actions reek of old-school tradition.

With all due respect, he didn't impose his views on me. It was I who gave him the message I was accepting of traditional practices. It was I who assumed the role and lived it out. He simply accepted what he was familiar with and received what I was willing to give. Prior, I had not expressed to him how I wanted to be regarded in the role of wife; whether traditional or otherwise. But he was simply willing to accept what I offered, and I offered what I thought was expected. I plunged into the unspoken vows and whole heartedly delivered as expected.

Women, isn't that what we generally do? We naively walk into a relationship thinking all will turn out as hoped when initially we don't specify our standards and requirements, for you or him. We do a lot of assuming and we take a lot for granted.

No doubt, my husband and I came into the marriage with the idea that a woman's task was the upkeep of the house and primary caregiver for the general needs of the children, and man's work was more on the outside, primarily upkeep of the grounds and property. Not that I didn't work outside at times, I did, or that my husband didn't work inside at times, he did. But we were familiar with traditional practices, so we simply operated within that realm. And since women have an ingrained desire to present a picture of a well-kept and attractive home, we tend to do what is necessary even when no one else is

willing to "help". We harbor this conviction and try to live up to it. Not that we particularly like it that way, but we accept the task.

Thinking back on my upbringing, I don't recollect seeing my dad do housework –ever. I'm sure he must have at some point in time, but to have done it enough for an image to be etched in my memory, it didn't. That was woman's work; his wife and his daughters. But I do remember seeing him busy at work on the outside - yards and home repairs, however needed. And that is the image that remained with me which I carried into my own marriage. I expected my husband to be busy with the upkeep of yards and maintenance.

At first, it was okay with my predetermined role. I was sort of proud of it actually; dutiful wife – cooking meals, cleaning house, mending and doing whatever was befitting for a woman of the home. But as years passed it just didn't have the same feel about it. Weariness came into play. I felt something was off-balanced. That feeling of pride turned into feelings of resentment. I was a traditional person, but a total traditional point of view was no longer working successfully for me. There were too many other variables to take into account. There were too many other things that required my attention.

Even though I worked a full-time job, I assumed the primary charge of household tasks. I had my self-imposed standards to live up to. But after a while, it grew old. Especially when watching my family watch me work while they were at leisure. Something just didn't feel right about it. And believe me, frustration and resentment built up. I began to realize I had to relieve myself of my own mandated standards. I wouldn't lower my standards per se, but I would adjust my attitude and routine, and to relieve my body of the stresses.

I knew that to a degree things would remain basically the same. I wouldn't switch-off completely. I knew I would continue to perform as the primary one in charge of keeping the house in order. But what would change was my perception about it all. I would no longer allow such mandates to be forged upon me; self-imposed or otherwise. I would not relinquish responsibilities, but I would handle matters differently – for me. I couldn't change my family's preconceived ideas, but I most certainly could change my own.

My first step in doing so -regarding household tasks, and in the regular routine of things -was to relieve myself of the unnecessary stress and pressure of feeling I was the primary responsible one to get things done. To accept if I decided, for whatever reason, to leave something undone, and, if no one else in the house saw the need to do it either, then that particular task could go undone for the time being. I could accept that if I did it, that's okay, and if I didn't that's okay too. And if I decided at some to do every household task – and that was my comfortable choice; then, that would be okay too,

Further, I would relieve myself of harboring resentment toward other family members when they didn't do it either. No longer would I keep score of who did what? We would get to it when we got to it. I needed to not be stressed about it. I have to admit though – old habits are hard to break.

This conversion didn't happen automatically. I had to work at it. There were urges to repeat what I was used to doing. At first, I found it a bit uncomfortable to relax while I watched someone else work. I felt I was supposed to be working as well. But I needed to relax in the fact, I could

actually, be the one watching television while others worked, without feeling guilty. And, if no one decided to complete that particular task, I would adjust my mindset to seeing a task go undone.

I could sense from the household though that my actions were being noticed. There were little remarks and sneers. They were so used to my old habits and practices. They were accustomed to a certain standard, but a standard kept basically at my expense. But I was determined to follow through with newness. I no longer wanted to be looked upon as the one supposed and expected to do; the one which would do when no one else was willing to do. I no longer wanted to be in a position of being taken for granted. I no longer wanted to continue in resentment, frustration and anger because I felt dumped on. I no longer wanted to debate the "helping me" issue. And, I no longer wanted to allow the traditional social order to dictate how I should or should not conduct myself.

I would view it as everyone's responsibility to maintain cleanliness and order within the household. Not as helpers, but as responsible parties. Not that I didn't already desire it to be that way, but I held to traditional views; women were expected to do regardless, and I expected myself to do regardless. But that particular traditional view was about to change for me. It really didn't matter to me if I continued to do a great deal of the housework, as long as I didn't feel dumped on, and as long as everyone else did their part. And then, each would have moments of busyness in the household and each would have moments of relaxation. And that would become understood.

As I unobtrusively continued my path toward change, an amazing thing began to happen. As I changed, my family changed; for the better for me. As I did less, they began to do more. Amazing huh! Then, I realized, it was me all along. I had performed in a manner which didn't require my family to do any differently. Why would they have changed something that worked well for them – especially when I was willing to do it all? This is what many women do. We take on the super woman persona, and then we blame family members for not doing enough. They will regard you as you require their regard.

My anew prospective is to be who I desire to be; a mixture; old-school, my training, and contemporary, my present; not totally one way or the other. I don't have to be one way or the other. I favor elements of old school – and basically that is my character and preference. Old-school grants certain character qualities which I am proud to possess. That's simply who I am. And that's quite okay. Always to strive for decency and in order of course; but I am to decide who I am, and how I choose to conduct myself. So, these days, in my new found way, I think of myself as a traditional individualist. Life is not to be scripted according to a predetermined mold.

Within this newly developed mindset, I've also gained a better understanding and acceptance of others; particularly my husband. I realized I didn't have the right to try to alter his essence either; to persuade him to perform like I wished him to for me. Although, previously, I spent a lot of time and effort in this endeavor; discussing and discussing; trying to get him to change his ways to accommodate me. And relentlessly, he remained true to himself and did as he felt he needed to do. He continued with what he viewed as important to him. He remained steadfast in spite of my complaints and requests to do otherwise. Then actually and ironically, in his doing so, he influenced me to respect and own up to my own individuality. I don't think that was his intent, but that is exactly what happened.

Men just seem to know how to express their freedoms – don't they? They really know how to do what it is they want to do; wife's consent or not. They just follow through with what they consider a priority at a given time. A man realizes that when his wife becomes upset, she will go through a period of sulking, and maybe fuss a bit, but in the end, everything returns to normal and life goes on. He has done as he wished, and eventually, wife will return to usual. This cycle happens over and over again.

Starting out in marriage, I felt I would have been more self-determining. Considering how I thought I was, I never imagined I would compromise my uniqueness as I tried to interlock our two personalities. But like in most cases, out of respect and expectation, a woman generally assumes a back seat to her husband. He becomes the driver of the relationship. Women are generally the more absorbent one in the relationship. She is simply expected to conform to her husband's manner of doing things. This has been the general practice over time. She conforms to his lead as head of household. But it shouldn't be a matter of conforming. Should it? Rather, one of blending. Blending makes it smooth; conforming puts a tug in the equation.

Prior to marriage, you must know each other's views regarding certain matters, and how those views will impact in the long run. You must pay attention to what is expressed, spoken and unspoken. To sincerely know the truths of your partner prior to the "I Do" is crucial for the success of the relationship and for each individual within the union.

We cannot change other people to suit our personal desires; we can only influence another. That's why it is so important to know the person and to understand what it is you can and cannot accept from them. Know your requirements and standards and even the deal breakers, and hold true to them. We place so much emphasis on the other person changing to meet our own personal needs; and women are known for doing so. I've found such a notion to be a misguided perception.

A wife so often depends on her husband to ensure her happiness, but that job belongs to her. She is to take ownership of securing her happiness. A husband should not be burdened with this responsibility. He's included in the equation, no doubt; otherwise, why marry. But ownership of one's own contentment and happiness lies upon the shoulders of that person. Each of us must take control of the compass leading to happiness. And actually, once you do, it's liberating.

A husband is to give of himself to secure his wife's personal happiness and contentment, and is accountable for certain aspects of her well-being. And a wife should want him accountable, but not to give him charge of it. He should be a supporter, an advocate, and an enhancement to your joyfulness.

Women remember, as we focus on the well-being of others, we must do the same for ourselves. Understand that you cannot truly create and provide a happy and healthy environment if the core of self is not well-nourished. How can you successfully extend outwardly what is not truly possessed inwardly? How can the extremities be any different than that of the core? The core is fundamental; the heartstring.

If a family wants a truly healthy home environment, then allow the woman of the house to be wholesomely healthy in self. Her bliss will radiate throughout and all will benefit. She will make certain of it. But if the wife/mother of the home, is burdened, over worked, underachieved and underappreciated; the home will experience the affects as well.

The family must become aware of the woman that lives within wife and mother and give back to her comparably to what is received from her. Not necessarily in the same manner, but in a manner in which she can feel loved and appreciated. A wife/mother who feels loved and appreciated will do all in her power to secure the stability and sanctity of her family. That is simply the way God designed her.

Ladies, if you are about to approach the altar, and commit to "I Do", you should think about the unspoken exchanges that are about to take place as you prepare to become wife. Go in to the marriage knowing who you are. Know who it is you are meeting at the altar. Know what you want out of marriage. Know who you desire to be as an individual within the marriage, and who you desire to become as a couple. Get a clear and concise understanding of your intents and what it is you expect of each other. Don't be timid in your communications and don't take things for granted. Communicate and communicate in order to make intelligent and informed decisions.

Along the way ladies, leading up to "I Do", see evidence from your intended that things can be delivered as best for you. It really doesn't matter whether you are traditional, contemporary, or whatever the case may be, just make sure you are sure of self, sure of what it is you desire, and that the potentially unspoken requests become spoken. Make it a priority to understand each other's expectations and perspectives. Don't overlook things you don't particularly appreciate thinking it will change later – because what is – actually is. What you may feel you can down the road. That same thing today which is tolerated may become burdensome later on. Don't focus on what could be, but rather, what is; that in fact, is what you are agreeing to live with.

If you have already met at the altar, and the "I Do" is already committed, and circumstance is not as desired; determine your status and make some decisions. If both are willing, then, the two of you must communicate, communicate some more, and communicate some more, if need be, until conditions become favorable and satisfying for both. It is a unified effort. It may be challenging, but a joy-filled existence in a marriage is so worth the effort; to make your home a joy-filled place to dwell.

It is most important that we as women get in touch and stay in touch with self essence, and grab hold of fullness as we live our lives performing our duties and responsibilities. You can't necessarily recapture what you have already missed out on, but you can surely give today a new meaning. Remember, you need not be super woman, and there is no one-size-fits-all mold to measure up to. We are all different and our circumstances vary. A one-size-fits-all mold is not viable to uniqueness.

Women, we must be an overall healthy force in our families, but not as the sacrificial one. We must embody contentment and radiate it outwardly. Do those things you enjoy, and live out the person that lies within. We can actually love, respect, and give of self to others and causes, yet maintain loyalty to self. Why live life and not live in self-authenticity?

No person or cause should have authority over you that rob you of your essence as an individual, not husband, children, or parents. No one! Neither should we relinquish that authority to another or others. If we give up self, our distinctiveness, then we are giving up too much. We should give **of** self, not give **up** self.

Regardless of what era, or what circumstance you find yourself, if you are facing issues which need to be dealt with, how you proceed from this point into the future is a decision only you can make. You decide whether you are willing to accept the status quo and continue as is, or walk a different path and establish newness.

In these modern times, and as so much has shifted in the lives of women, we must find what fits and what is needed individually. We need to be able to articulate it prior to "I Do". But one doesn't know what fits until one knows self. You have to know what you need and desire before extending yourself to anyone. This is where many women fall short, whether traditional, role-equal, passive dependent or whatever. Without the needed time invested in self, either can fall into the category of hiding. If you don't know how to assert self, then how are you to know how to communicate it to another? How does that person coming into your life satisfy you in ways you aren't certain of yourself? It becomes a maze. Then what happens is someone else guides you, looking through their lens; a view which may be significantly different than your vision. Consequently, you will find yourself being led in directions opposite of where you actually desire to go; hiding.

Again, I don't have a voice for every woman's situation, nor will every woman understand or agree with my opinion, but to the woman in "hiding" or to the woman that finds herself on this path, I know you clearly understand. And be reminded, it takes courage, perseverance, and most of all truth to change your course.

Even though it may sound cliché, the truth does set you free, but you must be willing to deal with the truths.

Realize we are treated by others as we allow ourselves to be treated. We give authority to others when we allow ourselves to be taken in a direction we don't desire to go. Or to be treated and regarded in a manner which we don't desire to be treated. Treat yourself as you want to be treated, then others will follow suit. Try it!

When I approached this same crossroad of transitioning, I took steps I now view as rather radical, but necessary for me at the time. I need not share exactly what my actions were, or what the exact determining factors that led me to that critical point. That is of no significance to you, my reader. I do not want my life choices to influence others to do as I did in that regard. We are all different in circumstance and in need. Each must find their own path leading to contentment and joyfulness. What may be good for one may be devastating for another. You owe it to yourself to seek and secure your own direction. Decently and in order of course!

What I will share however is, I was at a pivotal point, and I needed to make some definite changes for my personal well-being. Had I not, I feel assured I would have remained in "hiding", living out the proverbial mold. I would also have remained overwhelmed in responsibilities, striving to maintain a super woman's status; living out only a shell of who I actually represented as a total person.

I was at a point in which I had to examine myself, my circumstances and life wishes. I had to realign my thoughts, feelings and desires. I needed to reconnect me to me. It wasn't about others. This journey was about me. I needed to tap into my inner-person; the one I had forsaken, and to reacquaint myself with that person. I had gone way too far

left and I was determined to make a U-turn, and reposition things in my life. I had to take a good look at myself and all involved in my life. Where did everything fit? How and where did I fit?

Though there were family and friends to listen and offer advice, they could not supply the answers I personally needed. It was a matter of coming face-to-face with me.

When you truly submit to your inner-voice, tap into that part of you which captures distinctiveness, then you will find yourself propelled in a direction which is right for you. You must be honest to your heart. Women seem to have a difficult time doing this, for it is challenging for us to escape from the model picture of who we think we are supposed to be and of how we think we are supposed to conduct ourselves. But, it's those moments of truth which will lead you step by step out from "hiding".

Remember, always, always, the starting point to making any significant change, is to start with self. Recognize who that person is, surrender to that person, and live enjoying that person; the person God created with all fibers of uniqueness.

I whole heartily feel marriage is to be the most blessed and gratifying experience; two people coming together to share the journey of life. But it must be a union of the right ingredients in order to capture what it can truly offer. However, it all begins before gathering at the altar - before the "I Do's"; time invested to know, and understand the other person, and to ascertain if that person is the right one for you. Then, when those two people in love and in appreciation of each other meet at the altar, they would have already established a head start into happiness.

Even with all this in place, people develop and change as time passes and life is experienced. But change is one of the beauties of life. Who wants to always remain the same? But as changes occur, keep up with each other. Learn to appreciate your mate's achievements and growth. Don't allow one to leave the other behind. Walk through life together. Cheer and support one another. Communicate, communicate and communicate. Through it all, provide understanding and an open mind. Be each other's cheerleader–sincerely. Remember, jealousy and competition have no place in a marriage. It divides rather than unifies.

Now, if you find yourself to be at this point in life requiring restructuring your relationship and family life, and as daunting as it may seem, you can make a U-turn or veer in direction. You can actually get on a different path if that is what's desired. It doesn't mean you will need to change everything about your lifestyle. You may not desire or need to change very much at all from without. Rather, it means you are going to primarily work on self, and start to change from within to extend without. Respect the other person with the same intensity which you want to be respected.

Be aware, it's a path that needs to be carefully walked. It is a critical point. You don't want to be too radical all at once. You need to proceed cautiously as you work to plot your course - together.

You don't need to seek any and everyone's advice or share your all with everyone. No one knows what you truly need but the two of you.

During this time, your time and energy should be channeled in directions that are healthy and wholesome. You are seeking to make circumstances better, not worse. Each of you need to become reacquainted with you; your

thoughts, feelings, and desires. It's like dating yourself! Pay attention!

Ladies - when things are not going as hoped, and it's in your power to do something about it, rearrange things. That is your privilege. If something is burdensome, causing you a hardship, anger or agitation, don't overlook these matters. If you have been overlooking certain matters and pretending as though it's not a problem – stop it. You don't want to exist in pretense. That's a lie, which means you would be living a lie. Stop settling for less than what is essentially needed. You must seek to achieve what is personally nourishing and gratifying. You owe it to yourself.

If marriage is what you seek, go for it, and make it good. And if you are already married, the "I Do" already said – still, make it good. Otherwise, what is the purpose?

Chapter Thirteen

For a Man Actually Loves Himself When He Loves His Wife

And further, you will submit to one another out of reverence for Christ. You wives will submit to your husband as you do to the Lord. For a husband is the head of his wife as Christ is the head of his body, the church; he gave his life to be her savior. As the church submits to Christ, so you wives must submit to your husbands in everything. And you husbands must love your wives with the same love Christ showed the church. He gave up his life for her to make her holy and clean, washed by baptism and God's word. He did this to present her to himself as a glorious church without a spot or wrinkle or any other blemish. Instead, she will be holy and without fault. In the same way, husbands ought to love their wives as they love their own bodies. For a man actually loves himself when he loves his wife.

Ephesians 5:22-28,
The Book, New Living Translation

What I am about to discuss in this chapter may at first appear to contradict much of which I've previously expressed. But bear with me as I explain my stance. Then, I believe all will become clear regarding my position. Understand I speak from a Christian standpoint; my beliefs and actions, or lack thereof, is of this testament.

Although I am definitely an advocate for woman expressing and pursuing individuality – exploring her interests, talents, dreams, and asserting her voice; but within a relationship of husband, wife and family, I also support and accept that someone should lead. It is my belief man has been placed in position as principal leader of his family; an order of leadership which I believe has been ordained and blessed by God. I believe a husband is to be respected as head of household, and a wife is to accept and submit to his leadership as the Scripture unfolds.

Like any structural situation, there needs to be a leader. In a marriage, I believe God has entrusted this position to man. For woman to submit doesn't mean she renounces what God has placed in her as an individual, nor does it mean that husband becomes superior and wife becomes inferior. Instead, she accepts and trusts her husband to lead the family through the wisdom of God; to lead his family in love and devotion. It is this Godly wisdom, love and devotion to which his wife submits.

When it comes to this passage of Scripture, we so often hear of woman's command to be submissive to her husband, and it's a part which is reverberated over and over. But when you read further, this passage addresses man's order of submissiveness as well; a part of Scripture which is often downplayed and disregarded. And when mentioned, it's generally not with the same degree of intensity as with the part concerning woman.

Scripture clearly defines an order of submission for both, man and woman; how leadership and submissiveness interlock; this interlocking of the two becoming a natural happening which fulfills both man and woman; making it all possible for the relationship to flourish, as leadership and submission comes together, connect, and birth a oneness.

Too often though, this Scripture is expressed as if man is to rule woman, and it is used to maintain woman in a submissive place. When misused in this manner, man often relishes in it as if he thinks it allows him power over her. While it is often used against woman, as Scripture states, it is in fact an order to protect her. This Scripture is about covering, love, respect and devotion; a love, respect and devotion which is to envelop both man and woman - together. It is a two-sided commitment, one in which both husband and wife have a side, different but equally as important. If adhered to, it enables their union to function at its best, therefore positioning them to receive the intended covering and blessing of God.

As a husband leads, he isn't to lead for selfish gain, control, or dominance; as if to be a dictator and authoritarian. Nor is he to lead as if he is the boss and his wife is subservient. Rather, he is to lead her and the family in love and dedication, regarding them with compassion and honor. And when there are those times for his "control", it is to govern the situation for the whole; a control which his wife will respect.

In return, he receives love and honor as the leader of the family and as a follower of our Lord. Therefore, as his wife submits to his lead and headship, she embraces his love and devotion; willing to accept his lead as he takes his position as the steering force of the family.

232

Basically, from what I observe, and even with those where this Scripture is not honored, most wives look upon their husband as head of household. It is not that a woman doesn't want to follow her husband's leadership, but she may not feel secure in following him in the manner in which he leads her. She wants to feel that he holds her in high regard, and that he's leading in a manner which is good for the family unit. When he doesn't, she cannot feel relaxed with his judgment as her leader. But, if a wife can trust her husband's judgment and his love for her mirrors the kind of love Christ describes, then what reason would a wife have to not submit to her husband's leadership.

Now, in submissiveness, how is it that individuality and submission can travel a concurrent path for a woman? How can a wife exert her own desires and demonstrate distinctiveness, yet submit and yield to the leadership of her husband? I understand to submit means to concede to another for decisions and consideration; to defer to another's judgment or decision" ... to guide, to direct the course, and to tend in a certain direction. So, how is self-exertion possible for a wife who believes in this Scripture? I think it quite possible actually.

I really don't believe God would have given woman a functioning brain, an intuitive sense, and personality traits of her very own to simply shut down following marriage. Or, that God would have gifted her with talents and interests for them to fall by the way side simply because she has married. I feel confident a wife should express individuality, indulge aspects that make her who she is, and yet honor her husband's leadership as scripture support it. *Psalm 139:14*

The unit of husband, wife and family can be compared to that of a vehicle with distinct functioning parts. As with a vehicle, the steering component is vital. It is a crucial element to the unit; it guides the way. The family as a unit, the husband/father serves as the steering component. Although each component has its individualized function, as important as it may be, yet it relies and is dependent upon the steering component. But as with any vehicle, the steering mechanism, as vital as it is, has no true meaning, no functional power if it stands alone. Therefore, the husband being the steering component, shouldn't stand alone as he leads, but work together with the other family components as an interconnected unit.

A wife, in my opinion, honestly wants her husband's guidance. Not that she is incapable of guiding herself; after all, she rendered independence prior to marriage. But following marriage, she lives a different lifestyle where the dynamics of her family structure changes and her position changes from independent to interdependent. So, if she's one to believe in the husband being the leader of the family, and he is to lead her, he needs to understand who she is and what best suits and fulfills her needs. He cannot operate solely on his own. How can he lead and do what is best for her, if he doesn't really know who she is? And why would a wife want to follow the lead of a husband who doesn't have her best interests at heart?

Surely a woman doesn't marry for the benefit of the husband, and that she is to simply follow along. What would be the need for her to come together with him? What would be her gain? Why would a woman want to marry and submit herself to be led in a direction where she is not considered a center focus?

If she is to submit to him; no doubt he must invest time to know her heart, her strengths, her weaknesses, her desires, and her true spirit. Which in turn grants him insight into her times of joy, sadness, anger, anxiousness and overload; granting him knowledge of how he is to lead her at any given point in time. Being the leader is not an easy job. Is it? A true leader serves equally if not more to being served.

It is not a question of his love; most men, I would imagine love their wives, especially if they have the love of God in their heart. And, a responsible man also works hard to provide for his family. So, it's not even a matter of provision; rather a matter of respect, understanding and sensitivity. He must understand who his wife is as an individual and who they are when they connect together; not just who he wants her to be for him. His leadership needs to be scripturally based, yet customized.

Unfortunately, too often a husband doesn't invest the effort required to get to a point of truly knowing and understanding his wife. He is often more preoccupied with what she has to offer him and will express such when he feels she's falling short of meeting those expectations. However, he doesn't seem to hold himself to the same standard. He has more of an expected role in his mind for her, than he supposes she has in mind for him. Therefore, in my opinion, and since culture and tradition yields him support, he feels justified in his expectation of her role.

Why does a husband expect his wife to overlook and ignore certain actions from him, and at the same time, frowns upon her when she exhibits similar actions? Why does he seem to need a certain kind of freedom for himself, releasing himself from certain responsibilities as it relates to submissiveness in this Scripture? Yet, he wants to hold his wife accountable for her end to the letter, as if gender alone places her in a subordinate category. Being in the lead position doesn't make the supporting person lesser.

If man however, would adhere to part B of this Scripture, as much as he wishes his wife to adhere to part A, then her position of following his lead would not be a problem at all. It would flow naturally. But when he wants to cancel his part, yet wants her to submit; then it presents

problems. There is something about the male ego and chauvinistic spirit which expects just that. But, if man would love his wife with definitive love as Christ has for the church, then his wife would willingly and admiringly walk in submission to his lead. She would view it as an honor to do so, and not consider it demeaning in any form.

As a matter of fact, to submit would actually afford her certain kinds of mental and emotional freedoms, such freedoms her heart yearns anyway. Certain matters she wouldn't even have to think about, nor would want to. She would know he has those matters under control. She would be able to rest in his leadership and trust his love and devotion as he remains obedient to the guidance of the Holy Spirit.

Not that she will be in agreement with all his decisions, but she will be willing to follow his lead because she rests in the fact that she is being affectionately considered, and that he is allowing himself to be spiritually guided. She rests in the fact that she is a center-focus. Of course, she wouldn't expect all his decisions to be centered upon her every want, but she would feel confident that whatever decisions her husband makes as head of household he would have the best interest of the family at heart.

As we look at the design of our own body, we have only one head. Without the head, other parts of the body lose the power to function. The same principle applies to the family, there needs to be a headship; it's the base. Having just one headship makes things operate more smoothly. It doesn't minimize the other parts of the body; they are all interrelated and each is vitally important; but a head is crucial. If there is more than one headship, then there will be a tug-of-war, which will cause a struggle.

Surely there will be conflict, and sometimes serious conflict which will have to be worked through; sometimes much working out. That is to be expected, and will most assuredly happen at one point or another. But for two people with each other's best interest at heart and mutual respect for each as an individual, they should work together to untangle the knots. Love, respect and devotion will abound. Life in itself presents much struggle, we don't need to war against each other.

Generally, wives don't wish to assume the leadership role within the family structure, even though husbands may believe otherwise. But, if need be, a woman can function in this role, and can function very productively. Sometimes, when taking on such a role, her leadership may override that of her husband. However, it's simply not her heart's desire to do so. At times, circumstance may force her to take on the leadership role and she goes with it as need be. But she would rather leave that place to a caring and loving husband.

I also believe most women really don't mind doing what is required to make sure husband, children and home are taken care of, a woman takes pride in those areas of her life. We look upon them (husband/children/home) as "ours", and we want to care for and showcase them. When wife/mother does all the things she does for her family, the doing in itself is not the problem; it's the lack of genuine appreciation shown to her for what she does that leads to the problems, even though words of "thank you" may be given. Simply as habit, a thank-you simply glides across the surface of the lips. So, the true essence of feeling appreciation escapes.

When a man loves and values his wife, influences their children to love and respect their mother, and view her as other than a mere servicer, then the wife/mother will not feel undervalued and taken for granted. She will gladly serve her family.

I believe when God placed man and woman together in a most beautiful, serene setting; the Garden of Eden, it signified the beautiful and peaceful relationship intended between husband and wife. There's no question regarding the true connectivity intended between man and woman. Scripture defines woman's position to man and man's position regarding her covering; a ribcage connection. Think of the framework of the ribcage, how it magnificently contains the vital parts of the body; how it encloses, protects, and strengthens the body's frame and safeguards its structure. In that sense, it can be compared to the type of covering a wife is to receive from her husband; form, strength, support and protection. The body needs that strong support. The same goes for the family, the man/husband/father becomes the ribcage, and the body (family) relies on it.

It's no wonder man has been commissioned to love his wife as he loves his own body; she is actually part of his own body. And no wonder woman requires his protective covering; it is woman's innate design. The fact that a woman requires such covering and protection shouldn't be looked upon by him as her weakness. It's natural. Her husband should see it as natural, and not a flaw. In this regard, a husband should embrace what his wife desires of him; and a wife should embrace her husband's desire to cover her. However, if both husband and wife would love as God has commissioned, and respect one another's position as God has ordained, there wouldn't be much room for division.

In my opinion, a husband's love and covering to a wife is to be like that of a secured fort in time of need; a fort in which to retreat from harm and vulnerabilities. His love would be her shield and refuge. His love would be like that of a best friend; her closest confidant. His love and affection would extend in a way that would inspire her to achieve, and develop into her own as an individual within the marriage. His love would strengthen her character. Because of the depth of his love, she would prove to be a shining jewel to and for him; his help meet, his lover, his bosom to rest upon, his friend, his nurturer, his homemaker, his business partner, and his cheerleader. With a true heart, she would surely deliver as God's design. Awesome isn't it!

Both husband and wife are accountable for the success of the relationship; man is accountable to woman, and woman accountable to man. If a couple sincerely wants the marriage to flourish and the family to be successful as a prosperous unit, both must adhere to God's design.

If two decide to wed, both must be willing to commit to an order of submission. God, your mate, family and other, prioritized. The influence of other people and causes cannot enter in to present division. The idea of marriage in the Garden of Eden in this context may be metaphorically used, and perhaps may sound a bit like a fairytale, but actually, it is Scripture. Marriage is intended to be good. It won't feel good at all times. That's almost a promise. But not feeling good at spots doesn't mean the foundation is not good. If the foundation is good the "feelings" can be revived and renewed.

It is very possible for woman to be assertive in her own actions as well as be submissive to her husband's leadership. Marriage shouldn't cause her to forsake who she is; but enhances and develops who she innately is. Her husband should want that for her as much as she wants it for herself. Within the marriage, a wife should grow and flourish.

Yes, I believe and accept a woman is to be submissive to her husband's leadership, but in doing so, he is to submit to godly guidance. He is to be her covering, her anchor, and the truest encourager for her to become all she can be. So, as he submits himself to spiritual guidance, she respectfully submits herself to his lead. What wife would not gladly submit to that awesomeness?

"In the same way, a husband should love his wife as much as he loves himself. A husband who loves his wife shows he loves himself". Ephesians 5:28

A Good Marriage

A good marriage must be created.
In the art of marriage,
the little things are the big things.
It is remembering to say
"I love you" at least once each day.
It is never going to sleep angry.
It is at no time taking
each other for granted;
the courtship should not end with the
honeymoon,
it should continue through all the years.
It is having a mutual sense of
values and common objectives.
It is standing together facing the world.
It is forming a circle
of love that gathers in the whole family.
It is doing things for each other, not in the
attitude of
duty or sacrifice but in the spirit of joy.
It is speaking words of appreciation and
demonstrating gratitude in thoughtful ways.
It is not looking for perfection in each other.
It is cultivating flexibility, patience, and
understanding
and a sense of humor.
It is having the capacity to forgive and forget.
It is giving each other an
atmosphere in which each can grow.
It is most important to find room for things of
the spirit.

It is a common search for the good and the beautiful.

Author Unknown

Chapter Fourteen
To Sum It All Up

(In Review)

As pointed out, over the ages women have been faced with particular struggles to attain certain rights and privileges. Many considered as trailblazers, fought to achieve what was believed to be rightfully due. Without the efforts of these trailblazing pioneers, chances are, many doors of opportunity open to women today would possibly still remain closed. Resulting, there is much to be applauded, respected and appreciated. Because of the sacrifices and efforts of the trailblazers and others, today's woman is empowered to seek and achieve whatever interests and career paths she desires.

As with the pioneers, and still, there are times to unite and fight collectively; cooperative efforts coming together to benefit all who need to receive. Without such unification, many issues would remain unresolved. However, just as important as times of unification, there are times when one must fight an individual battle - to press forward to achieve individual rights and privileges; a time when one must conquer for self; to ascertain that which enables to be distinguished as an individual. One must capture what is needed and desired for one's own sense of peace and contentment

Even though I encourage the attainment of rights and privileges and empowerment, I must reiterate the fact that my writing's undertaking and focus has not been intended to be a shout-out for the movement of Women's

Liberation. However, I do not minimize the movement's validity or integrity. Even though my position borders on a related premise of privilege, but to compare and measure self to another or others is NOT at all the point and focus of which I address.

The journey I speak on, "to blossom out from hiding" is of a personal focus and issue. To determine who you are, apart from all others, not in comparison. If there's to be any measurement of comparison at all, it is for you to measure and compare the present self to the ideal self; tapping into your innermost feelings; remembering fallen dreams, aspirations and passions; to revive qualities of a fundamental nature which may have been forsaken; retracing and recapturing hidden essence; to reincorporate those elements into the present, developing and enhancing a revised version of self; one which breathes exuberance into the soul. Grasping that amid all others, you are to maintain a sense of personal exclusivity; to value what it is you desire for self. To realize you deserve to achieve and live out that which you desire (in the realm of decency and order of course). You deserve to represent the innateness of self. Your innate traits weren't placed inside you to be forsaken or hidden.

It is important to understand, to do what is necessary to achieve a healthy and content you, are not to be considered selfish actions. And you should not feel guilty or allow others to impose guilt upon you for pursuing what it is that gives you joy. To achieve for self is simply to gain in self – to self-nurture; to bring together parts of self to allow God-given elements to culminate into a wholesome whole – a wholesomeness which can be recognized and appreciated as the authentic you.

From personal experience, discussions, and observations, I recognize how common it is for a woman to place herself in a box; therefore, falling short to experience the fullness of life. It is this shortfall to attain fullness for which I advocate. To understand it is one's privilege to live the best life available to them.

Women have tendency to feel since they have trodden a course for a long period of time, and time and energy have been invested, they must continue on that course. As if it's too late to make a change. So, they give in to what is, instead of pursuing the desires of the heart. But if one has the ability and circumstance allows it, it's never too late.

In midst of securing distinctiveness, know that it is absolutely okay and fitting for a woman to commit to those she loves and cares, and to be willing to sacrifice for them at points in time. Generally, a woman accepts the responsibility of certain charges with pride and without issue. It's not at all debasing to her to accept what comes naturally. But what she does consider debasing is when her efforts are taken for granted, and she's expected to adhere to the double standards and cultural idiosyncrasies simply because of gender; that who she is as an individual is simply supposed to go away.

Woman however is not totally blameless that she finds herself in this position, inadvertently perhaps, but she somewhat consents. This is a truth about herself which she must realize. How is she part blame? Because, as she consistently accepts what she doesn't want to accept, do much of what she doesn't want to do, and overlooks much of what she doesn't want to overlook, it echoes - I'm willing, in spite of. And since she appears willing, it then becomes the expected. Then as she continues, in spite of, she loses sight of who she is and who she started out to become. Her voice becomes soften. To the family, she's the doer more so than a benefactor.

Although today's woman has her focus on family and home, unlike that of yesterday-minded woman, she has a world of opportunity waiting to be explored and conquered. So, she figures why not handle both worlds. Why not take it all on? With this notion has surfaced the attitude of superwoman. I can do it all, I can have it all, and I can handle it all - well. I am a superpower.

At the onset, as she supposes to handle it all, there's one aspect she fails to figure into the equation; future overload. She tries to incorporate so much. And her family looks at her as a bottomless pit of resource and service. The supposed "must do's" take front and center as she - the doer - lives life stretched in various directions. If she's employed, she lives in the center of two different worlds, trying to operate proficiently in both. The individual she started out being, one of self-purpose and direction, slowly turns into someone undistinguishable; for more is being expelled than being taken in to fortify her core.

Although I have spoken mostly of the nuances of the traditional-minded woman, which is my personal point of reference, those experiencing hiding are more inclusive. The range is far-reaching. There are also those who are abused, battered, misused and violated; those who are scorned and operate within fear. Those who have retreated within self, and fear and hopelessness paralyze their actions. Their self-esteem and self-value have been shattered. They suffer tremendous loss of self. For them to come out from under the clutches of "hiding", requires a great deal of effort, courage and focus, and possibly special professional help. But, if there's a way, then exercise the will, and put determination in action.

However, the affects stemming from hiding - regardless of the circumstance, regardless of the particulars, and regardless of the initiation point, is similar in nature. The severity may vary, yet there is commonality; the neglect of self. And when you neglect core elements of self, attributes which represent who you are - you abandon YOU. Having abandoned YOU is not a content place to reside.

Although there're definitely times when you need to delve into the whys of matters, there are times when we must go forth and leave what has been alone. You can become lost and burdened trying to figure out the whys. While some of the whys are readily revealed, others may require a lot of digging to disclose. Some things are better left alone. What is crucial is to determine what it is you need to do to move forward

Allow yourself to come clean with yourself. Release yourself to live out YOU. Come up with a plan. For without a plan to change, you will remain the same. You'll be spending wheels and going nowhere. If a change is desired, a plan has to be executed and determination put into force. It really is okay to release the old weights and make the needed changes for the better. Take heart, take courage and do it.

This book has been entitled "To Blossom out from Hiding", a title I meticulously chose to represent what I feel epitomizes a state-of-existence and a state of need many women today; too many actually. Even though a woman is at a place today where opportunities are afforded, yet many remain restricted – emotionally and perceptually. However, much of that is self-inflicted. Many have chased the infamous "model role", one which is considered the "coded" rite of passage; the measurement of a real woman, imposed, implied and expected. A role which not only shapes and molds perception and mindset, it dictates actions. Personal choice becomes an element neglected.

There isn't an ironclad path to "hiding". As stated previously, there are many attributing variables. It grabs hold of those in all walks of life, various cultures, nationalities, and religions. Since "hiding" is a process evolving over time, and is an unintended happening, its clutches simply steal its way into existence and into your life. But due to its clutch on your person, eventually, and at a point, you realize much of self is being denied.

The message conveyed in, "To Blossom out from Hiding", is not for every woman; nor will every woman agree or understand the concept I offer. But for those particular ones, those which share a common mindset and perception; those which have been somewhat immobilized and dictated by traditional practices and mores; those which have been under suppression for one reason or another, those which compromise the essence of self for others; and those which can attest to the silent scream – "Who am I", then for those women, its content can be liberating, comforting and healing; soothing to the soul.

249

Why? Because its message witnesses to the innermost parts of self, it speaks to undisclosed sensitivities, it validates feelings and longings, and it provides a view of a pathway to recovery.

Years ago, I was once this woman. And because I was, I am able to recognize the traits in others. My spirit has become as a detector. It doesn't matter how successful a woman may be, how productive she is, how educated she is, or even how skillfully masked she has become, there's something about her persona which is like an open book, and I can decode the signs. Those signs point her out. As well as identifying her, I understand her, and most importantly, I reach out to her.

Understand that because she seeks to revive her individuality, doesn't mean she doesn't appreciate and respect her life as a whole, enjoying family and honoring responsibilities; she does, and is proud of it. But after living daily forsaking self, and as years have gone by, life assessment factors in. She assesses her position in life, pondering could've, should've, and only ifs. These factors weigh on the mind and heart. She sees her clock ticking, time is on a count-down, and life has yet to be lived in a manner desired.

Understand you don't have to give up anything to make changes in your life unless there's something that needs to be given up. You don't have to be drastic in changes of yourself or your circumstances. You don't even have to relinquish responsibilities as you know them. But there are some must do's; be honest with self, pay attention to your heart, take charge of your actions, and make changes accordingly. Subsequently, rearranging and realigning things in your day-to-day and valuing yourself as a priority. Respect yourself as you desire to be respected; then others in your life will follow suit. It doesn't mean you should minimize your respect and responsibilities to others, it only means you don't minimize your respect and responsibility to self.

Only you know the yearnings of the innermost-self. Only you know what gives joy-fullness. Only you know what is hidden within. Only you know the aspects of self which are waiting to sprout and blossom. Only you know what God has placed within you. Release it! Live it! Enjoy it! Don't be discouraged or afraid to live as YOU. And don't allow others and circumstances to continue to rob you.

My appeal is to all who need to receive this message and for those readers needing to receive, I wish for you to clearly recognize who you are. Grab hold of it, consume it, and move forward. Be encouraged and be empowered. Don't ingest the information and not digest it. Don't walk away unchanged.

Some changes may be subtle in nature, while others may require more radical actions. Ask yourself, what is hidden within that you would like to unveil? What was stifled, that you would now like to release? What talents do you possess that you would like to unleash?

Reactivate those elements. Rediscover your voice, and express it. Put in action that which is already present in the mind and heart. Once you determine what those things are, don't be afraid to chase after them. And once you chase it, capture it.

I know much of what I've addressed pertains to man as well as woman, but I do not know what it's like to walk in a man's shoes. I can only bear witness to that of a woman, especially that of a traditional-minded one; one who views herself, as most traditional women do, the rescuer for those she loves and to whom she is committed. As for many, while they are rescuing others, they overlook rescuing self.

My writing as I see it, addresses a truth – a truth in the lives of many women, and a truth which is often overlooked and often disguised to appear otherwise. It has been my intent to bring attention to this truth, and to for its advocate its transformation; enriching lives.

Ladies, if you have reached a point in life where you feel the need to do things differently, then do so. It's your life. Make the needed changes. Don't be afraid, nor feel as though it's too late. If you're still breathing, still well, and still capable, it's not too late. Sure, some things in life have passed; never to be seen again, we live in seasons. But, there's always newness to claim at your present moment. You can capture joyfulness and contentment in self as well as circumstance. There can be new dreams and aspirations if past ones cannot be actualized.

If you want to go back to school, go. If you want to lose weight, lose it. If you want to reinvent your vocation, reinvent it. If you want to start a business, start it. If you want to spend time in areas of interest, spend it. If you want to get from under the mundane of everyday life, then create new and interesting things to do. If you need to close a few doors, close them. And if you need to open a few, open them. Whatever you need to do to allow vigor and passion into your life, do so. You owe it to your life.

Don't go through life any longer and not experience YOU! If you have forsaken the essence of what makes you the person that embodies your true spirit, then you are not experiencing the authentic representation of self.

Begin your journey to allow the true essence of YOU to blossom out from hiding. At whatever point you are in life, young or older, LIVE. In decency and in order of course!

Chapter fifteen
Now, What?

Now, let's get down to business. After having prompted you to probe your mind, feelings, circumstances and relationships, it's likely you have gone through an in-depth self-assessment - examining your views, actions and mannerisms; your lifestyle. You're probably thinking – so, I've become aware of some things, but now what? You're likely thinking, why does it all matter at this point in life anyways, and even if it does; what am I going to do about it?

You probably faced a few facts you would rather not have faced, some which you were already aware, but had pushed back, and you probably uncovered a few surprises. But, in the midst of feelings of uncertainty and unease, hopefully you are encouraged as well; charged up and ready to go forward into a journey leading to self-renewal; excited to see what the future uncovers.

Even if you are inspired and encouraged, chances are you have thoughts and feelings which are all jumbled. Varied thoughts are passing through your mind. Or, you may be overwhelmed with thoughts and feelings and see yourself at a point of impasse; many emotions released. And, after all the self-probing, self-assessing, and thought-provoking undertakings; you still wonder, now what?

If you have determined you are a woman in "hiding", or feel you are headed in this direction, it is my hope that amongst the sea of emotions you are experiencing, you are motivated and are positioning yourself to make a U-turn, a detour, or whatever the case may be to get on a course toward change. Be encouraged. There are answers to your quandaries. You just have to sort through some things.

Don't allow yourself to remain locked in a state of desolation, or to remain commonplace in an undesirable situation. Rather, become inspired to make whatever changes are needed to establish a lifestyle that grants a satisfactory measure of peace, joy and contentment. It is hoped you will allow yourself the opportunity to receive and establish a fresh wind and fresh fire to begin your journey to recovery of true self.

Don't talk yourself out of it. If necessary, talk to someone close to you that will hold you accountable for what you say you want to do. Someone to support, encourage and love you through it. If you require counseling to talk it through, then seek the proper counselor. There's no shame in asking for help. Just be careful whose help you solicit. Sometimes, girlfriends are just not the ones to give the advice, even if they are your BFF.

Grasp an understanding of what you need at this point in life. Don't settle any longer for circumstance you don't want when you know it really is not a healthy situation. Envision what and how you want things to be for yourself and get on that path. Realize you are deserving of it. See yourself as a priority in your own life. Don't allow others' expectations to override that of your own. Don't permit what others think of you to impede your actions. It's okay to chase after what makes you content in self. Realize that! Accept it! Embrace it! Start now!

We don't simply discard other people and responsibilities, of course, but we can rearrange some things. Start mentally, then actually; small steps and gradually let things unfold.

Be mindful of the fact that you need to invoke your own sustaining motivation. Remember, surfing on someone else's vigor and enthusiasm will gradually slip from under you. Someone else's motivation can jump-start you, but eventually you must ride on your own willpower. You must become rooted in your own self-determination. Just think how many times we have listened to a motivational speech, or read a motivational book, became all fired-up to whatever the cause may be; motivating thoughts and energy flowing, only later to become weary and lose that energetic charge, eventually reverting back to a point of doing the same old thing the same old way. Another's testimony may inspire you, but if you expect someone else's energy to continually carry you through, it's likely that it won't.

You must establish your own sustaining fire. You must establish a purpose and a vision for self. If you become rooted in your own self-determination, you will become more focused on your goal and desired outcome. You must be convinced and committed to your cause to be steadfast to follow through on course.

Now, you may be considering all that has been said, and have decided to make a few changes, yet you tug with how to start the process. Encouragement and discouragement are running on parallel tracks. Pride, fear, and disillusionment are pressing hard to defeat you. So, what do you do? How do you nudge yourself from one position to another?

In order to initiate change of any kind, you must decide to take a first step. You must determine a starting point; however small it may be. What simple change can you make today?

Start by doing one thing different which gives you a sense of empowerment and accomplishment in self. Just one different action can jumpstart you. It may be something as

simple as following true to your feeling to say "no" to someone, when you're so used to saying "yes". Or even to say "yes" to something or someone when you have been saying "no". Regardless, just do something DIFFERENT! TODAY!

As you continue, pay close attention to daily activities and how you generally handle and manage things. Figure out what it is you desire to change. Figure out what it is you desire to do, or not do. Go within self. Be honest in accepting what you discover. Take those pieces you find, and place them in a comfortable order.

You don't have to be like anyone else – don't compare – just be you. After you have tapped into that inner-person and come up with some answers; begin to rearrange different aspects of your life, one step at a time. Prayerfully, astutely, patiently, and cautiously go forward. Don't self-talk out of it!

If family meetings are feasible, then have those meetings. Your family has already taken note of the change in your behavior and is already wondering what is going on with you. Meet with them and share your dilemma. Include all of the immediate family, and at some point, in time, meet with friends, siblings and parents if you deem it necessary. They can offer encouragement, direction, and lend an ear of objectivity. Share your concerns with whoever is important and close to you.

When you meet with family, do not walk away from the meeting without establishing a sense of accomplishment. Family members may not completely understand what it is you desire of them, but if they want what's important to you, then they are likely to give their support. Someone that loves and cares for you should want you to be happy -right?

If not, then you will have to figure out how you are going to proceed without their direct support. While you don't want to alienate your loved ones, you will have to figure out reasonable solutions. You don't want to cause discontent in one area while you are pursuing your own contentment in another.

Assure them you will not neglect commitments and responsibilities, but will be making a few changes to better ensure your own well-being. Don't sit on it. Once you start making personal changes, they will begin to take note. Even though they might not appreciate it at first, eventually, they will make some adjustments themselves.

In the meantime, remember not to be too critical toward them. It's not their fault you find yourself in this position. It's a position you accepted upon yourself. You are the one who allowed yourself to become the sacrificial one. Regardless of how you have handled things in the past, it is your prerogative to change.

You may only require subtle changes. You don't want to change who you are, rather you want to enhance who you are. You don't want to get CRAZY in your actions. Keep everything decent and in order. But whatever the need is, simple or not so simple, go forward. Don't be afraid. And don't remain so comfortable in your cocoon. Step out!

A first step I suggest however, is for you to spend moments in meditation. Reclaim knowing self in the spirit and truth. A process to help you understand what it is you want and what it is you need. Understand too, what you need and desire today may be totally different than what it was five, ten, fifteen, or more years ago; we change and develop daily.

Don't get lost in past dreams if they cannot be actualized today. Make new ones. Figure out who you are at this present time, and work from there. Embrace who you are; years lived, lessons learned, trials experienced and mistakes made; all of it – embrace it. Then begin to reshape it. Don't allow age to deter you. Live until you're not living.

I also suggest you keep a daily journal for a period of time. Talk less and observe more of self and others. Don't debate and argue your points of view. Debating time, for the moment, is over. This is to be a time of observation and discovery. Begin to record daily happenings that stimulate liveliness; what calms your spirit; what drains your spirit; what gives you enjoyment; what makes you laugh, and what or who kills your laughter. What makes you feel at home with self and others? Pay attention to these things. Be honest in your responses. Breathe! Breathe deep.

Another aspect to examine is relationships. Strengthen those which you treasure and reestablish friendships which you desire to rekindle. As for other relationships, put them all in proper perspective; you have to know when to hold and when to fold. You want to receive a positive charge from people in your circle of family and friends; surround yourself with people that appreciate and celebrate your presence in their lives.

Another important phase of the journey is to identify your stressors and what triggers these stressors? Record that information. Take a true look at the facts and dissect them. Let your gut be the guide. What can you do to either eliminate or minimize the negatives? These are the areas that tear your body down. These are the areas that attack your well-being. If it is possible to change the situation, change it. If not, you just may have to fine-tune and adjust your mindset regarding the matter, and realign yourself around it. What may appear important at the present time just might not be as important after you dissect the situation.

Don't be too hasty to go in a direction unless you are certain. Go slowly. Don't rush into anything. Let the process be as if you are viewing a compelling movie, frame by frame. Unlike TV, with this movie, you can edit it at any point. You are the director. View it, edit it and rewrite where necessary. Don't play the role of an extra in a movie you are writing, and producing which you are one of the main stars.

Only you have knowledge of what is needed to satisfy your inner-self. Bring heart and head together to establish a well-balanced you. No longer allow the inner-person to remain hidden within. Live out joyfulness in self. Having joy breeds good health - emotionally, mentally, physically and most of all spiritually. A content you, supports every vital organ in your body. A smile on your face supports heart health. A joyous presence makes your skin glow. An unstressed body relaxes your mind and muscles. A feeling of being appreciated fosters a sense of worth. Enjoying activities of interests gives you passion. And to engage the talents and gifts which God has placed within you provides a sense of meaning and purpose.

Be encouraged and bravely move forward on your journey to blossom out from hiding. Establish some goals, and keep your eye on the goal. It is not going to be an easy feat to make life altering changes, while having to consider the feelings and well-being of others. But a feat you need to take on.

Grab hold of the best life for self. Bring forth the essence which God has placed within you. It is a gift to be received. Receive it. Step by step, moment by moment; get to know who you are and where you desire to go. Begin to feel the fibers of your essence return to you. Embrace it as if giving yourself a great big hug; as if a missing loved one is returning home, and you are so elated to see that loved one. That loved one is -You!

So now what? Get going, that's what; newness awaits you. Make the first step, then another, and another. Be bold in your endeavors. But mostly, understand what it is you want to happen. Know what you want, set goals, put plans in action, and step out.

Chapter Sixteen
Become Naked

There are times when we fail to be honest with self. In self-talk, we often tell ourselves things that are not quite accurate; we appease with distortions and exaggerations. So actually, we lie to ourselves.

We learn to accept these distortions and exaggerations and they feed into our minds as truths. Perhaps, it's a coping strategy to help us better deal with certain situations. It softens the perceived adverse effect. The truth sometimes stings, so we sugar-coat which in turn allows us to feel better about ourselves or a situation. It shields us from hurt and disappointments. Sometimes the lie is better faced than truth. However, it becomes a false sense of reality, and that false sense is what we often choose to live out.

Eventually, and at a point in time when we want to move from one critical point to another, we have to own up to the lies we feed into our minds. We must disclose and become totally naked to self. We cannot go forward in certainty and peace unless we confront and deal with the distortions, exaggerations and untruths.

As you journey to blossom out from hiding, allow yourself to experience moments of nakedness. I suggest you experience such moments sooner than later. For these unveiling, self-disclosing moments will provide opportunity to further explore self; to strip off layers and to examine each layer one by one; allowing self to bare and expose in a very private nature - soulfully, physically and spiritually - to self.

Know this phase requires guts; you must own up to pretenses and cover-ups and compel self to come out into the open; to uncover disguised and hidden elements; delve into the soul; no pretenses, no masks, and no lies; to acknowledge truth in the form of raw nakedness; a moment in time to be totally real to self. Be mindful though, you just may travel to a place where you have never allowed self to travel before.

On occasions when I've instructed classes of young adults, and at times when I've determined it to be of benefit, I've asked my students to engage in a mirror-facing activity; a simple activity which allows one the opportunity to self-disclose and examine self face-to-face. You simply face the mirror.

In this group activity I offer a quiet setting for all to be seated at a table. Each has either a small table-top or hand-held mirror; one wide enough to comfortably view the entire face at a glance. Other materials needed include paper and pen to record thoughts and findings. Each student relaxes in the setting and tries to eliminate mental distractions as much as possible. They sit quietly for moments facing the mirror, studying the features and expressions of the face. Usually, students are a bit skeptical initially, but quickly relax into the exercise, and sit quietly observing and probing.

Most times the young women in the class start off noticing surface features such as hair, blemishes, shape of the nose and so on; usually noting what they perceive as the negatives. But the longer they observe, the deeper they travel into self, going beyond surface and traveling intensely into the eyes. The mood would then become quieted and expressions began to change as they experienced a deeper look. Once allowing self to travel inwardly, to actually examine the story within the eyes, they were often surprised about what was actually revealed to them.

At the end of the exercise, if desired, students would share their findings amongst each other. It was always a highly moving experience for the listener as well as for the

participant. As revelations were discussed, there was a range of emotions released – some in cries, some in laughter of amazement, some in shock by surprising discovery, and others, inability to recognize the eyes in the mirror that stared back at them. Just an array of feelings and emotions were expressed. However, everyone was able to walk away from the experience having benefited, and surprisingly glad to have participated.

One amazing aspect worth noting is, most of the ladies wrote down points sensationalizing the negatives and downplaying the positives. When they shared those expressed negatives with fellow students, almost always, others had not focused on those attributes in the same manner. In many regards, others didn't consider those attributes negatives even after being pointed out.

Typically, people admire positive traits in others. It's the positive which stands out. And with this particular exercise, positive traits in one another were pointed out which the individual had not recognized in self as admirable quality. Most students left the exercise feeling more positive about themselves, and more hopeful. And at times when there were negatives which merited discussion, students were better in an element to listen and to process what was pointed out; understanding that the exercise was done in best intention for all.

No doubt, we all have a few critical people around to focus on our negatives, and it can be disheartening if we allow it. But, realize those few people should not represent the majority in our circle of family, friends and acquaintances. So, we don't need to dwell on negative energy which those few people bring, but focus on the majority, those in our lives who bring positive energy.

There are times in life though, when we need others to point out things about us that require our attention. We need to actually hear constructive criticism and comments which are meant for our good; we need to accept helpful hints. At those times, we need to be receptive even if it pinches our ego a bit. It is those types of things which help us build character and face our truths. So, when those who love and celebrate you point out some things they think you may need to hear, listen and consider. They don't mean you harm, but good. Unfortunately, everyone's intent is not for our good. There are times when we are opposed by others, and you may view it as an attack. Even then, before you dismiss it, consider what has been said, process it and determine if you can benefit from it.

If you choose to participate in this mirror-facing activity and you are not in a group setting, you may want to have a trusted person to share in this experience and to bounce feelings off of. But if you prefer to be alone in your nakedness to face yourself alone, that's okay too.

Either way, as you face the mirror, first write down what you see on the surface; your hair color, style, and texture; your eye shape and color; pimples; your smile or lack thereof; etc., whatever you see. Then note your thoughts about these features. Meditate on them for a short while. You don't want to spend much time here.

Once relaxed and engaged, pay close attention to the presence of the person staring back at you. Who is that person looking at you? Do you recognize that person? What is being revealed through the story of your eyes? Look deep, much deeper. What is being unveiled? Answer these questions; for your eyes reveal your truth. Your true feelings are all present and reflected in the expression of your eyes. So, what are your eyes expressing to you?

Verbally you may have been expressing one thing, but now your eyes may be telling you a totally different story. The eyes reveal all. They don't lie. Allow yourself to receive what is revealed and your truth will jump out at you. Does the story in your eyes and the reality of your world match? And even more importantly, does the story in your eyes and the heart match?

When I first participated in this particular activity, and noticed the expression in my own eyes, I was surprised at what was revealed to me. I didn't like what I saw. My eyes did not express real joy. I saw gratefulness, but not cheerfulness. The healthy sparkle was missing. As I looked deeper, I noticed a hint of melancholy. I did not know exactly how, when, or why, but somehow, I had let go of my zeal and it reflected in my eyes. The more I looked into my eyes, the cover-ups became uncovered and my nakedness became exposed – to me.

I knew at that point, I wanted to change the story my eyes revealed. I wanted to recover my zeal and that sparkle. I wanted to renew life passion – authentically. I wanted it to be evident in the story in my eyes. But first, I had to face my truths and take ownership. I had to go deep inside and claim me, and allow myself to release me. I no longer wanted to travel through life in a fog of lost zeal. Regardless of how productive I was in activities, in employment, and for my family, I had to regain me.

So far in mirror facing, we have discussed what I consider the initial phase. But this experience goes deeper – physical nakedness. This aspect however is not done in a group environment, or at least I don't suggest it be done in a group. This phase should be in total privacy. This phase is not metaphorical nakedness, it's the real thing. You are going to strip of your clothing.

This may sound a bit laughable at first, but go with me. It's really a serious matter. You will still need a mirror, but this time a full-length mirror, one which allows you to see yourself from head to toe. When in a private and comfortable setting, and not hurried, position yourself in front of the full-length mirror, standing upright. While viewing yourself, begin to take off all of your clothing, piece by piece, allowing yourself to view and examine your physical nakedness bit by bit. After becoming completely naked, allow yourself to view your body as if you were viewing a work of art – which you are by the way.

You may be pleased with your physical appearance, and this will not be a challenging task at all. Or, you may not be as pleased, and you don't care to look at yourself. Whatever your category, allow yourself to take a good look at your body. Take note of who you are naked. Don't think about how another may view you. Take note of yourself for self. Relax in looking at you. This is your body – own it.

If pleased and confident with what you see physically, you may just want to get redressed, and be on your way, you are finished with this phase of the nakedness experience. No doubt, you have a few helpful hints to give to the rest of us who may not have done as well in this department. However, even if you are okay with actual appearance, but deal with special issues concerning what your body may have been exposed to; experiences which you have allowed or experiences which may have been imposed. If this is the case, don't be too hasty in redressing. Just look. Remember, raw honesty is the key. If you are struggling emotionally concerning specific issues in regard to your body, then allow yourself to accept you. This is your body. Reclaim ownership, and appreciate you at this moment. As always, if special help is needed to work through specific issues, seek appropriate counsel. Strive to turn your mirror-facing activity into a positive one.

Now, for you who are not as pleased with your physical appearance, don't look away, continue to look. This body belongs to you, embrace it. Hug yourself and tell self, "I love you". You're alone, no one is watching. As you continue in this physical nakedness experience, and as you face the mirror to view your body from all angles, be kind. Love your body regardless of how you perceive it to look. This body keeps you alive. This body serves you every day. This body is your personal Godly temple. So, love it, even if its appearance is not what you like at the moment. Appearances can be altered and redone; but embrace you at this moment and mean it.

After loving on yourself, gently note what changes you desire to make. If you determine you need to get your body back to a healthier shape, make a plan to start working on it. Make attainable short-term goals. If you need to increase muscle tone, plan to start doing appropriate exercises; there are all sorts and means available. If you need to lose weight, consult your physician and start a weight reduction plan, go small at first. Even if you need to gain a few pounds, make the necessary healthy adjustments. If you want a simple make-over. Do it. Whatever your physical cosmetic desire may be, within reason, begin working on it. It may appear to be a long road ahead, but if you don't make a start, you'll never get there.

We say that it's all about the inner-spirit, and the inner-spirit is most important - it is in large. But if we are real, we'll admit females love it when they feel they look pretty. So, if pretty or beautiful is what you want, do what it takes to make you feel pretty and beautiful. Remember beauty comes in all shapes, forms, and ages.

In the meantime, you are not to compare yourself to any other. If you do, that will bring on additional stress and self judgement. You are aiming for joy and contentment, not another stressful endeavor.

Make up your mind to work on enhancing whatever features you desire to enhance. It's about how you feel about yourself. However, no one is perfect, nor do we need to be perfect. If you think about it, by whose standard are we to classify perfection? We just need to be comfortable in our own body. Remember, the feeling of attractiveness starts on the inside, then spills over onto the outside. So, mindset may be the first thing you need to change.

No doubt, women have always desired to look beautiful- on surface. To feel and look beautiful starts when we are little girls. We rejoiced in being told we were pretty. As women, most invest much time and money in this effort. And culture imposes quite a bit of pressure too. So, to look beautiful is not a new trend – it been forever. But today, as you look at yourself in the mirror ask, "What do I need to do starting today to become reasonably pleased with my own appearance?" Not what someone else wants of you, but what do you want for yourself. What is beautiful to you for you?

Now don't go crazy and get all radical. Extreme is not necessary. Take your time and plan. Feel proud about it as you go. Don't beat yourself up, and by all means, keep the stress out of it. Just understand why you want what you want. It doesn't need to be a tug-of-war in your head.

Case in point - I began to gray prematurely; in my thirties actually. It didn't come as a shock when it began to happen because my mother had experienced the same. But still, it was unwanted gray hair. So, I began to use hair color to tone it down a bit. As the years passed and I got older, and since gray hair often accompanies getting older, I tried to persuade myself to let nature take its course.

Bring the grey on. .I thought that was how I was supposed to handle it - traditionally. Scripture tells us gray hair represents evidence of wisdom. So, since I had arrived at that point, wasn't I supposed to let evidence of wisdom show? So, I would go back and forth with the argument to color or not to color; self-battling. As I looked around and noticed many of my peers beginning to gray and going natural, I thought maybe I was to do the same. Still, it just wasn't what I wanted for myself.

From time to time in this going-back-and-forth process, I would express it to my hairdresser. One day during this discussion, she firmly said to me, "Why take yourself through this? Why deny yourself something so simple, and most importantly, something which you feel enhances your appearance?" When she spoke those words, it was as if a light switched on. I immediately began to see the issue differently. Those questions changed my whole outlook regarding that particular matter; thinking - if there are enhancements available, appropriate and not harmful, why not take advantage of them? Why not do what it takes to make you feel attractive and comfortable in self. It's a choice; your choice. I chose to color and I feel good about it – still.

Features change as we mature, that's a fact. Sometimes we become stressed over what's naturally altered by time. But in the process, we can be proactive in doing what is needed to help us feel good about ourselves even though nature is in command. We still have a measure of control. We just have to embrace those changes as they occur and work with them. Sometimes, it really doesn't take a lot to enhance. But in the end, it's what you desire for yourself.

I once heard a well-known minister speak on positive thinking. To paraphrase his sentiment, he expressed - people generally spend much time on the negatives; often dwelling on what is not, more so than the positives of what actually is. We hear this sentiment all the time –right? But what he went on to express is-even when there is a negative, often times there are simple fixes and remedies. Why not take advantage of the simple fixes?

As an example - he expressed - if you have missing teeth and are not pleased with your appearance as a result of it, simply go to the dentist and get yourself some teeth, and the dilemma is solved. If your hair is thinning or maybe you're going bald, and it troubles you, then just go buy yourself a wig or get a weave, and the dilemma is solved. Why stress over issues which can be easily solved. In other words, fix what can be fixed and go merrily on your way. Minimize the stressors and feel good about yourself at the same time.

In your nakedness, allow yourself to reveal all to you. And then make some resolves. There may be some simple fixes, and then, some not so simple. Again, where there's a will, there's likely a way. Go for it!

Don't let mirror-facing be a onetime occurrence. Keep facing yourself in the mirror as a check-point to asse development as you work and progress from point to point. And remember; honest nakedness. And as you do, continue to pay attention to the story in your eyes. The eyes speak volume and truth. It's your tell-tell sign. Release yourself to live life so a sparkle is reflected in the eyes. And what's amazing, others will see that reflection and it can actually become contagious.

Chapter Seventeen
Ultimate Nakedness

There's yet another phase of nakedness in which I suggest you participate. It's a phase which stands alone, one which has its own special place, and one which merits much reverence – spiritual nakedness.

Spiritual mindfulness has guided and guarded my actions throughout life. Yet, there were time when I sort of lived life with God being in the wing. I was aware of His presence, and aware of His sovereignty, but largely, I viewed Him as help in time in times of need. I honored Him in worship, and lived within convictions of my faith; still, I sort of followed my own standard of righteousness, allowing my own thoughts and ideas to justify my actions and steer my direction.

Even when we have received and accepted Jesus as Lord and Savior and guiding source, we can sometimes straddle the fence. On one hand we may truly believe, yet on the other hand, we blindly follow our own ways; believing we are okay. And sometimes, even knowing that we are not right in our actions, still, we follow our own selfish desires; justifying why we do what we do.

It's a wonderful thing that God has a plan for our lives.

And because of His amazing grace, He doesn't let go of His own as we go off onto our own path and are led by our own righteous standards. So, even during times of waywardness, being aware of His presence and His covering, I remained God-conscious. And as I matured in life and in worship, and because of God's love, He without fail, kept His hand on me. I was guided to realize that God consciousness isn't enough. I realized there were more, and I wanted more of Him, and I would seek more.

I would observe others of faith who seemed to possess something I didn't possess, to express something I didn't know how to express, to demonstrate a spiritual boldness I didn't demonstrate, and to have a certain peace I didn't seem to have. I never was one good at pretending; I am transparent in my feelings. What actually is - is what shows. So I didn't pretend to be what I wasn't or feel what I didn't feel. But I knew I wanted to express more spiritual joy and experience more spiritual freedom. There was a yearning to have a different kind of relationship with God and Lord, but there was blockage. He was present, He was in view, but the relationship was somehow blocked. I knew there was to be a deeper walk with Him, but yet there was a barrier.

This feeling could be compared to that of walking around with shades on your eyes. While the sun is shining and in focus, seeing its brightness and enjoying the sun, yet the view is obstructed; it's shaded over. I was seeing God through an obstructed view. I was wearing shades. For a while that view seemed okay. I was accustomed to that view. But as life happened, and as I learned more of Him, I wanted to capture the full view. Whatever the blockage was I wanted it removed. I wanted to see clearly. I wanted the sun (Son) to be in full view.

For many reasons, we walk around wearing a type of shade, dimming our view, vision and perception; hindering our relationship with God, operating in dusk instead of daybreak. Sometimes, we are aware that our vision is obstructed, and sometimes not. Regardless, the affect is the same; the view is obstructed and the benefit of receiving fullness is hampered. We allow ourselves to become comfortable with an obstructed view and settle in to it. So, we continue to wear our shades.

I believe we allow ourselves to wear shades which obscure our view because we don't want to see our messes and we don't want to be held accountable. Sometimes we just don't know how wrong our actions are, because we haven't fortified a relationship with the Lord to strengthen our knowledge and understanding of His Word. Therefore, we can't clearly see and understand His Way for our lives. But as long as we remain shaded, we go merrily on our way in our own righteousness.

There comes a time however when the shades must be removed. And if we don't submit to God's nudging to remove them, He has a way of removing them for us. This could be a subtle nudge or one more intense. Either, He raises our awareness and brings us face-to-face with what it is we actually need of Him, and of what it is He requires of us – sooner or later. We should want it to be sooner. And sometimes because of our own self-indulgencies, we choose later. Be mindful though, along with choosing later we choose to experience the consequences of our actions.

I remember how the elders used to instruct when trying to guide and shield younger ones from life woes. We youngsters in our narrow mindedness, feeling we already knew what was best for ourselves, would often respond to them as if they were speaking a foreign language, showing little regard for the wisdom life had imparted them. In their wisdom and in response to our dismissal of their instructions, they would simply say and with sort of a smirk, "Just keep on living, and wait on time".

Time and experience actually do reveal much. The elders knew that eventually life would teach us just as it had taught them, and if we didn't adhere their instructions,

all that needed to happen was simply to wait on the element of time. They knew that the clarity of their words would eventually surface, and that time mixed with experience would become our teacher; a teacher we wouldn't be able to ignore or dismiss. And it is easier to listen to the words of the wise than to experience the school of hard knocks.

Doesn't it work similarly with God when we don't adhere to his written Word and instructions? He mercifully allows us time to go astray, to do our own thing, to endure life and follow a path we design for ourselves; while we wear shades obstructing our view. As we do, even though He remains hovering, He permits us to experience our own way along with the adversities that follows.

Because of His love, patience and grace, at the appointed time and hopefully before we are far gone in obscurity, He allows us moments to face ourselves in His mirror. Then, if we are willing, He'll usher us back unto Him. He will deliver us out of the murkiness of obscurity, and guide us into the light of clarity. He will rescue you – no matter what, and regardless of circumstance. He will remove the shades from your eyes so you may see Him clearly. He loves us just that much; unconditionally.

I've reverenced God all of my years as far back as I can remember. But I've come to realize there's so much more to a relationship with Him than to reverence. I now understand how much of an in-depth fellowship with Him is available to us, and to what extent a most intimate relationship can be established if you allow ourselves to face His mirror. His mirror is most revealing.

In narrow-mindedness, we place ourselves in a different category than others when we don't consider our habits and vices to be as bad as someone else's. That is an obscured view. All people don't have the same struggles, yet, wrong is wrong and sin is sin. There is no level of degree when it comes to sin. Regardless of the type of struggle, severe or not as severe, when fellowship with God is broken, it's broken.

We have all dealt with struggles which hamper our relationship with God. We sometimes consentingly allow mess in our lives, our actions, attitudes, views, motives, and people who are not best for us. So, we all have struggles to overcome. In God's sight, no one is better than the other.

We all have to decide to let go of certain things because it is not God's way. It doesn't matter to God what the struggle is, great or small as we may determine it; but what does matter is that we allow Him in to release it, to save us and to place our feet on solid ground; His path.

Sometimes we don't even realize we are messy thinking because we rate our deeds according to our own perceptions and self-righteousness, fooling ourselves and others. We can see wrong in others, but we don't want to accept it in self. But wrong is wrong, mess is mess, and sin is sin regardless of who's doing it or what the wrong, mess, or sin may be. When we allow ourselves to face God's mirror; His Scripture, teachings, instructions and Holy Guiding, we clearly see our mess.

It takes a genuine relationship with Christ to realize the personal role we play in our own mess. Without Christ and His workings in us, we will continue in it and continue to fool ourselves, wearing shades covering our view.

To have a genuine, intimate relationship with God through Christ, we must become naked before Him and surrender to his Will. He knows all about us anyway, there aren't any secrets unknown to Him. So, why not surrender to the Almighty who knows all, divinely loves you, and has a divine purpose for your existence? Why not surrender to an Almighty that protects and guides you? Why not surrender to an Almighty that has all riches and desires to share with you? Why not surrender to an Almighty that will never hurt you, never forsake you, but will love, cover and keep you? Why not?

At a point, I too needed to rid myself of the mess, surrender to the power of the Lord and allow the Holy Spirit to take control of my mind, heart and actions. There comes a time, at least it did for me, when you must shed weights, let go of misconceptions, let go of self-guiding, and stop being judgmental toward others as if to be their judge and jury. There comes a time to simply rest at the Lord's feet and surrender. Then, the Holy Spirit will immediately nudge you when you are in the wrong, and your heart will condemn your actions and you will desire correction.

Even if we are a "good" person, and really strive to conduct yourself in a "good" manner, and you are trying to follow the Lord's lead, we are not perfect people, and we all fall short at points in time. Our thoughts, tongues and actions are going to go left at times. But because we have a forgiving God, He's merciful to forgive even at those times.

The Lord is present and available to supply needs, heal wounds and hurts, and provide love, grace, mercy and

salvation. He's there to daily walk and to talk with us as His spirit indwells us. However, He doesn't coerce us to allow Him in, he only invites us. But He does bring us face-to-face with truth, whether we're accepting or not.

Before we can enter His inner-courts to enjoy the truest sense of His fellowship, we must become naked before Him. We must come to a point that we simply strip before Him, ask Him to rid us of our mess, and to clean us up according to His will and purpose for our lives. Not only to rid us of our personal mess, but the mess which we allow others to bring into our lives as well. At times, He has to prune and purge our involvements and relationships, and we must be willing to allow Him to do so. He knows what is best.

Allow God to mold and bless the path He intended for you. Just surrender, breathe and exhale. Feel the weights simply fall from your body as joy begins to flood your soul. Share all with God and become naked as if to be a newborn babe in your newborn natural suit. Once you do, and allow Him in, you will begin to view things differently. Many things you view as utterly important won't seem as important after all. Life takes on a different meaning. Amazingly, you will find yourself smiling more, even to yourself. Others will surely take note.

I believe God wants each of us to be dynamic as we live the journey of life. But regardless of the talents, gifts, and resources we may have, which are all true blessings given to us; it's only through relationship and fellowship with Jesus Christ we can receive the truest sense of joy.

Even then, should we expect to be euphorically happy all the time? We won't. Should we expect to be exempt from hardships, trials and tribulations? We most certainly won't be. But if you trust the Lord, and allow Him to guide

and cover you, I can guarantee you will be shielded in those trying times. You can expect to receive an inward peace and joy that surpasses all other. You can expect the assurance of the Holy Spirit to direct you. You can expect to receive the revelation of your purpose and of His will. First, you must face yourself in His mirror. Allow yourself to face the truths about yourself. Allow yourself to become naked before the Almighty; the ultimate nakedness.

As I have journeyed to blossom out from hiding, I blossomed in relationship with the Lord. I allowed myself to become naked before Him. Prior, I couldn't have imagined the joy which a true relationship with Him provides. Not a mere God-consciousness, as was for me at one time, but a true relationship based on His standards, His love and my need. Real joy; indescribable. As I used to witness in others, now I too can express boldness and excitement in spiritual joy.

Shedding my weights and surrendering mu heart to my God and Lord, will forever outweigh any other experience on this side of life. Everything, I mean everything, works so much more smoothly and in order when you allow Jesus in and walk with Him daily. It's almost like coasting in air and depending on auto pilot to take you wherever you need to go. No doubt there will be turbulent spots at times, but I know that when you arrive at your point of destination, all is well.

I am most humbled and grateful to God for giving me a sense and heart to follow His guiding. I am grateful to Him for His patience given along the way as I was lost in doing things my own way. Maybe thinking I was right in many regards, but I wasn't right. Once I allowed Jesus in and allowed Him to remove the shades from my eyes, which in many regards was my messy thinking, I was then able to

see the sun (SON) clearly. I was blind (really) but now I see.

There are words to a familiar song which I would like to share; words which express my soul's sentiment regarding the goodness of the Lord. It expresses my gratefulness for the privilege I have been given, allowing me to experience an intimate relationship with Him; gratefulness for the joyfulness I carry each day from within to without.

It Makes Me Want to Shout
When I think about the Lord
How He saved me, how He raised me
How He filled me with the Holy Ghost
How He healed me to the uttermost
When I think about the Lord
How He picked me up and turned me around,
How He placed my feet on solid ground
It makes me want to shout,
Hallelujah, thank you Jesus,
Lord you're worthy of all the glory,
And all of the honor, and all of the praise
It makes me want to shout hallelujah!"

So now, as you become naked in all forms, allow yourself to walk in your truths. Once you do, you don't have to keep looking backward and dragging all the weights you may be carrying from the past. Let go! Let God take over. And when you come face-to-face in the mirror, contented and joy-filled eyes will be looking back at you. Evidence is always in the eyes.

Chapter Eighteen
Love Self

Throughout my writing I have given personal testimony, reported testimony, and other accounts why a woman may find herself in a state of what I perceive as "hiding". However, what good is it to bring attention to a concern without offering some type of solution or direction of how to better the situation. How are you to achieve that which I propose? What is the How To(s)?

As I bring my writing to a close, I would like to end with a few suggestions of How To; at least how to as I see it, and how to as it has worked for me. I believe them to be how to(s) which can work for you as well in your journey as you position to blossom.

What I offer is a simple formula. Yet it is one which requires courage, strength, and determination to apply in your daily walk. You will need to have a made-up mind to follow through in order to be successful in your endeavor. That's a fact. You may desire change, but to transfer from mind to action, then from action to renewed reality can be easier said than done, especially if you are used to doing things a certain way and for so long. But change does not occur without change. To change what appears to have been etched in stone requires determination; unfailingly.

You must grab hold to a sustaining motivation, which is actually the desire and hopefulness that lies in the pit of your gut. Along with that, you will need sustaining stamina to take you through the processes of getting from step A, to B, to C and so on. Be encouraged, as you progress from step to step you will find new thoughts awakening, transferring into actions and transforming your mindset and perceptions. Newness will begin to emerge.

To aid in this transformation, I offer a simple principle, one which I believe can be instrumental; a simple acrostic tool – LOVE SELF. I use Love Self because I believe loving self, in its truest form, is an element of devotion ignored by many women. And to love self is a level of self-respect which enables to claim ownership of self as an individual.

I believe if this simple tool is used in the context in which I offer, it can serve to trigger consciousness – reminding you to maintain self as a priority and center-focus; reminding you to respect your own personal thoughts, desires, hopes, dreams, ambitions, and most importantly, voice; reminding you the self which resides within deserves to be the self who lives outwardly; and reminding you that, that which God has placed within you – talents, spiritual gifts, interests, and passions represent the distinct individual He designed you to be; elements which are not to be forsaken or hidden.

Amongst all the hustle, bustle and responsibilities, women must be reminded to respect self as a priority in their own lives – not to become self-centered, but self-focused. Output cannot far outweigh input. If that imbalance persists continuously, day to day, month to month and year to year, depletion is right there on standby – inevitably to happen; mentally, emotionally, physically and spiritually.

Now, let's break down the formula LOVE SELF as I propose. Hopefully it will be received in a way that is meaningful and applicable to your life. Keep these points in mind and allow them to work in your favor to bring mind and heart in unity; to encourage and to remind you to

maintain a wholesome balance. You must still remain accountable to others of course, but you must also accept ownership and answerability to self as well.

Keep in mind as you journey, the focus is to release and increase. Release restraints, misconceptions, imposed expectations, and stresses. Increase joyfulness, contentment, and well-being – physically, emotionally and soulfully. Each aspect outlined in the formula is to point you in this direction.

Keep in mind I speak to a particular woman; a particular mindset. You know who you are. Again, don't just read and nod in agreement with what is being said, and remain unchanged. Instead, receive it and allow it to make a difference in your life. Learn to love self – respectfully, honestly and genuinely! To love self is so vital to your joyfulness. To love self is so vital to well-health. Learn to affectionately regard who you are, what you are and how you are.

I have broken down the acrostic into two parts. The first I regard as personal housekeeping; ways in which to decrease. This section is where you clean up, clear out, and rearrange – leading to the refresh. Then we move to part two, the increase; where you restore, revive and reinvent. However, all aspects work together to guide you on a path to blossom out from hiding. All points lead you to loving self.

LOVE SELF - Let's begin to break it all down.

L – Lay it all out on the table

At this point you've taken a look at your life as you see it; your personal assessment is done and hopefully, you have a vision in focus. Now, I ask that you think on the different aspects of your life, make mental notes, and then formulate them so you can name the different facets one by one. Not figuratively but actually. Call them out – name the different facets – pros and cons.

Write each of them down on a separate piece of paper; spread them out on a table and arrange them so you can view each piece individually; the good and the not so good and the positive and the negative. Even write down the broken areas – home, relationships, employment, family matters, personal issues; wishes and desires, whatever. Just lay out everything that comes to mind. Take a good look at what lies before you; this is your life at this present time. Think on them. Examine them.

Now, the things you love about your life, place them in a keeper pile. These are your strengths. These are the ones which carry you forward. Next, pick out the things you would like to change in whatever form that may be, put them in the make-over pile. These are the ones to become future goals; ones which you want to change, enhance or reinvent. Next, focus on the ones you would like to abandon; the regrets disappointments, hurts, and sorrows, and put these in the to-be-abandoned pile. These are the ones which you are to let go of; they are your weights. You want to unload weights and lighten your load. It may take a while, but you will unload them one by one, moment by moment, and opportunity by opportunity. Lastly, write down your heart dreams and aspirations and place them in the vision pile. This category is what will propel you to blossom out from hiding. These are the ones that will breathe exuberance into your being. These are your personal life-thriving desires.

Laying it all out so you can visually see the pieces of your life gives you a full view at a glance of what is going

on in your life. At some point we need to take a good look at who, where, and what in our lives. When we lay it all out – honestly – we can see what actually is and cannot ignore the hard facts.

Don't put these pieces of paper aside to be forgotten. Allow them to serve as a personal indicator. Don't be too hasty in your observation and actions if you have space enough, you might want to leave them scattered on the table for a few days. You want to have intermittent views. Allow it all to soak in and then begin to do what is needed to start a plan to bring about the desired results. Don't get stuck in the negatives and don't engage in a pity party. This is simply a tool to use to give you a visual of the moment – to show you what areas you want to keep as is, what areas you want to adjust or modify, and what areas you wish to delete.

After laying it all out, a few days or so later, or when you are ready, let's move further into the next part of the acrostic.

O – Oppressors - minimize them ASAP – Oppressors are tormentors, causing anguish and distress. There are situations and circumstances in our lives in which we have minimal to no control. Some are a part of us for a season and others may be ongoing. Some things we just have to deal with and make the best of it. We try to make lemonade out of the lemons. We do the best we can, and go on. Then, there are other types of oppressors in our lives which we simply allow; those which are not a must, and those over which we have control. We actually have the power to do something about them.

In laying it all out on the table, you have identified the oppressors. They are hidden within the make-over and the to-be-abandon piles. Recognize the ones over which you

have control – the ones which you allow upon yourself, the ones which drain you of energy, the ones which keep you awake at night, and the ones which are saddled on your back and weigh you down. Now, begin the process to unsaddle them. First you must undergo a mind adjustment because you are used to carrying the mental weights. But if you can come to terms with the fact that this is something you don't have to endure, it's a weight you don't have to carry, and it's a battle you don't have to fight, then – you will be able to let it go. It's a process though; we don't empty our minds readily. It takes practice. Once something filters in, you have to immediately push it back out, and repeat the cycle until you achieve the goal. It doesn't mean that you necessarily rid of everything, but you don't continue to allow certain matters to have the same aggravating effect on you.

If you think about it, how can you actually blossom if you are oppressed? And why allow such in your daily living when it's not a must that you do. It doesn't mean you will be less concerned about matters, but why get bogged down with the unnecessary? Perhaps a cliché but true, we really do need to choose our battles. Some battles we actually don't have to engage. It's important to relieve self of as many emotional and mental oppressors as possible. It will allow your days to be lighter and brighter. Stop trying to control everything! Let go of unnecessary mental and emotional weights. Minimize oppressors ASAP.

Following the identification of the oppressors, what you will need to do next is …

V – Vomit and Purge – This may sound a bit gross, but it's a necessary step.

When you vomit, you eject unwanted and harmful substances from the body; the impurities and foreign

matter. To purge, you eliminate and clean out the clutter and the unnecessary. Purging prunes, clarifies, and unloads; and the two, vomiting and purging work together. In life, there may come a time when to vomit and purge the unwanted and harmful; those things, matters, and individuals which cause more harm than good.

Think about times when you've had a bad stomach ache and there's something in your stomach you need to get out as quickly as possible; it is painful, cramping and sickening. You vomit, and afterwards you feel better, immediately. This may be what you need to do at this present point, rid yourself of the contaminants so you can feel better, immediately. It's important you **vomit up the impurities and purge the unwanted.**

Figuratively, throw up all the unnecessary mess, stressors and undesirables that engross you – anxieties, hurts, disappointments, and resentments, whatever it may be. If you allow yourself to think, you can just start expelling them one by one. You can feel your body feeling lighter in the process. Now, go through the motion as if you actually are vomiting. Don't take it back after you've thrown it up. Once it's out of your system, let it be out. Your stomach will feel better immediately; for in that throw up you'll find particles of impurities which have been keeping your stomach tied in knots. That which is in the throw-up is the culprit of your headaches, reflux, IBS and ulcers. Vomiting is good for the physical body.

Along with vomiting and relieving yourself of impurities, you will need to purge in several areas. Starting with your living area you are to clean house - literally. Take a long, hard look around you. Note if your environment is crowded and cluttered with things, things and more things? Believe it, when you **purge your environment** of

unnecessary things, unused things and things in excess, you will feel more in control of self and your environment. Items can become weights even if they are useful things. Being useful doesn't mean you should keep everything. Clutter takes away from mind clarity. Things in excess crowd and give a feel of being smothered. Purging allows you to relieve yourself of entanglements, and restores a better feel of order and simplicity.

Relieve yourself, whether you give things away, sell them, or throw them away. After which, notice how you will begin to feel calmer and more organized. Surprisingly, even memory will improve because you are also detangling your mind as well as your space.

Let's move a bit deeper into purging. It also extends to relationships. There are definitely times when we need to **purge relationships**. Each of us at one point or another is likely to experience toxicity in a relationship- a relationship which is unproductive and/or destructive.

Sometimes, we hold on to a relationship even when we know it's toxic. Toxins of any kind will cause serious harm if not eradicated. Therefore, it's important to identify relationships, especially those of your inner-circle which cause you duress, stress, hurt and pain. Take note of the ones which wear and tear you down. Take note of those individuals you enjoy seeing come and those you delight in seeing go. Then, those you need to rearrange; rearrange. Those you need to keep at a distance; keep at a distance. And those you need to totally disconnect; take courage and disconnect. Why submerge yourself in toxins? Ask yourself, why am I holding on?

Relationships are needed in our lives. We depend on them; family, life partners, friends and acquaintances. For that reason, as best you can, surround yourself with

individuals who offer positive energy and have your best interest at heart; ones which nurture, support, and embrace you; and ones which add goodness to your existence. Keep in mind, positive increases and negative decreases. Are you being increased or decreased by a relationship?

Certain people and situations in our lives are fixed and there isn't much we can do about those individuals or situations. But for those, over which you do have control, purge yourself of the toxic strains. You will find, in releasing the relationship contaminants, your body will become stronger, healthier and more joyful. Remember, your body is your detector. Your body will let you know when contaminants are present. Pay attention to your body's indicators. You cannot be at your best if toxins are present in your body.

Continuing in the purge, there's yet another phase - **mind purge**. We must purge the mind of cobwebs and stinking-thinking; whatever the negative blockers may be which clog the mind and hinder well-being. Clear out as much of it as possible and shake it off. Daily, go through the practice of shaking off. What good does it do anyways to hold onto these types of thoughts and feelings? What has happened has happened. The past is the past; it is what it is. We cannot change one thing of what has already happened. But we can change our present stance and outlook. We can influence and change the now.

Learn from past experiences. Be stronger for it. When we hold on to debilitating emotions, it causes personal injury. And such thoughts take control of your life. We so often allow the negatives of the past to govern our present, and the negatives of today to stifle the future.

What can we do about the mistakes and troubles of yesterday but do better today? Purge your mind of your present crippling thoughts and replace them with more healthy ones.

Letting go generally isn't easy. The body adjusts to being tense, worried and overwhelmed. Letting go takes practice. You sometimes have to start small and then go bigger. You may start by letting go of just one negative thought when it enters the mind. Quickly think about something positive. Feel renewed strength in your mind and body as you do. And when that negative thought resurfaces; immediately take control. Adjust your body and mind to being in control of it. You really can do it if you determinedly apply it. Don't remain a captive of the negatives. Sometimes what's in the mind isn't actually the case at all. Much of what we think could or will happen, doesn't.

You can't always take control of external circumstances, but you do have control of the mind and what filters through it. Even if a negative by-pass your filter and enters the mind anyway, you can reroute it out; but it takes practice. So, practice until it becomes normal.

Again, realize it isn't easy to just let go of past hurt, pain and disappointments. In some cases, you don't understand the why of what has happened, or the why of what is currently happening. You seek reasoning. To let go of what we don't understand is difficult

Then, there may be times when you feel too wounded to let go; the pain seems so great you can't seem to pull yourself out from under it. Too, you may feel your resentment toward another deserves to be held on to, as if holding on to it causes pain to the other person. Actually, it is you who are internalizing those feelings. You have to muster the strength to let go of it. Face it one moment at a time, one day at a time and one step at a time.

Sometimes we work through pain and disappointment by confronting the issue. Confronting could be a matter of acknowledging what actually is to properly deal with it; to confront whatever the situation is so you will be able to go forward in peace. You may need to talk it out with another. Understand, sometimes we just can't do it alone, and need another's helps to work through it. Who do you trust in spiritual wisdom? Who do you trust to disclose to? If clinical help is needed, don't be too afraid or too proud to seek proper help.

Your goal must be to usher in peace, joy and contentment. We don't have to invest time and actions in retaliation, trying to get back at those we feel have caused us injury. Reprisal belongs to God. It is Scripture. He will take care of it. Trust Him. Trust Him! Work to get yourself in order, strive to achieve your own contentment, and do what is required to accomplish this feat. It is your life.

A final focus on mind purging, yet one equally as important is to **release the mind of self-blame** – to forgive self of past regrettable actions. It's not always what someone else has done unto us; sometimes it's what we feel we have done to ourselves, or even what we feel we have done to another. So, our minds remain burdened with guilt.

We refuse to let go of past mistakes. We continuously beat self up over it; regret and more regret. But what can we do about past errors? We can't retract them. What we can correct, we should of course. Where we need to seek forgiveness, we should ask for forgiveness. If neither is possible, holding on to it won't make matters better; actually, it makes things worse.

If you continue to hold self-contempt in your mind, it paralyzes you from doing your best for self as well as others. It drains your energy and robs you of motivation. If you sincerely want to do better, feel better and perform better, forgive yourself of past errors, and purge your mind of self-disdain.

Things happen in life, intentional and unintentional. Some happenings are because we are uniformed and ignorant of facts, and misguided. And somethings because of selfish thinking and deeds. In remorse, we must take that unfortunate happening, channel it in a different direction and pay it forward positively. I reiterate, we cannot do anything about yesterday, but the present can be a different story. You can use that negative channel into a positive outcome.

Just like it is necessary at times to forgive others for their actions, it is also necessary at times to forgive self, especially if your good will is being held hostage. We are not perfect creatures; none of us. Of course, some mistakes are greater than others and the burden of it can be great. But know, you are worthy of forgiveness and love.

God forgives you for your actions when you are sincerely remorseful and sincerely ask Him for forgiveness. Are you better than He? If you can right the wrong, do so. If that is not possible, learn from your mistakes, pay forward to another, and peacefully start anew. Don't beat yourself up any longer.

At this point we are coming to a close of the housekeeping part of the LOVE formula; the decrease aspect. The final focus is......

E – Exterminate and Exhale – There are a few things in our lives which we must completely wipe out. No if, and, or but about it. And once we do, we must take a deep breath and let go. Take a step forward and keep going.

Let's look at these things as the rodents in our lives. Rodents generally consistently bite and gnaw, gradually

eroding and diminishing its substance. In this case, you are the substance. Ask yourself - what and who are the rodents in your life that are continually biting and gnawing at you?

Since you have laid it all on the table, unloaded oppressors, vomited and purged the unwanted, it's time to exterminate – wipe out the rodents, and manage their intrusion.

The need to exterminate signifies, I am tired of it, I no longer want it in my presence, and I'm going to rid myself of its intrusion.

We all know how uncomfortable it feels to have rodents moving around in our personal space. It becomes unnerving. We want to exterminate and bring the matter under control. The rodents in this case however are not actual bugs and pests, they are whatever unnerving matters and agitators which happen to be in your personal space;

be it person, place or thing. And it needs to be exterminated.

What is in your personal space you would rather not be there, or even more so, you know shouldn't be there? A job you hate, a friend that really isn't a friend, a love interest that really isn't love, a love interest that really isn't yours, a family member that continuously mooches; an adult child that simply will not leave the nest, whatever. Purging prunes, but exterminating extinguishes.

We must decide what stays and what goes. It's called taking charge. If unnerving circumstance persists in your life, and you have the power to do something about it, then you must. Why work on a job you hate, when you can change jobs. It might require additional training or education, but do what is required. Time is going to pass anyway, so why not let it pass making a change? If it's a relationship which causes persistent distress, then you already know what you need to do about it. If it can be fixed, fix it.

Don't throw away a relationship which is worthwhile keeping. Put the work in it to make it work. But if it's not working, it's not working. You may hold on hoping it will magically work out, but is the magic taking place? And if it's harming you emotionally, physically and/or mentally, then you have a decision to make, don't you? Don't be too hasty, but do be decisive.

Whatever the adverse situation is that gnaws and bites at you; you must decide what you're going to do about it? Or, do you continue to allow the gnawing and biting to destroy its substance –you.

Make up your mind and muster up some guts. EXTERMINATE! Love self enough to do what needs to be done to put you in a better frame of mind, your body in a healthier condition, and your circumstance in a more content standing.

Once you exterminate, and you begin to feel lighter, brighter and more in control, then EXHALE; allow yourself to breathe comfortably as you release your mind of all that has held you captive. Once you come to the point of exhaling, you are definitely on you way to blossom out from hiding. You just may not know what comfortable breathing is until you exhale.

So far, we've dealt with the LOVE segment of the acrostic – which signifies loving self where as you clean up and clear out elements which are debilitating and robbing of contentment and joyfulness. In order to regain wellness, we must come to an understanding of what it is that has been allowed to weaken us more so than to strengthen. Once coming to this realization, we must do what is required to restore and nurture an overall well-being.

I trust you will allow yourself to come to this realization, and then, to do what is necessary to foster an over-all well you.

Now let's move into the SELF portion of the acrostic – signifying the building, sustaining and liberating aspects; drawing out the fundamental nature of your essence; the aspect of you which embodies your interests, aspirations, dreams and passions; aspects which characterize you as a distinct individual; the aspect that breathes joy and contentment into the body and soul – SELF.

Let's start with a most crucial aspect…

S – Spirituality– Feed you spiritually every day. No exception and no compromise. Whether you choose to pray, meditate, read Scripture, read inspirational quotes, engage a spiritual partner, or whatever your meaningful preference may be. Whichever you choose – feed self spiritually each day.

Although spirituality, it's positioned later in the acrostic formula; it is the most essential aspect of all. It is the root, core and foundation of everything else. It's where one should get the truest sense of strength, courage, guidance and anchoring. It is the cohesive entity and sanctity which draws all other together in unity. It is the present and future. It is the guarding factor of all we do and all we hope. It is our help in time of need. It is the ultimate joy. It is our salvation!

I am a Christian, believing in the Father, the Son and the Holy Spirit; God the Father who created me, Jesus the Son who redeemed me, and the Holy Spirit the Comforter who sustains me. My faith is my Solid Rock and guiding force; a lamp unto my feet which stabilizes me, and a light unto my path which directs me. I believe one cannot blossom to their fullest and understand purpose without establishing a solid-footing spiritually. Having a solid faith-base is your cornerstone. And it is here you began to understand true joy.

If you are not anchored spiritually, I strongly and sincerely hope you will find the way; which I believe there is only one – Jesus Christ. *"Jesus is the way, the truth and the life."* John 14:6 if you need direction in finding the way, and have a heart to do so, the answer is found in Romans 10:9-10. Please read, believe and receive, and it is yours. Realize – if we confess our sins, He (God) is faithful and just to forgive us our sins (no matter what the circumstance), and to cleanse us from all unrighteousness. 1 John 1:10 Awesome!

If you already know Jesus, but feel you have regressed in your relationship and have fallen out of fellowship, then examine your heart and recognize what it is that has distracted you, or what biblical principles you may have compromised. Ask the Lord for renewal and allow Him to restore your fellowship. Be mindful, there may be ways you must mend, some things you may need to forsake, or some things for which you desire forgiveness. But know for sure, He is a merciful God. He never leaves nor forsakes His own. Hebrews 13:5. He's willing and waiting for you to come unto Him, with lovingly out-stretched arms.

Even if you are one who is solid in your faith and your fellowship, yet needs an anew measure of strength, focus and direction, then it's praying time. Open scripture and allow the Lord to speak to you through His Word. But along with prayer, and through faith, we must put works in action.

I believe we cannot live out all we are meant to be without having a true relationship with God through Jesus Christ. How else are to understand His plan for our lives?

How else are we to understand how to bring together mind, heart and purpose, other than to establish a relationship with the Almighty, one who knows all, has all, and knows everything about you – past, present and future. How do we truly blossom without being connected to the Vine which is connected to the Root?

Whatever it is you feel you must do, whatever it is you feel you need direction in doing, whatever it is that pains you, whatever it is you need to let go of, whatever goal you strive to achieve, whatever adverse situation you may be facing, whatever guilt, whatever... discuss it all with the Lord. Turn it over to Him and allow Him to guide, shield and bless you. He is the Great Solver, He has all solutions; He is the Great Physician, He heals; He is The Great Compass, He guides you where you need to go; He is the Greatest Friend, He listens to anything and everything without judgment and condemnation. He is God – omnipotent, omnipresent, and omniscient – all powerful, all present, and all knowing.

Grow strong in spirituality. Feed yourself spiritually every day! No exceptions! Surround yourself with people of like faith. Anchor yourself in a bible teaching and honoring church. Allow God to lead you in this season of your life. He is unfailingly AWESOME!

Now, continuing in the formula of SELF. Let's take a look at...

E – Embrace, Enhance, Expand and Empower – Love who you are, respect who you are, and become empowered in who you are. Then expand – broaden your horizons, increase your territory and fascinate your mind.

It's important you embrace who you are at this very point in time. Be confident in it; perceived flaws and all. Don't think time has forsaken you, it hasn't. You may have

to tweak a bit, realign some things, but, embrace, enhance, expand, empower and experience what yet remains.

It doesn't mean you are going to be totally together. Who is? But work on what needs work. Enhance what needs enhancing, repair what needs repairing, and reinvent what needs reinventing. Yet, love yourself in the now. Tell yourself you are wonderfully crafted, for you have all sorts of wonders within you. Believe it. Then hold yourself accountable to experience it. Revel in it!

To demonstrate a point, indulge in doing a quick little exercise. Stand up and stretch out your arms – one to each side of you, extend them as far as they will reach - stretch.

Breathe deep a few times. Do you feel that sensation? Do you feel the expansion of self? Isn't it kind of exhilarating and empowering? Doesn't it feel liberating? Don't you feel the extension of self? Those are the type feelings you want to experience in life as routine.

Fascinate your mind. Do something out of the norm. Try something different and new. Live, laugh, be interesting and be interested! Expand your adventures. Go places you've never gone, see faces you've never seen, and walk walks you've never walked. It gives you vitality, youthfulness and inspiration. Resurrect old desires and establish new ones. Enjoy old friends and establish a few new ones. Spend time with your loved ones and enjoy togetherness. Don't take time for granted. Don't take loves ones for granted.

Don't indulge in self-defeating self-talks, talking yourself out of doing things you would like to do. Lay aside the fears. Be bold in your attempt and courageous in your efforts. Live a life which embodies joy and contentment; if it's less than, you are settling. Don't settle.

Place things of interests and excitement on your calendar and hold yourself accountable to follow through. Don't wait on others to initiate, you do it. If you desire to do things with your significant other, and he is not interested at the moment, then find ways to excite him so he'll join you. Let him see your newness and renewed vigor. But if for some reason he won't oblige, and as long as you're in decency and order, go forth on your own.

Don't let days, weeks or months go by without granting yourself pleasurable times. Don't be boring to yourself. You are the one who is responsible for bringing excitement into your life. Capture your desires. Know what you want and establish a plan to achieve your dreams and goals. We are never too old to dream, and never too gone to achieve.

Maybe you've sold yourself out to the hustle and bustle of life's obligations, and forgotten what it is that actually pleases you. Maybe it's time to give self a refresher course. Just start doing a few things and see what captivates you.

Become familiar with charming yourself. When a woman feels charming, she feels empowered. Usually, we do things to charm others. And that's okay. Or, we wait for others to charm us. But what I suggest at this point, especially since you identify as a woman in "hiding"; one accustomed to neglecting self, is that you learn to charm yourself.

Charm yourself in ways you would want someone else to charm you, even if you have someone special in your life that provides these things. Still, I suggest you make yourself feel good, appealing, and attractive for your own sake. Move about as if you are special. Stand erect. Walk with a bit of swagger.

Put aside clothes that are unflattering to your appeal. Particularly focus on wearing clothes you feel attractive in.

If you're not particularly savvy in coordinating outfits, go window shopping and notice what matches well. Learn how to coordinate what you already have in your closet. If you can, buy a few pieces and mix old and new for a different and appealing look. We feel good when dressed in clothing we feel looks good on us. It flatters our ego, doesn't it? Well then, flatter your ego.

Do something different with your hair even if you like your current hairstyle. Change your style a bit to a different flattering style. Watch how others are going to notice and express the difference – positively.

Occasionally indulge yourself. Buy yourself flowers. Enjoy their beauty. Take yourself to a special restaurant, and look pretty while you dine. Buy yourself some nice body moisturizers and lavish your body. Rub and pamper your own body. That's okay – it's yours. Learn new things, a different language for instance. Get involved in things you can appreciate and be appreciated. Make friends with someone unlike you. Expand!

Embrace, enhance, expand and empower – let that be your focus. Not just for today, but the next, and the next, and the next. Don't exist as a spectator, observing others doing what you wish to do. Do!

Now moving on…

L – Live a Healthy Lifestyle – Adjust your palate, get off the couch and get moving. A healthy body experiences life better, and differently. A well body connects positively to every other aspect of life. It enables everything else in life to be more enjoyable and appreciated. We cannot skimp in this area. We only have one body, and we must commit to taking care of it – well. If we serve the body well, I believe the body will return the favor.

Along with routine check-ups and following through with medical instructions and recommendations, where we depend on others' expertise, there are a few areas where we can depend on self to aid in the endeavor of living a healthy lifestyle.

We must view a healthy mind and body as the foundation and building blocks for wellness. Wellness in the body situates you to cope better with all other things that come up in life. We must treat our body with kindness. We cannot put anything and everything in it. We cannot abuse it with substances, food or anything which can become harmful.

Healthy living is actually a learning process and it requires endurance. We like to do what feels good at the moment instead of doing what is actually good for the long-run. We like the easy and now. And we can be lazy people.

Lazy feels good. But, if we want quality living, we must do what is needed to achieve quality.

One important practice in doing so is to nurture the body in getting proper rest and relaxation. Your body needs it. Rest and relaxation promote a calm presence. Simply getting sleep doesn't necessarily mean the body is rested or relaxed. Even while sleeping, the mind still processes things which cause unrest. So, you wake up feeling just as tired as when you laid down. In the morning you get right back on life's merry-go-round and start all over again – tired, day after day.

If that is you, stop it! Focus on scheduling your evening so you will get at least seven to eight hours of consistent rest and sleep. Even if you cannot sleep that length of time during the night, make sure the body is resting that amount of time. You cannot operate to your fullest if the mind and body are tired. Restful sleep rejuvenates a tired mind and body. There are always exceptions, life happens. But as best you can, rest the body for a consistent seven to eight hours.

To aid in this effort, stay away from becoming aggravated right before going to bed, whether it's a TV program, a conversation, thinking about bills, thinking about tomorrow's schedule or whatever the case may be. These things disturb restful sleep. Instead, find ways to calm the mind before going to sleep; reading, music, meditation, intimacy, or whatever your desired tranquil means may be. Make a practice of calming yourself prior to sleep. Then, you're more likely to go to sleep with more of a serene feeling, and you're likely to have a more restful night; thus, be more rested upon rising, and have a calmer and more productive day.

Sleep is a wonderful tool God has given us to refresh and rejuvenate the body. It is healing. Whatever you have experienced in that day, sufficient sleep and rest allows the body the opportunity to recover and be physically prepared for the next day.

I've learned the body cannot skimp on sleep; regardless of how young you may be or how strong you may think you are. If you are one to skimp on sleep, you may not realize it now, but ill-effect is taking place in your body right now. Eventually those ill effects are going to surface one way or another.

For the longest time, I thought I could operate on five hours of sleep. In a way I did. I stayed up late doing busy work, got up early and went to my job facing a busy schedule. I performed at what I thought was my best. But what I didn't realize, I wasn't operating at my optimal level. During those times, I suffered with headaches. A headache tablet was one of my best friends. For years I took headache medication. It became a way of life. I underwent certain tests searching for the cause of the headaches. Fortunately, test results were negative. But, because there was periodic mentioning of my sleep habits, I began to pay better attention, and started the practice of getting more sleep.

I began to notice I was more energized, more alert, clearer thinking, more productive, less annoyed and agitated; my overall body felt stronger. And I wasn't yawning throughout the day. Eventually, I noticed I was taking fewer headache tablets. Subsequently, a headache tablet became an every-now-and-then need, to almost none. Getting seven to eight hours of sleep and rest made a world of difference for me. I learned to appreciate adequate sleep and rest.

I was aware of the recommended eight hours of sleep, but for some reason I never really took it personally. I felt I was okay with the five hours since I was functioning alright. I thought I had this built-in resilience that allowed me to go on and on, regardless; and I did – unfortunately.

Now, I realize all those years of taking headache medications and undergoing tests when all I needed was more sleep and rest. Seven to eight hours of sleep on a nightly basis, strengthen my mind and body. It's amazing what quality sleep can do for the body and mind.

The body can't continuously endure tiredness when going to bed and tiredness upon awaking without experiencing negative repercussions. Each body's need may differ, and one can endure more than another, but I've learned that the amount of sleep a body requires for it to function at its best doesn't differ much from one person to another.

Another aspect of a healthy lifestyle is to make time for you each day to enjoy simple pleasures. Do something just for you, if only for a few moments. Spend quality moments – a telephone conversation with a friend, pleasure reading, listening to music, meditating, taking a walk, enjoying a TV program, taking a nap, or hiding yourself in the bathroom, (which is one of my favorites get-away). And by all means, don't forget laughter. Laughter is good for the body and soul. It's relaxing. If laughter doesn't surround you in some form on a regular basis, you may need to examine your company.

Something else to think about is to make your environment pleasing to your view. What does this have to do with a healthy lifestyle; a lot? Your environment can serve as a soother; a haven. So, surround yourself with things in your home which delight you, and gives you pleasure. Have at least one area in the house in which you can retreat to receive relaxing soothing moments. Do not fail to spend time there. A few moments may be all you need, but do it.

Next, don't overwork the body when you don't have to. So often we push our bodies to the limit, time after time as if it is made of concrete, and as if the body is totally resilient no matter what. Well, it isn't. The body can stretch a distance, but if stretched over its limit, similar to a rubber-band, it will snap. Never to return to its original form even if repaired. We shouldn't expect the body to bounce back regardless of how roughly treat it. We can't continuously overwork it. We must respect the body and its limits.

Two final important focuses in the area of promoting a healthy lifestyle, ones which most of us grapple with, are healthy eating and routine exercise. We all know how

important it is to eat healthy and to exercise the body to maintain physical well-being. We also know these two elements work together. So, why don't we do as we know we should regarding this matter? What stops us, other than commitment and respect for our body? Most of us know what medical experts recommend, and we also know we feel better when we actually engage in physical exercise and eat balanced and well-prepared foods. So, why are we so slothful in doing what is needed?

Generally, for ladies, the result of dieting means you can fit and look nice in clothing. There's nothing wrong with desiring to look nice in clothing, but shouldn't we be equally concerned with putting the right foods in the body to produce a healthy and fit body. If we adjust our mindset to eating well and exercising regularly, the weight will take care of itself – right –and then, the desired look will naturally happen.

Make a habit of keeping junk and processed foods out of the body. We minimize our chances of eating this food if we don't place them in our homes. Most of us are not strong enough to ignore something we want if it is in our possession. But, if we want a healthy functioning body, then we must eat quality foods. The body becomes a by-product of what we put in it. The old saying "we are what we eat" – we are. Certain ailments don't just happen to our bodies, we contribute.

It doesn't mean we have to totally eliminate certain foods which we enjoy. We all splurge now-and-then. That's to be expected. But we can't base our diet on the unhealthy foods and expect it to be healthy. The healthy must far outnumber the unhealthy.

Also, it is important to be educated on nutritional value. Once you realize the health advantages in certain foods,

and how they actually nourish the body, you will begin to migrate toward those particular ones. Don't torture yourself by eating foods you dislike, since there's enough variations for you to select ones, you can enjoy and appreciate. I don't particularly like eating broccoli or avocados, but because of their nutritional benefit, I blend them into a smoothie along with fruits and will actually enjoy drinking them.

Reading labels are also of great benefit. It helps us to know the ingredients included in the foods we select. You may not be able to avoid all risk factors, which is almost impossible to do anyway, but at least you can become more knowledgeable regarding what you choose to put in your body; therefore, more informed to make wise choices.

A well-nourished body aids in getting restful sleep. Restful sleep aids in having a relaxed body. A relaxed body aids in total well-being. Well-being aids in being a content and joy-filled individual. To eat nutritionally definitely requires commitment, but it's one that each of us needs to make.

Now, let's give attention to the exercise aspect of living a healthy lifestyle. Whatever method of exercise you choose, it needs to be one which you can appreciate and enjoy. Just realizing you need to exercise may not be enough of a sustaining factor to keep you on track. If you can enjoy the exercise, it kind of takes the work factor out of it and you're more apt to continue it. Otherwise, it may become another stressful chore. And the one thing that is not desired is another chore in an already busy schedule. If it becomes added stress, you're not going to do it.

There are many methods and techniques of exercise available today, so exercise doesn't have to be a grueling activity; but you must discover a method which is pleasurable, or at least one you can stick to. Exercising

doesn't have to be in long stretches of time, it can be broken up into mini sessions. Still, it must be effective, regular, and you must commit to at least a few days weekly. But actually, you can do a few minutes of something every day without even leaving your house.

If you need a partner to stay motivated, team up with someone so you can socialize and exercise at the same time. If time is a factor, go to bed earlier and get up a bit earlier, giving yourself a few extra minutes in the morning, or simply cut corners in another area to allow yourself a little extra time. If you like structure, attend a structured class or go to a gym. You may choose to swim, dance, walk, run, ride a bike or whatever your pleasure, just do it routinely. The point is, do something to move your body on a routine basis. Even if you are already at an ideal weight, you still need to exercise. Exercise remains crucial, even for skinny people.

If we would view the body as our most valuable possession, I believe we would do a better job of caring for it. We shouldn't experience poor health because of neglect. We may not be perfect in this area, but we must be willing to treat our bodies with respect.

Under normal circumstances, the body would take care of us if we take care of it. We think, act, work and relate better when the body is well taken care of. At some point, in one way or another, we will meet medical challenges. But, if we work to produce a healthy body, we will be better fit to cope and to overcome such challenges when we are faced with them.

Rest, relaxation, healthy eating, and exercise are crucial to wellness. Just as we accept unquestionable responsibilities in other areas, we must also accept unquestionable responsibility in doing what is necessary to

nourish and nurture the total body – consistently. We can't expect the body to perform at its best unless we nourish and nurture it to be its best. We must desire that our body function at its optimal level and do what is necessary to achieve optimal level performance. If we want to be at our best, take care of the body temple.

How are we to achieve all the things we desire to achieve if the body is not well taken care of? Take ownership in doing what is needed in this area. Get off the couch, close the bag of chips, and go walking.

Lastly of the SELF component of the Love Self acrostic formula, a drawing together of all other aspects is...

F – Faith and Focus – regardless of what you plan and whatever the goals, you must have faith in self and focus to achieve.

Spiritual faith is to be your primary anchor and root. There's no getting around needing to be rooted spiritually. Yet, vitally important is your faith in self. Regardless of past or present circumstance, believe you are an achiever equipped with God-given abilities. You can do whatever it is you aspire to do. And you must believe you deserve to receive whatever you aspire to achieve.

Whatever your destiny, walk toward it. Establish goals, and muster up a determined faith in yourself. Know that you are fearfully and wonderfully made - *Psalm139:14.* You may wish all you want, but if you don't have faith in self to achieve, chances are you won't.

You know better than anyone what's in your heart. You know what direction you desire to go, what it is you desire to do, and what it is you need to do. You know all about your fallen dreams, ones you once wished for and desired to happen. Well, isn't it time to make them happen?

Even though things don't always work out as hoped, we should never stop dreaming, never stop wishing and never stop hoping. A dream shouldn't stay in the mind; we actually have the power to do something about it. But it takes faith and focus. And it must be strong enough that we don't become easily distracted. And then, there're haters out there, waiting for you to fail. Don't.

Put aside negative thoughts and focus on the positives of what can be. The past is the past, and there's nothing we can do about it. Time gone is time gone, and there's nothing we can do about that either. But we have the present. Focus on a plan for the present that will impact the future. There's a saying "When we fail to plan, we plan to fail".

Have confidence, trust, assurance and belief in yourself. Resurrect some of those fallen dreams, and also create new ones. Walk out in faith in God and in self. You've already been endowed with much – innate and through experiences. No longer allow it to hide. Use it and allow it to blossom and flourish. Perhaps you can't bring to fruition all your heart desires, but you can bring to fruition enough so that you are content in self and content in life. No one can stop you but you.

Tap into what God has placed in you. Blossom and be content and joyful in the one life God has granted you. I believe He wants nothing less for you.

Each life should experience the essence of who you are. Life happens and it can disturb and change the course of where we were headed, once bright-eyed and bushy-tailed, but we can still redirect our course. So, redirect if need be, and enjoy YOU. Life is beautiful and a contented soul is splendor.

Return to self and experience self! Remember - LOVE SELF.

In Closing

Since you realize through the acrostic of LOVE SELF, its demonstrating love of self, and, in positioning to move forward to blossom out from hiding, you are first to clean house - to face some things by laying it all out on the table, minimize oppressors which weigh you down, vomit impurities which contaminate your system, exterminate the unwanted and unneeded which gnaws and bites at you; then, to refresh and strengthen you need to become spiritually rooted, enhance and expand by broadening your horizons and enlarging your territory, commit to living a healthy lifestyle, demonstrate faith in self, understanding you are an achiever, and to focus on your goals, establishing a plans to attain heart wishes.

Now, having all of that under belt, let's close with another dimension. It is not a part of the acrostic formula but it is most important in the formula of life...

T – Thankfulness - gratefulness, appreciation and humility. We are better overall when we develop and maintain an attitude of thankfulness. It minimizes negative thoughts and feelings and maximizes the positive ones. It works on our behalf rather than against us. If we are embodied by an attitude of thankfulness, we feel better, perform better, and are received better; we have fewer thoughts of what we don't have and more appreciation and gratefulness for what we do. We become cognizant of what we consider the small things. But if you think about it, even the small is great. All are blessings.

Just think. Who are we void of thankfulness – to God, family and others? Even though I advocate self-contentment, how can we truly be joyous and content in self without expressing thankfulness for all we have, all we are, and to all who contribute into our lives? The song and adage that states "Count Your Many Blessings", - count them; name them one by one, and realize what God has done. And be grateful to those who love and promote you. And it would be wise to let them know.

Upon waking each day, quickly name five things for which you are grateful. Watch how your morning will automatically start off on a positive note. The next thing you know your list of things will increase from morning to morning because your attitude of gratefulness heightens.

I offer this LOVE SELF formula as what I view as workable tool to assist on your out from hiding journey. And however, this principle may apply, claim it, use it and live it.

RESPECT yourself today in loving yourself. Don't let time continue to pass you by without claiming the purest essence of self. We want to be healthy in the mind, body, soul and spirit. And we also should want to be prosperous and productive in engaging all aspect of self. It is our responsibility to achieve it. In doing so, you are to be your greatest cheerleader!

All who have read and needed to have received what is contained in this book; I hope that it inspires, encourage and strengthen you. And, that it takes root in your heart to move forward. It has been my heart which I have shared with you. And know, I'm cheering for you to blossom out from hiding.

In Thankfulness

I would like to thank each of you for taking the time to read "To Blossom out from Hiding".

I hope by coming forward and sharing my thoughts, feelings and testimony it impresses upon you to recognize and to accept certain happenings in your own life, and to take action to do what is required to assure a contented you.

You owe it to yourself to blossom into the most magnificent being; a beautiful and flourishing individual. Just like a budding flower which unfolds and develops into a stunning presence; budding and unfolding into greatness.

Whichever doors you have allowed to close yet yearn for them to open again; find a way to open them. For those doors which you have never allowed yourself to enter, yet have a yearning to, strive to open them. And for those doors which need be closed, take courage and close them.

I wish for you to exude that beautiful innateness of God's special, unique design – you. I believe it is all possible, but not merely possible, rather commissioned by the Almighty God. Self-contentment, joyfulness, and exuberance are yours to partake.

As you journey, I wish God's blessing upon you as you grow in the experience of YOU as you go forth "To Blossom out from Hiding".

Woman

Woman, a unique being designed and crafted by Almighty God; a creation delicately and intricately molded and crafted in her own as an individual, yet so similar to all others. She is designed and detailed in such awesome beauty which attracts and appeals to the eye – a beautiful silhouette of God's design.

Woman, a delicate creation; she's mild and meek, yet bold; a tower of strength, yet fragile. When necessary, she can attack as a roaring lion, yet be as gentle as a lamb or a kitten desiring to cuddle.

Woman, she is energetic, hard-working, clothed in virtue and dedication; endowed with talents, skills and abilities; usefulness to extend to others needing to receive. A gem this creation of God.

Woman, miraculously drawn from the rib of man, connecting her to him; a rib answerable to her covering, shielding, supporting, and protecting; connectivity which she desires, admires, and depends.

Woman, if she desires to find him, he who allows himself to know her – her beauty illuminates, alluring the blossoming of a beautiful flower, a sweet fragrant destined to flourish. She seeks him – the rib she believes designed especially for her - her resting nook; a place where she may be positioned in the beautiful, bountiful Garden of Eden. After all, that is God's design.

Woman - lover and helpmate to man as God has ordained. Man, often misunderstands her as she strives to claim her rightful place beside him, for he often mistakes her strength and intuitive guide as lead and control; a misunderstanding which causes a tug between them. But her heart only desires his love and respect as she inherently submits herself to him.

Woman, responsible for bringing all human life into the world; mothering, nurturing all human life as it develops from a seed into actual life. What an awesome responsibility God has entrusted upon her; yet, she grabs hold of it with honor and will defend to the end.

Woman, she doesn't require greatly, but that which she requires is essential to her soul; it defines her essence; an essence that longs to be fulfilled. She appears mysterious, but is actually transparent; appearing complex, yet her needs are so simple in nature. But that which she needs – she needs.

Woman, she seeks to explore that which God has placed within her; to release that which burns within. She will know when she captures it, so she seeks to attain that special, restful, peaceful place as she sojourns.

So, Woman, lifeline to man, mother to our world, anchor to our families, manager to our homes – a jewel- and a sweet, sweet savor to our world.

Woman, this magnificent creation of God!

Gloria Mangum Glasgow

Serenity Prayer

*God grant me the serenity to accept
the things I cannot change;
Courage to change the things I can;
and the wisdom to know the difference.*

Reinhold Niebuhr

Author's Biography

Gloria Mangum Glasgow is an educator, human services professional and entrepreneur. She is a graduate of Point Park University, Pittsburgh, Pennsylvania, where she received a degree in psychology and secondary education. She continued her education in the area of business education and financial services.

Gloria was born and raised in South Carolina, where she now resides. She is a devoted wife, mother, and grandmother.

Gloria has dedicated many years as educator, social worker, counselor and life coach to many. It is her heartfelt desire to offer her skills and counsel to aid in enriching lives.

Gloria speaks to women, believing that many live their lives sacrificing themselves for the sake of those they love and are committed. But in its midst, forsakes distinctiveness, losing a sense of true self. She understands it is most important- crucial actually – to exercise who you are as an individual – to know, respect and, engage self whereas true essence may continue to blossom. And she advocates on this behalf.

Gloria's aspires to speak to the heart of women who experience a similar plight; one which involves a particular mindset. Her aim is to inspire to explore heart and mind connection; to unite both to unveil the true one who resides inside self. To know, God has gifted each with a special design, and that special design is to be pursued, captured and lived.

Gloria believes that to love, respect, and develop self is a testament to God – to exert that which He has placed in you as an individual.

Her advice to all is to honor and love God; love and respect self; and love and respect others – in that order. Loving God first, allows you to put all other in proper prospective, and to love and respect self places you in a right order to extend yourself to others in a wholesome manner affording you an existence of peace, joy and contentment.

www.ingramcontent.com/pod-product-compliance
Lightning Source LLC
Chambersburg PA
CBHW051133120626
46547CB00012B/780